DEERSTALKER!

Holmes and Watson

on Screen

by

RON HAYDOCK

The Scarecrow Press, Inc.
Metuchen, N.J. & London
1978

Library of Congress Cataloging in Publication Data

Haydock, Ron.
Deerstalker!

Bibliography: p.
Includes index.
1. Sherlock Holmes films. I. Title.
PN1995.9.S5H3   791.43'7   77-24465
ISBN 0-8108-1061-1

CONTENTS

Credits and Acknowledgments   v

Foreword (by Keith McConnell)   vii

1   The First Sherlock Holmes, and What Came
      Afterwards   1

2   A Hound It Was   20

3   The Valley of Fear and William Gillette   38

4   The Further Adventures of Sherlock Holmes   54

5   Enter the All-Talking Detective   72

6   Arthur Wontner Carries On   86

7   Rathbone and Bruce Arrive on the Scene   107

8   The Mystery Masters at Universal Pictures   126

9   Baker Street: Transition to Television   150

10 "You Have Been in Afghanistan, I Perceive. . . "   170

11 The Television Casebook of Sherlock Holmes   184

12 Peter Cushing and Christopher Lee at
      Baker Street   203

13 Jack and the Deerstalker   222

14 The Million Dollar Sleuth   237

15 The Rivals of Sherlock Holmes   252

16 The Game Is Afoot   272

Bibliography   283

Index (by Donald F. Glut)   289

The original Sherlock Holmes: Dr. Joseph Bell, a contemporary upon whom in the 1880's Sir Arthur Conan Doyle modeled his world famous detective. (Courtesy Eddie Brandt's Saturday Matinee.)

CREDITS and ACKNOWLEDGMENTS

ABC Television; the Academy of Motion Picture Arts and Sciences; Betty Ashley; BBC Television; Robert Bloch; Eddie Brandt's Saturday Matinee, North Hollywood; Leonard Brown and Malcolm Willets of the Collectors Bookstore, Hollywood; Constance Campbell of Prime TV Films, Inc.; John Robert Christopher.

Herman Cohen; Columbia Pictures; Jerry Courneya; Ronald Burt De Waal; Dean Dickensheet; Steve Edrington and Jim McDonald of Bond Street Books, Hollywood; John Farrell of the Los Angeles Sherlock Holmes Society, the Non-Canonical Calabashes; Charles E. Fritch; Robert Fuller of CBS Radio; Vic Ghidalia; Gale Gifford; Ed and Anita Goldstein; Bob Greenberg; Jeanne Marie Grimaldi; Leo H. Gutman of the Sherlock Company.

Jim Harmon; Mrs. Jean Haydock; Eric Hoffman; Peggy Hynes of the Eastern Educational Television Network; Ronnie James; Christopher Lee; John Leyland of Blackhawk Films; Carl Macek of the American Comic Book Company, North Hollywood; Lynne Maynor of Specialty Films; Keith McConnell; Thom Montgomery; George Morgan; NBC TV.

Frank Neill; Jack Nicholas; Luther Norris; Paramount Pictures; Mark Phillips of the Non-Canonical Calabashes; Karen Randrup; the late Basil Rathbone; Frank Rodriguez; Captain Cecil A. Ryder, Jr.; Frank Saletri; Al Satian; Salvatore Scorza; Gene Shepherd; Ray Dennis Steckler; 20th Century-Fox; Rick Talcove; United Artists Film Corp.; Universal Pictures; Bill Warren; Dr. Julian Wolff of the Baker Street Irregulars, New York City; and Jerry Yung. But I don't know whether to thank Donald F. Glut, or not...

The photos and illustrations herein are courtesy of the respective studios and/or individuals as indicated in the captions accompanying each photo or illustration.

R. H., January 1977

FOREWORD

by Keith McConnell

Sherlock Holmes is one of the most haunting characters ever created in fiction. I remember Basil Rathbone
once telling me how the character possessed him, literally
haunted him.

Rathbone had been doing a series of Sherlock Holmes
films which although made on a low budget were very well
done. Rathbone, who had been an international star for many
years before becoming synonymous with Holmes, wanted now
to give up the character. But the producers kept begging him
to do another and yet another film, and he ended up doing all
in all about fourteen pictures.

Ultimately when Rathbone finally managed to break
away from the character he created, it was too late, and he
could not get employment in Hollywood for anything else.
Weary of the situation, he went to New York where he did
plays and radio work, but he really never was able to dis-
associate himself from the character that he had made so
famous in films. He told me quite honestly that had he
known that "Holmes" was going to become such a trademark
for him, he would never have tried so hard to escape him
and would have continued to play the part for the rest of his
career.

Shortly before his death at 75, Rathbone was quoted
in a New York paper as saying, "Surely there's at least
some part for an actor of my background to play...."

It was a tragic ending to the brilliant career of a
wonderful actor.

Sherlock Holmes' character also affected William
Gillette in a very similar manner. At first he was pleased
to take on Holmes' characterization, but after a while he

Keith McConnell as Sherlock Holmes, World's Greatest Detective, in <u>Murder in Northumberland</u> (West End 1974).

---

didn't quite know <u>which</u> character he was, Gillette or Holmes! It was an incredible merging he didn't know how to cope with.

I understand this very well, having played Holmes several times myself. I know how the character can affect your whole way of thinking. Suddenly I found myself deducing things, automatically starting to evaluate and observe matters as if I really were Holmes--"the observation of small things," as I believe Conan Doyle once explained it.

As a matter of fact, I can honestly say I liked playing Holmes. But then as an actor who's been around for a long time with only moderate success, I thought it would be great fun to hang my hat on the Holmes character; unlike Rathbone, who, as an international star with enormous popularity, was understandably annoyed for being identified with the same character over and over again.

I remember that Barry Fitzgerald's brother, Arthur
Shields, went through the same experience. We were doing
a play at the Los Angeles Civic Theatre, "The Plow and the
Stars," which had made him famous at the Abbey Theatre in
Dublin. A few months earlier, however, Shields had done a
wine commercial on television. But now--after 55 years as
a director and an actor--while he was again doing this famous
play by Sean O'Casey, he was approached one evening in a
restaurant by a group of people asking him for his autograph.
But ironically enough, not for his performance in the play
but because of the wine commercial.

It infuriated him so much he refused the fans' requests
and told them quietly, "No, no, that's not me...."

Speaking strictly as an actor, I feel I've been enriched
by playing Holmes, and I'd like playing him more because I
rather enjoy the blending of Holmes' character with my personality. He somehow does get into your blood, and if for
some reason you miss a Sherlock Holmes part, you get terribly incensed and disappointed because it is a Holmes part
you missed, unlike just missing other parts, which happens
to any actor.

Perhaps the most Holmes-haunted individual of all,
though, was Arthur Conan Doyle himself; and you can draw
an interesting analogy between Conan Doyle and Sir Arthur
Sullivan, who wrote all of the music for the Gilbert and Sullivan operettas, which enjoyed such tremendous fame during
the same period.

Conan Doyle and Sir Arthur Sullivan were contempor-
aries in many ways. Very interesting are the similarities
between them. They were both knighted; were both of Irish
origin, although Conan Doyle was Scottish born (at least they
were both Gaelic); and both had a dislike for the things that
made them famous. Arthur Sullivan wrote symphony after
symphony that never lived on, and Conan Doyle's histories
and other works, which he wrote so meticulously, are rarely
read; it's an extraordinary paradox that they both still enjoy
tremendous fame through the particular talents they really
despised. Doyle's son Adrian, in fact, once told me that no
one was permitted at the dinner table ever to mention Holmes'
name or his father would go into a fury.

In his later life Conan Doyle became an advocate of
spiritualism, attempting in every way to prove life after

death, and in a strange way the "figure" of Holmes has perhaps injected his influence more on Arthur Conan Doyle than
he ever imagined. In fact, he had killed off Sherlock Holmes,
you may remember, in Switzerland, but after running out of
money through his explorations into spiritualism, Doyle re-
surrected Holmes to generate new income.

I think it was quite deliberate that Conan Doyle never
brought Holmes into the occult in any of his stories. Con-
versely, it is ironic that "Holmes" in reverse had done exactly that for Conan Doyle. Not only did Holmes support
Conan Doyle's experimentations into spiritualism, but perhaps
in his own ways has kept Conan Doyle alive in the minds of
successive generations of the public.

Yes, you might say that despite Conan Doyle's obvious
dislike of Sherlock Holmes, it is directly through Holmes
that Doyle has achieved his greatest goal. Inasmuch as he
could never prove life after death in his own lifetime, it is
through Holmes, who is always with us in one art form or
another--books, plays, films and so on--that Conan Doyle
has shown there is, if not life after death, life without
death...

One

THE FIRST SHERLOCK HOLMES,
AND WHAT CAME AFTERWARDS

It began with a robbery at Baker Street. Armed with
a large sack, a thief had sneaked into the living room at
221B and immediately started looting the room of its valuables. Before the rascal could get away, though, Sherlock
Holmes stepped into the scene and a motion picture legend
was born.

The year was 1900, the very turn of the century, and
the film in which this sequence occurred was Sherlock Holmes
Baffled. Produced by Thomas Alva Edison's American Mutoscope & Biograph Company in New York City, the film had a
running time of only some thirty-five seconds, and technically, it wasn't a movie at all. Though it is true it had been
shot with a movie camera, Sherlock Holmes Baffled had originally been designed to show not in theatres but only in the
popular storefront and amusement center Mutoscope machines
of the era, and it has only been over the past few years that
this first of all Sherlock Holmes pictures has been recon-
verted back to movie film for more modern viewing with projectors. At that, if it hadn't been discovered that the Library of Congress in Washington, D.C., still actually had in
its archives a paper-print copy of this film, Edison's his-
toric Sherlock Holmes venture would still be considered lost.

Which is, unfortunately, the main problem with most
of the early Sherlock Holmes pictures: they are lost to the
ages. Today many exist only as titles, or perhaps story
synopses. Critical reviews of some have been unearthed by
dedicated scholars like Michael Pointer, William K. Everson,
Ronald Burt De Waal, Anthony Howlett, Cecil Ryder, and
Ray Cabana: clippings and bits of sometimes informative
print culled from the now yellowed, often brittle, and all-but-
forgotten pages of film magazines and show business trade
journals of the time.

1

Researching the Sherlock Holmes films made since 1900 has become like trying to reconstruct the history of Ancient Egypt or even the prehistoric past: some artifacts remain, but the life itself is long vanished.

Ironically though, for all the Holmes films that are lost, this very first Sherlock Holmes picture does exist and if one had the unenviable task of having to select only one of all the early, pre-talking Holmes films to let survive, it would have to be this one, Sherlock Holmes Baffled. It is, after all, the first of its kind, the first time Holmes ever stepped in front of a movie camera, and short in length though it may be, its very brevity makes it act like a sort of unique teaser to all the filmed adventures to come: still-existing film exploits made through the years with Moriarty, Spider Women, Loch Ness Monsters, and other terrors that have stalked the Holmesian screen since that debut year of the 20th century.

Besides being clearly the first screen appearance of Sherlock Holmes (and regardless of the fact it even predates the historically important Great Train Robbery film by three years), Edison's Holmes picture is also important because it's a very early example of motion picture trick photography. Confronting the thief at Baker Street, Sherlock Holmes and the audience are both equally startled to suddenly see the masked thief vanish from sight in the blink of an eye, and then just as suddenly reappear elsewhere in the living room at Baker Street. Then again the wily intruder pulls his vanishing act, but this time for good.

And faced, then, with this rather singular problem of a man who can appear and disappear at will, Sherlock Holmes, just before the end of the picture, turns to the camera at last to justify the title of the film: Holmes wears a very puzzled expression.

Directed by Arthur Marvin, Edison's Sherlock Holmes film was shot with only one set, and one straight-on, full-shot camera angle, and can be viewed time and again without boredom. It's fast, entertaining, and over before you would like it to be. It seems an elementary enough deduction to say that Edison, in fact, probably got the idea to make the film directly from William Gillette's stageplay, Sherlock Holmes: A Drama in Four Acts.

Written by Sir Arthur Conan Doyle and Gillette him-

William Gillette in Sherlock Holmes: A Drama in Four Acts, written by Gillette and Sir Arthur Conan Doyle, and first produced in 1899. (Courtesy Bond Street Books.)

self, the play had opened the year before at the Star Theatre
in Buffalo, New York, on October 23, 1899. Within two
weeks, however, Gillette had brought his play to New York
City, opening it at the Garrick Theatre where it immediately
began its long and sensationally popular big city run. Undoubtedly Edison, located right there in New York, simply
took notice of the play's enormous success and drawing power and decided, then, to also use Sherlock Holmes as a subject for drama, now for a moving picture. One particularly
strong point in favor of this argument is the fact that when
Holmes appears in Edison's film, he is wearing a long dressing gown that is highly reminiscent of the Baker Street wardrobe as introduced by William Gillette on stage.

Nowadays, the name of Basil Rathbone is synonymous
to the world with that of Sherlock Holmes, and most people
actually think Rathbone was the first movie Holmes (just as
most people think Johnny Weissmuller was the first movie
Tarzan, when he was in fact sixth). Rathbone, for all his
everlasting fame as the Great Detective, was hardly the first
film actor ever to take up a magnifying glass in pursuit of
criminals. That distinction of course falls on the shoulders
of the star of Sherlock Holmes Baffled--whoever he was.
Actually, no one knows his name. Edison's film contains
absolutely no cast credits whatsoever. We know the identity
of the second movie Holmes--Maurice Costello, in Vitagraph's
Adventures of Sherlock Holmes five years later--but exten-
sive research in the field has so far failed to bring to light
the name of the actor in the dressing gown in the Edison
film. That this first of all Sherlock Holmeses of the screen
should therefore be relegated to everlasting anonymity is--
like the thief robbing Baker Street in the film--also something very much of a crime.

Vitagraph's Adventures of Sherlock Holmes was released in 1905. Directed by J. Stuart Blackton, I Adventures
of Sherlock Holmes (subtitled Held for Ransom) was written
by Theodore Liebler and was eight minutes long. It starred
Maurice Costello, who went on to become a very popular
leading actor of the silent screen, and had Sherlock Holmes
rescuing a young woman from kidnappers. But if the film
was intended at all to be the first entry in a series of Sherlock Holmes films, the project was short-lived because Vitagraph, which was also located with Edison in New York City,
never did make any sequels. In fact, two years later when
they returned to the Holmes stories to film Caught, which
they based on the famous "Red-Headed League" adventure,

Maurice Costello starred in Vitagraph's Adventures of Sherlock Holmes--Held for Ransom (1905).   (Courtesy Jerry
Yung.)

---

they completely eliminated Sherlock Holmes from their script,
and instead substituted members of the New York Police Department for the Baker Street sleuth.

    The creation of an actual Sherlock Holmes film series,
then, was left to the Nordisk Film Company of Denmark,
who in 1908 began producing the first titles in the first
Holmes series of all.

    RELEASED BETWEEN 1908 and 1911, Nordisk's prec-
edent-setting series of Sherlock Holmes thrillers comprised
13 one- and two-reel adventures that gained for themselves
a wide popularity wherever they played in the world.

The first six Nordisk films were Sherlock Holmes in
Deathly Danger [also called Sherlock Holmes Risks His Life],
Raffles Escapes from Prison, The Secret Document [also
called both Sherlock Holmes in the Gas Cellar or The Theft
of the State Document], The Singer's Diamonds [also called
The Theft of the Diamonds] (1909), Cab No. 519 (1909), and
The Gray Dame (1909). All were written and directed by,
and starred, Viggo Larsen. A formidable-appearing man
who really looked not unlike William Gillette, Viggo Larsen
is actually the first actor of importance to become associated
with the role of Sherlock Holmes on screen; a part he was
eventually to play 14 times in all.

In general the 13 Nordisk adventures of Sherlock
Holmes were all highly melodramatic affairs, fast paced for
an action concept, and Viggo Larsen's first three films were
actually a kind of series within a series because they featured E. W. Hornung's master jewel thief Raffles as the
main villain. In the opener, Sherlock Holmes in Deathly
Danger, Raffles (played by Forrest Holger-Madsen) even
teamed up with Holmes' archenemy, Professor Moriarty
(Otto Dethlefsen), to do away with Holmes' interference once
and forever, but by the end of the story Holmes had captured
them both and sent them off to jail. Others in the cast of
this (and future Larsen films) included Elith Pio as Billy,
the Baker Street pageboy; Paul Gregaard, Gustav Lund, Aage
Brandt, and August Blom. Watson, though, was curiously
absent from the action, and in fact never did appear in any
of the Nordisk films.

"The photography of [Sherlock Holmes in Deathly
Danger] is of a superior quality, and the scenic effects [are]
quite ingenious and novel," the New York Dramatic Mirror
reviewed (December 19, 1908). "The plot is also interesting
and is developed with considerable skill and with reasonable
lucidity.... Too much, perhaps, is left to the spectator's
knowledge regarding the personalities of Sherlock Holmes,
Raffles and Moriarty [but] the story [nevertheless] holds the
attention strongly...." Comparing the acting styles of French
and American film actors with that on view in the Nordisk
film, the Mirror added that the "acting appears oddly stiff
... but it is mostly pleasantly devoid of the ridiculous over-
acting and contortions resorted to by so many pantomimists.
When Raffles is arrested, he does not throw a succession of
acrobatic fits and when Moriarty is taken, he is only reasonably violent in the hands of the officer...."

When Nordisk made their next Holmes film, <u>Raffles</u>
<u>Escapes from Prison</u>, they picked up the storyline from
<u>Sherlock Holmes in Deathly Danger</u> and showed Raffles break-
ing out of prison to plot anew. Professor Moriarty wasn't
in the adventure, however, and so the wily cracksman had to
go it alone against Holmes. But as may be expected, Raffles'
freedom was short-lived and by the end of the picture Holmes
captured him again, and then sent him back to jail. But in
the next film, <u>The Secret Document</u>, Raffles once more broke
out of prison, and so the game between Raffles and Holmes
was afoot again.

Besides E. W. Hornung and his character, Raffles,
Viggo Larsen's Nordisk films were also influenced to a great
degree by the William Gillette stageplay. In <u>The Secret</u>
<u>Document</u>, for example, Holmes was seen trapped by Raffles
and his gloating henchmen in a lethal gas chamber--a scene
that was famous in the Gillette play. Regardless, after the
adventure of <u>The Secret Document</u> Raffles was retired and
Holmes began taking on one-time villains like John Baxter,
the culprit in the fourth film, <u>The Singer's Diamonds</u>.

A ne'er-do-well whose parents had died when he was
a very young man, leaving him in turn a sizable fortune,
John Baxter (played by Paul Gregaard) went through his inheritance recklessly and when he discovered he was broke
he went to his uncle (August Blom) for help. His uncle refused to give him any money, but then foolishly showed him
a valuable diamond bracelet that he was going to present to
a famous opera singer (Aage Brandt). Naturally Baxter decided to steal the bracelet and later, getting into the singer's
house by climbing down an outside rope he'd hung from the
roof, Baxter hid behind a balcony door to wait for the girl
and the bracelet. But when "the singer enters the room ...
although she notices the figure behind the door, [she] keeps
very cool and collected, and walking to the telephone she
rings up Sherlock Holmes; but she has only time to call out
her name and scream before John has knocked her down.
He tears the bracelet from her arm ..." (<u>Bioscope</u>, January
27, 1910) and escapes up the rope. Driving to the singer's
house as quickly as possible, Sherlock Holmes "sees at once
what has been done, and without hesitating he climbs up the
rope to follow the thief. The latter cuts the rope, but Sherlock Holmes arrests him after a hot pursuit over several
roofs of houses...."

<u>Cab No. 519</u> was another action episode, but Larsen's

sixth and final Nordisk-Holmes film, The Grey Dame, was a
mystery of the supernatural variety about an ancient home-
stead where "there is the legend that whoever sees the Grey
Lady dies almost immediately. A nephew who wishes to obtain his uncle's title and property, dresses up as a ghostly
grey lady and appears before his uncle, who shortly afterward
dies. The inmates of the house are greatly alarmed, and as
the old man's son also sees the mysterious grey lady, Sherlock Holmes is summoned. Sir Arthur Conan Doyle's super-
human magician soon sets to work, and (unassisted by Watson) quickly obtains a clue. Secret doors and chambers reveal themselves to the wonderful wizard ..." (Bioscope,
September 2, 1909). Like all the Nordisk films, The Grey
Dame was also well received--it was "full of exciting move-
ments, and the plot is worked out with decision and sureness
of attack. There is not a lingering moment in the story,
which moves rapidly, tensely and convincingly, as all detective stories should. Above all it is exceedingly well acted
and then it has been very nicely set and mounted ..." (The
Moving Picture World, 1909, p. 344).

When Viggo Larsen left the Nordisk series after The
Grey Dame, Otto Lagoni took over as the new Holmes for
three more adventures: Sherlock Holmes in the Claws of the
Confidence Men [also called The Confidence Trick or The
Stolen Wallet], Sherlock Holmes Captured [also called The
Bogus Governess] and The Diamond Swindler, all released in
1910. Otto Lagoni had first played Holmes on stage in Wil-
liam Gillette's play in Denmark, in 1902.

The Lagoni films returned Sherlock Holmes to Nordisk's basic crime-action type of storyline, but without the
continuing villainies of the rascally Raffles. Elith Pio stayed
on as Billy the pageboy, with new players like Axel Boelsen
and Ellen Kornbech added to the casts, and the Lagoni films
(as well as all the remaining Holmes films in the series)
saw the sleuth going up against unconnected, one-time criminals like kidnappers, murderers, secret organizations and,
in general, thieves and turn-of-the-century outlaws of a
quality less dapper than that debonair cracksman, Raffles.
Throughout the series, though, the company retained their
trademark of usually fast moving action, and the films were
well received by audiences and critics alike.

In 1911 Nordisk released The Million Dollar Bond
[also called Sherlock Holmes' Masterpiece] with a new Holmes,
Alwin Neuss. Neuss also appeared in The Disguised Nurse,

but then left the series. Like Viggo Larsen, however, Neuss
went on to play Holmes in many more films for other studios,
and also carved himself a sizable fame as an early Sherlock
Holmes of the movies. His replacement at Nordisk was Holger Rasmussen, who finished out the series with The Murder
at Baker Street [also called The Conspirators or The Member
of the Black Hand] and then Sherlock Holmes' Last Exploit
[also called The Hotel Mystery].

But after releasing the Last Exploit film, Nordisk was
still not quite through with the Holmes stories. In 1912 they
returned to Baker Street to borrow "The Adventure of the
Norwood Builder" for The Hypnotic Detective, which introduced a new screen sleuth, Professor Locksley, who replaced
Holmes in the script. Professor Locksley's face, though,
was a familiar one to Holmesian doings because he was
played by none other than the studio's last Holmes, Holger
Rasmussen. Then in 1913 Nordisk featured Locksley in another tale borrowed from Baker Street, The Stolen Treaty,
which was based on "The Naval Treaty." Of all the Nordisk
films, however, only The Stolen Treaty seems to have survived the passage of time.

There were other Sherlock Holmes films appearing on
screen in 1908, the year the Nordisk organization in Denmark
initiated the first Holmes movie series. There were, in fact,
such films as Sherlock Holmes' Enemy, Sherlock Holmes in
the Great Murder Mystery, Sherlock Holmes, and the first of
all Holmesian comedies, Miss Sherlock Holmes. Actually the
year was a banner year for Holmes on screen, and marked
the detective's first emergence as a genuine superstar of films.

The first of the other 1908 releases was Sherlock
Holmes' Enemy [also called Rival Sherlock Holmes]. Produced by Ambrosia Films, an Italian company, Sherlock
Holmes' Enemy received a wide distribution and was well received in the United States, "a pictorial detective story of
merit, with many lightning changes of disguise by the detective in his pursuit of the lawbreakers. Exciting scenes and
physical encounters are numerous. A sensational subject of
superb dramatic effect ..." (The Moving Picture World,
May 2, 1908). Then came Sherlock Holmes, a Hungarian
film that seems to have been released only in Europe. It
starred Bauman Karoly as the Great Detective. The most
important of these three other 1908 Holmes films was, however, Sherlock Holmes in the Great Murder Mystery: important to the saga of Holmes on screen not only because

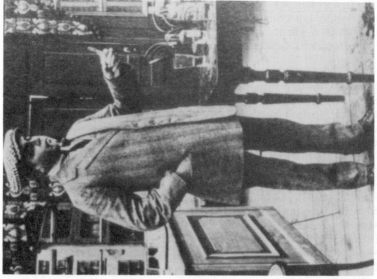

it is the first known appearance of Watson in any of the films,
but also because the picture was a literary crossover with,
ironically enough, a detective story that had greatly influenced
Conan Doyle when he first began creating the private inquiry
agent he finally named Sherlock Holmes. [2]

Released in America by Crescent Films, Sherlock
Holmes in the Great Murder Mystery was a Danish film
based on Edgar Allan Poe's "The Murders in the Rue Morgue."
The picture saw Holmes taking on the part played by Poe's
detective, C. Auguste Dupin, in the tale, and then solving
Poe's classic mystery about a series of brutal murders that
Holmes, now, shortly discovers to be the work of an escaped
gorilla. "Through circumstantial evidence a young man is
accused [of the murders] and is just about to be convicted
when through the aid of our hero, Sherlock Holmes, he is
freed just in time ..." (The Moving Picture World, November 28, 1908). In Crescent's film adaptation of the story,
it was Watson himself who directed Holmes to initially try
his hand at cracking the rather inexplicable mystery.

As in the case of the actor who played Holmes in
Edison's Sherlock Holmes Baffled, the name of the actor
playing Watson in Sherlock Holmes in the Great Murder
Mystery is lost to the ages. In the early days of picture-
making, studios practically never gave billing to the actors
and actresses in their films, believing that audiences were
only interested in the film as a whole and cared little who
was playing whom. Films were still considered a novelty,
and the star system had not yet been born.

About the Holmesian comedy of 1908, though, it is
interesting to note that Edison, who was the first to bring
Sherlock Holmes to the screen, was also the first to use
Sherlock Holmes, or at least the sleuth's name, for comedy
purposes too. Edison's Miss Sherlock Holmes that year told
of the humorous exploits of a lady detective who single-hand-
edly took on a gang of crooks, and later Edison was again
(and again) to resort to such Holmesian parodies for the screen;
even more so, in fact, with his films about the Biograph Sleuths.

Opposite, left: Otto Lagoni in Sherlock Holmes Captured
(Nordisk 1910). Right: The Disguised Nurse (Nordisk 1911)
starred Alwin Neuss as Holmes and Elith Pio as Billy, the
Baker Street pageboy. (Both photos courtesy of Eddie
Brandt's Saturday Matinee.)

The first series of Holmesian comedies was produced
the following year. Released by Cosmo Pictures in England,
The Exploits of Three-Fingered Kate and Three-Fingered
Kate, Her Second Victim were directed by H. O. Martinek,
and starred Charles Calvert as Sheerluck Finch, a detective
who was forever tracking down the villainous Three-Fingered
Kate, played by Ivy Martinek. In the first film, Kate and
her accomplice Mary (Alice Moseley) stole jewels, and in the
second film they were trying to pass counterfeit money.

It was a popular series that continued with Three-
Fingered Kate, Her Victim the Banker and The Episode of
the Sacred Elephants in 1910, and The Wedding Presents,
The Case of the Chemical Fumes, and The Pseudo-Quartette
in 1912.

Italy's Sherlock Holmes and France's The Latest Triumph of Sherlock Holmes were also released in 1909. The
former was produced by the Italia Film Company, who also
made their own Holmes comedy that year, The Little Sherlock Holmes. There was also another Edison comedy, A
Squeedunk Sherlock Holmes, and a British Clarendon one-
reeler called Bobby the Boy Scout; or, The Boy Detective.
Directed by Percy Stowe, the latter was about a valiant boy
scout named Bobby, who, playing sleuth, went after a gang
of burglars and eventually managed to round them up.

The year also saw the first film adventures of Sexton
Blake and Nick Carter. Created by Harry Blyth in 1893 as
a sort of Sherlock Holmes for boy readers, Sexton Blake was
very much modeled after the Baker Street sleuth and, in
fact, even lived on Baker Street. Blake had a landlady
named Mrs. Bardell, a bloodhound named Pedro, and an assistant named Tinker, who usually accompanied Blake on his
many exploits. Unlike Dr. Watson, however, Tinker wasn't
an assistant roughly Blake's age but a young chap for all the
boys in the audience to identify with. Tinker was, actually,
rather like Robin the Boy Wonder in Batman comic books.

A character whose popularity continues today, though
as always primarily in England, Sexton Blake made his film
debut in Gaumont's 1909 Sexton Blake, a two-reel adventure
written and directed by C. Douglas Carlile, who also starred
as the detective. Sexton Blake saw the intrepid sleuth rescuing a squire's daughter from unknowingly marrying a criminal, Roger Blackburn, played by Russell Barry, and the
film was followed by another Blake adventure two months

later. Produced by the London Cinematograph Company, The
Council of Three was directed by S. Wormald and again starred C. Douglas Carlile as Blake. This time Blake saved a
kidnapped girl from a trio of blackguards who had formed an
extortion ring.

America's Nick Carter has also had an incredibly long
life. In more recent times, Carter in novels has become a
super-spy in the tradition of James Bond, but when he was
created by editor Ormond G. Smith and writer John Russell
Corydell in 1886 he was a private detective whose exploits
were filled with amazing action and deduction, though never
enough deduction to slow down the fast-paced stories. Nick
Carter actually predates Sherlock Holmes by one year,[3] and
if Carter has one particularly outstanding trademark in his
many stories, dime novels and later pulp magazines, besides
furious action and hairbreadth escapes, it was that he was
really the unequalled master of disguise. Nick Carter could
make himself up to look like anybody, anytime, anywhere,
and he first burst to life on the screen in 1909. It was a
serial, The Adventures of Nick Carter, made in France and
starring Andre Liabel, who then continued playing Carter in
later cliffhangers.

FILMED IN GERMANY in 1910, Vitascope's Arsene
Lupin vs Sherlock Holmes was a series of one- and two-
reelers that returned Viggo Larsen to the role of Holmes,
which he had left after six films with the Nordisk company
of Denmark two years earlier. Based on the book by Maurice LeBlanc, the five separate films that made up the Arsene Lupin vs Sherlock Holmes series costarred Paul Otto
as Lupin, and saw Holmes coming to Paris to combat the
various schemes of France's national thief.

A great admirer of Conan Doyle and Sherlock Holmes,
Maurice LeBlanc had originally written Holmes into a Lupin
short story called "Herlock Sholmes Comes Too Late," published in the book Arsene Lupin, Gentleman Burglar in 1907.
But after realizing what a good time he'd had introducing
Sherlock Holmes into his Lupin story, LeBlanc decided to
follow it up with a whole book about Holmes and Lupin: Arsene Lupin vs Herlock Sholmes, published the next year.
The stories were eventually purchased by Vitascope Pictures
in Germany, and then made into the series Arsene Lupin vs
Sherlock Holmes. LeBlanc would probably have loved to have
used Holmes' real name instead of the humorous play on the

name in his own stories, but copyright laws concerning published works were quite strict even in those days.   Copyright
laws concerning movies and film adaptations, however, were
anything but strict back then, if in many portions of the
world they existed at all; and so when Vitascope turned the
Holmes-Lupin stories into films they reverted right straight
back to LeBlanc's original inspirations and called their film,
and its Baker Street sleuth, by their proper names.

        Directed by Viggo Larsen himself, the <u>Arsene Lupin</u>
<u>vs Sherlock Holmes</u> series was actually quite a bit like the
Holmes-Raffles films Larsen had made while he was at Nordisk in Denmark.   Caught in one episode, or at least foiled
in his plans, Arsene Lupin was only to be seen returning to
light-hearted criminal activity in the next, once more challenging the prowess of England's Sherlock Holmes.   The episodes were <u>The Old Secretaire,</u> <u>The Blue Diamond,</u> <u>The Fake</u>
<u>Rembrandts,</u> <u>Arsene Lupin's Escape,</u> and <u>The Finish of Ar-</u>
<u>sene Lupin</u>, and they quite smoothly followed LeBlanc's orig-
inal stories: <u>The Old Secretaire</u> had Holmes chasing Lupin
after the thief had stolen an antique secretaire that also contained a prize-winning lottery ticket;   <u>The Blue Diamond</u> had
Madame Real, Lupin's comely associate, robbing Ambassador
Baron d'Hautrec of a famous blue diamond that formed part
of the royal crown of France; and <u>The Fake Rembrandts</u> had
Holmes taking after Lupin after the thief had stolen valuable
paintings and then substituted phony ones.

        <u>Arsene Lupin's Escape</u> saw Holmes thinking he'd
trapped Lupin in a house in Paris, but the thief cleverly escaped, and the final adventure, <u>The Finish of Arsene Lupin,</u>
saw Holmes at last locking Lupin up behind bars, at least
for a little while.

        Like the LeBlanc stories themselves, the films about
Arsene Lupin battling Sherlock Holmes were also very popular, and in 1912 they even inspired the production of a stageplay in Madrid.   Years later, in 1945, urged on by the new
successes of the Universal Pictures series of Sherlock Holmes
thrillers starring Basil Rathbone and Nigel Bruce,[4] and also
recalling the famous Holmes-Lupin stories that had once so
fascinated not only France, England and Germany, but most
of the rest of the world as well, Pereda Films in Mexico
returned to those combats with <u>Arsene Lupin,</u> a feature about
the master thief that included, as one of its elements, an
adaptation of LeBlanc's first Holmes-Lupin story, "Herlock
Sholmes Comes Too Late."   Where Holmes arrived too late

was a castle that Lupin had already successfully looted of its family treasures.

But after finishing the last title in their Arsene Lupin vs Sherlock Holmes film series, neither Vitascope nor Viggo Larsen ever made any followup pictures about Holmes and Lupin. Vitascope and Larsen did reunite later in 1911, though, for Sherlock Holmes vs Professor Moriarty, which marked another very early screen appearance of the Napoleon of Crime. But in a very great way Sherlock Holmes vs Professor Moriarty was still something of a return to the Holmes-Lupin films: Moriarty was played here by none other than Paul Otto, Arsene Lupin himself.

Hemlock Hoax, the Detective was also released in 1910. A one-reeler from America's Lubin Pictures, Hemlock Hoax was another in the long and ever-growing line of comedies that were having fun with sleuths whose names were similar to Holmes; in this case, a detective whose sleuthing was something of a joke to the people in the little town where he lived. The misadventure was about a couple of local boys who decided they were going to have some laughs at Hoax' expense, and so they ran to him with news of a terrible murder. Going to the scene of the "crime," Hoax saw the dead body and then after following up a clue, he arrested a tramp. But when he took the tramp back to the murder site, Hoax discovered to his amazement that the dead body was "merely a dummy stuffed with leaves" (Bioscope, May 26, 1910), after which he punished the boys properly for pulling such a stunt.

The year 1910 also saw the release of two more Sexton Blake films. Produced by the London Cinematograph Company, Lady Candale's Diamonds was written and directed by S. Wormald and returned C. Douglas Carlile to the role of Blake again. In this third film, Blake was up against a band of jewel thieves who had stolen the Lady Candale's diamonds from her home, and although the next Carlile-Blake film sounded like the second part of the Candale adventure, or at least a sequel to it, it wasn't. Produced by Gaumont in 1910, The Jewel Thieves Run to Earth by Sexton Blake was an entirely different film, although this picture too saw Blake chasing jewel thieves. In this fourth film adventure, Blake was tracking a gang of jewel thieves who had robbed a jeweler and then left the man's helpless clerk facing cold-blooded death by a clock mechanism that fired a gun.

The popular Holmes-Lupin films, however, inspired other moviemakers to start making Sherlock Holmes films, with France, Lupin's home country, in fact producing two new Holmes thrillers before even that year of 1911 was out. These films were Sherlock Holmes Cheated by Rigadin (who was a thief in the style of Arsene Lupin) and Adventures of Sherlock Holmes, starring Henri Gouget. Both films were made by the Eclair Company, a studio that was shortly to begin a very important association with Sherlock Holmes.

The year 1911 also saw the release of Sherlock Holmes Jr., a Rex Films comedy starring Helen Anderson, and other Holmesian parodies like Britain's A Case for Sherlock Holmes, directed by A. E. Coleby, and Italy's The Stolen Necklace, produced by the Ambrosia company. The most important Holmesian comedies released that year were, however, $500 Reward, Trailing the Counterfeiter, Their First Divorce Case, and Caught with the Goods--the first four Biograph Pictures entries in what proved to be a long-running series of very popular comedies directed by and starring a man who was shortly to become known the world over as the most famous silent movie comedy producer-director of all time. His name was Mack Sennett.

THE BIOGRAPH SLEUTHS, as they were originally called, were played by Mack Sennett and Fred Mace, who throughout their 11 Holmes-inspired comedies dressed up in deerstalkers and long touring-car coats, and smoked big, curving pipes. In every one of their one-reel misadventures they almost catch their man, the $500 Reward in 1911 setting the standard for all the zany exploits to come.

In $500 Reward, the Biograph Sleuths were hot on the trail of a notorious burglar, whom they wanted to catch so they could collect the $500 reward money. But instead of capturing the crook, the two manage to arrest not only one of the thief's own victims but also another detective working on the case. At the climax, an ordinary policeman finally collars the elusive villain and wins the prize.

The Biograph Sleuths continued their bungling exploits that year with Trailing the Counterfeiter, in which they blew a hole in a police station because they thought it was the counterfeiter's hideout; Their First Divorce Case, which had them trailing the wrong woman (they were tracking the wife who had hired them, and not her husband's secret girlfriend); and Caught with the Goods, where they successfully rounded

Mack Sennett (right) and Fred Mace as the Biograph Sleuths
in Their First Divorce Case (1911).   (Courtesy Eddie Brandt's
Saturday Matinee.)

---

up the town's Vice Committee, mistakenly thinking the Committee to be the crooks they were chasing.

These films were all produced in New York City by
Edison's Biograph company, but after making one more
Sleuths film for Edison, Their First Kidnapping Case in 1912,
Mack Sennett and Fred Mace left the east coast for Califor-
nia, where Sennett started making his own pictures.   In
California he founded Keystone Films, now a legendary name
in motion picture comedy history, and almost immediately
started making some more new Sleuths films.

At It Again and A Bear Escape continued the Sleuths'
saga in 1912, and the only real differences between the new
films and the earlier ones--besides the obvious one that the
two detectives were no longer called "The Biograph Sleuths"
but simply "The Sleuths"--were that Sennett was now his own

producer and had his own studio, and there were some new
faces in the supporting casts (including Ford Sterling and
Mabel Normand) as well as fresh, California locales. Besides making these Sleuths films, though, Mack Sennett was
also turning out many other kinds of comedies in his slap-
stick style; films that justifiably started earning him the all-
around nickname of King of Comedy. But it still wasn't until the following year that Sennett made his last group of
Sleuth epics: The Stolen Purse, The Sleuths' Last Stand
(with the two detectives disguised as Indian squaws), The
Sleuths at the Floral Parade, and Their First Execution.
Then Sennett went on with other comedic conquests.

The sweeping success of the Sleuths films urged many
other studios also to burlesque Sherlock Holmes. Even right
in the midst of Sennett's series in 1912 there was Imp Pictures' The Flag of Distress, which was a Sherlocko and Rueben Wilson comedy starring H. S. Mack and J. W. Compson;
Powers Films' Baby Sherlock, Thanhouser's Surelock Jones,
and Champion's The Robbery at the Railroad Station, another
film using the comic name of Sherlocko for its lead character. In The Robbery at the Railroad Station, however, Sherlocko's companion in mystery detection was not a Rueben
Wilson, but simply a Dr. Watso.

Other 1912 comedies or takeoffs on Holmes included
Pathé's A Midget Sherlock Holmes, and Britain's Urbana
Trading Company's production of A Canine Sherlock Holmes,
directed by Stuart Kinder and starring Spot, the famous Urbana dog, on the scent of silent movie crime. There was
also a series of Charlie Colms films, while the following
year, 1913, saw the birth of yet another series of Holmesian
lampoons: the Burstup Homes pictures. Produced by Solax
Films, the series included Burstup Homes, Burstup Homes'
Murder Case, The Mystery of the Lost Cat, and The Case
of the Missing Girl.

That year 1913 also saw famous movie heroines like
Pearl White and Bliss Milford getting into the act. Miss
White, the serial queen, starred in both The Amateur Sleuth
and Homlock Shermes, while Miss Milford's comedy, The
Sherlock Holmes Girl, another Edison misadventure, saw her
playing yet another female investigator tracking down crooks.

NOTES

[1] In 1922, Blackton directed England's first color feature film,
The Glorious Adventure, about a great fire in London.
The film was produced by Stoll Films, who at that
time was having great success with an Adventures of
Sherlock Holmes movie series. One of the cast of
players featured in Blackton's The Glorious Adventure
was Cecil Humphreys, who was also appearing in
quite a number of the Stoll Sherlock Holmes films.

[2] At one point in the beginning of it all, Conan Doyle had considered naming his detective "Sherringford Holmes,"
while Dr. Watson had been jotted down in the author's
notebook under the name of one "Ormond Sacker."

[3] Nick Carter first appeared in print in The New York Weekly
newspaper, on September 18, 1886. Sherlock Holmes
first appeared in print in Beeton's Christmas Annual
for 1887.

[4] In 1944 in the midst of their Sherlock Holmes films with
Rathbone and Bruce, Universal Pictures also produced
an Arsene Lupin film. Directed by Ford Beebe,
Enter Arsene Lupin starred Charles Korvin as Lupin,
and J. Carroll Naish as Police Inspector Ganimard,
Lupin's traditional foe. Enter Arsene Lupin was
written by Bertram Millhauser, who wrote many of
the studio's better Holmes films, and featured in the
cast was Gale Sondergaard, who had recently finished
starring as the infamous Adrea Spedding in Universal's
Holmes film, The Spider Woman.

Two

A HOUND IT WAS

Without question the most famous of all Sherlock
Holmes stories is the one about The Hound of the Baskervilles, that phantom devil dog of the West Country of Devonshire whose curse of violent death had for centuries fallen
upon the Baskerville family during those dark hours of the
night when the powers of evil are exalted. A classic of
mystery and horror, it seems certain, in fact, that if Conan
Doyle had never written another Sherlock Holmes adventure,
the names of both Conan Doyle and Sherlock would be world
renowned for this one alone.

The first screen version of The Hound of the Baskervilles was produced in 1914, only 13 years after Conan Doyle
had first published the story in serial form in The Strand
Magazine, and to date there have been as many as nine other
productions: seven for the theatre screen, and two for the
home screen. (There was also Murder at the Baskervilles,
but this was not a true adaptation of the novel. See Chapter
Six.) How Conan Doyle ever came to write this legendary
novel about a legendary hound of horror, is as interesting as
the story itself, which was not entirely a product of the author's own vivid imagination but actually a tale based on a
real-enough Devonshire legend.

It was B. Fletcher Robinson who first told Conan
Doyle about the legend of a hell-hound that was supposedly
roaming the West Country. A promising young journalist and
a friend of Conan Doyle's through literary circles, Robinson
was in 1901 living near Ippleton in Devonshire, and when
Conan Doyle vacationed at Robinson's home, Parkhill, that
year, the two of them spent many an hour driving by horse
and carriage over the surrounding countryside and moors.
During their drives, Robinson started telling the author various tales of local legend and, in particular, Conan Doyle
was struck by one such legend about a giant hound.

20

Basil Rathbone in the 1939 <u>Hound of the Baskervilles</u> (Fox).
(Courtesy George Morgan Collection.)

According to Robinson, the legend had begun in the
17th century.   Sir Richard Cabell, Lord of the Manor of
Brooke and a man of the West Country whose evil reputation
was very well known, was an extremely jealous husband.
Cabell had one night accused his wife of having an affair with
a man of Buckfastleigh, and though Lady Cabell denied it,
Cabell became vicious with her, thrashing her mercilessly.
Breaking away from him, and escaping their house, she
started fleeing for her life across the surrounding moors,
swept by chill winds from the even bleaker regions of nearby
Dartmoor.   Moments later Cabell overtook her and in a rage
murdered her with one of his hunting knives.

Then came the hound.

Recounting the legend to Conan Doyle as they drove
over the very same desolate moors where the legend had begun, B. Fletcher Robinson said that the hound was Lady Cabell's own, a large and faithful dog that had leaped after
Cabell when he ran out after his wife on the moor.   As

Cabell slew her, the hound madly attacked and killed him.
In the fierce struggle, however, the hound itself was fatally
wounded by Cabell's slashing knife, and the next day on the
moor the people of the village found the animal lying dead
alongside its slain mistress.

Since that time, Robinson recounted, local legend had
it that the ghost of Lady Cabell's hound often stalked the
moors on nights of the full moon, howling for its slain mistress.   Many superstitious locals, in fact, claimed they had
actually seen the phantom hound; others said that although
they hadn't ever seen the hound themselves, they had most
certainly heard its wailing bay of torment echoing out over the
countryside.

Such, at any rate, was the legend of the hound that
Robinson told Conan Doyle, and creatively excited by this
strange tale the author started writing his own version of the
story, now involving Sherlock Holmes and Dr. Watson in the
singular adventure of the Baskerville family, whose men for
centuries had been variously plagued and murdered by a hor-
rifying devil hound that glowed in the night; a family whose
youngest and sole-surviving male, Sir Henry Baskerville, was
even then, right in Holmes' own time, also confronted with
the hound's terrible curse of death.

Conan Doyle's inspiration for the name of Baskerville
also came while he was vacationing at Fletcher Robinson's
family home at Ippleton in Devonshire.

With the gracious permission of Harry Baskerville--
who was Robinson's very own groom, and who had been driving Conan Doyle and Robinson by horse and carriage over the
moors--Conan Doyle borrowed the name to use for the cursed
family in what has certainly become his most celebrated novel
of all.

GERMANY'S VITASCOPE PICTURES company produced
the first <u>Hound of the Baskervilles</u> film, in 1914.   Directed
by Rudolph Meinert, the picture starred Alwin Neuss as Sherlock Holmes, but there was no Watson in the story.   Neuss
had originally played Holmes at Nordisk in Denmark three
years earlier.   Others in the cast of this <u>Hound</u> four-reeler
included Erwin Fichtner as Lord Henry Baskerville, Friedrich Kuhne as Stapleton, Andreas Van Horne as Barrymore
the butler, and Hanni Weiss as Laura Lyons.   Richard

Oswald wrote the script and though it followed Conan Doyle's novel rather closely, there were some changes made.

The film had it that according to local legend, the Baskerville family was everlastingly linked with the ghostly appearances of a huge black hound that was sometimes seen racing over the countryside. Whenever the hound appeared, it was supposed to mean danger for the family and so when Sir Charles Baskerville was found dead with his throat torn out by the fangs of a savage animal, no one at Baskerville Hall was greatly surprised and immediately the fearsome, spectral Hound was blamed for Sir Charles' death. But because the man's heir, Lord Henry Baskerville, was nevertheless greatly concerned about such goings-on, he took it upon himself to call in Mr. Sherlock Holmes. He did this by writing a letter to Holmes; a letter which he gave to Stapleton, his caretaker, to post.

But Stapleton "destroys the letter," according to Clifford H. Pangburn in Motion Picture News (March 6, 1915) "and appears [to Lord Henry] disguised as Sherlock Holmes. Unfortunately for [Stapleton], the real detective reads a notice of his supposed presence at Baskerville, and proceeds to investigate. The great detective at once discovers that the man who is impersonating him is the caretaker. After an astonishing series of adventures in which the criminal nearly does away with the detective ... many concealed doors, trick chairs, and underground passages ... the real Hound of the Baskervilles is discovered in his secret den, where Stapleton had kept him. He is killed and the murderer arrested, when it is further discovered that he is the disinherited nephew of the former Earl, and that his elaborate schemes had all been in an attempt to obtain the estate by killing off the rightful owners."

The Hound itself was "a monstrous Great Dane, with flaming eyes and fire oozing from its mouth" (Motography, March 6, 1915), and the film was a great success. Such a success, in fact, that Vitascope went right ahead that same year and made a sequel film that really was a sequel: The Isolated House picked up exactly where the original film had left off.

Featuring Alwin Neuss as Holmes again, and returning others to the same roles they'd played in the first film, The Isolated House began with Stapleton's (actually Roger Baskerville) being condemned to death for the crimes he'd committed

in the previous film.   But he managed to overpower his guard,
escape prison, and take up residence near Baskerville Hall.
Then he disguised himself and went to Baskerville Castle
where he introduced himself as Loris Collamore, a new
neighbor.   By this time Lord Henry had taken a wife, the
former Laura Lyons, and shortly Stapleton succeeded in lur-
ing them both to a unique submersible house he'd built in a
nearby lake.   He made them his prisoners, then returned to
Baskerville Castle saying he was Lord Henry's relative, and
that he was taking over now.   But the servants were suspicious of him, and called in Sherlock Holmes, who traced
Lord and Lady Baskerville to the submersible house.

Quite an invention, the submersible house could be
sunk beneath the surface of the lake or raised above the surface by two controlling levers.   But when Holmes broke into
the place to rescue the prisoners, Stapleton was on hand and
sank the house beneath the water.   A fight ensued, a window
was broken, and water started coming in.

Stapleton wanted "them all to drown like rats in a trap,
but Holmes finds the lever that raises the house and rescues
the Baskervilles," George D. Proctor said, reviewing the sequel in Motion Picture News, July 17, 1915.   "When they are
on dry land he tries to go back to arrest the steward [Staple-
ton], but the house with the steward inside sinks back under
the water before his eyes.   This affords excellent melodrama.
The disappearing house is very interesting.   In addition, the
picture is well produced and has fine photography."

Nor was The Isolated House the last of the films inspired by the success of Vitascope's original The Hound of
the Baskervilles.   More sequels were made over the next
few years, original Holmes screen stories that carried over
the characters and basic settings from the Conan Doyle novel.

How the Hound of the Baskervilles Returned and The
Uncanny Room continued the saga in 1915.   Stapleton returned
to life in these new adventures, always plotting more evil.
After The Uncanny Room, however, Alwin Neuss left what
had become a Hound movie series to make other Holmes films
at other studios.   Eugene Burge then took on the role of
Holmes in The Dark Castle, but was replaced by Erich Kaisertitz in the next film, Dr. MacDonald's Sanitarium.   Kaisertitz also played Holmes in the final Hound adventure, The
House Without Any Windows, released in 1916.   The directors
and writers, and some of the cast, also switched around in
the later films.

Richard Oswald, who had only written the first few films, both wrote and directed How the Hound of the Basker-villes Returned and The Uncanny Room before leaving to make other Holmes films elsewhere. The Dark Castle was then written by Robert Liebman and directed by Willy Zehn. Zehn stayed with the series for the last two entries, Dr. MacDon-ald's Sanitarium and The House Without Any Windows, but Paul Rosenhaym replaced Robert Liebmann as writer on both films. Along the way, Friedrich Kuhne (Barrymore) and An-dreas Van Horne (Lady Baskerville née Laura Lyons), among others, also dropped out and were replaced in the final films.

Overall though, the Hound series was unique and can be likened to television's Dark Shadows series, where strange events and even stranger characters kept turning up time and again at Collinwood, the mansion in Dark Shadows that was the focal point of all the goings-on. Besides the importance of the first Hound film, and the series in general, to the story of Sherlock Holmes on screen, Vitascope's original 1914 production of The Hound of the Baskervilles is also ex-tremely noteworthy because it represents one of the earliest Holmes films actually to come from an original Conan Doyle story. For years studios around the world had been creating their own original screen tales for Sherlock Holmes, and not paying much attention at all to the published stories. But the decade that saw the first filming of The Hound of the Basker-villes actually became characterized by just such adaptations. Some of these screen versions, like the Vitascope film, were not authorized versions, but many others were. The very first of the Conan Doyle adaptations that emerged during these years were, in fact, not only fully authorized productions, but enjoyed the participation of the creator himself of the world's most famous consulting detective.

STOKE MORAN, the ancestral home of the villainous Dr. Grimesby Roylott on the western border of Surrey, was the foreboding locale for The Speckled Band, the opening en-try in the first series of Conan Doyle film adaptations. The year was 1912, the series itself was called simply Sherlock Holmes, and it was produced by the Franco-British Film Company. M. Georges Treville starred as Sherlock Holmes, Mr. Moyse played Watson, and there were eight two-reelers in all.

"The most interesting fact in connection with these ad-ventures of the greatest detective in modern fiction is that

Dr. A. Conan Doyle, the popular creator, himself supervised
the production," G. F. Blaisdell wrote that year (The Moving
Picture World, November 23, 1912). "This will give satis-
faction to the thousands of readers of these absorbing tales
who at this time may not be followers of motion pictures. That
these reproductions on the screen of some of the more important
incidents in the career of the mythical detective-scientist will
bring to the picture houses a new clientele goes without saying.
If the others in the series are of the same standard as that main-
tained through 'The Speckled Band' the new-comers in filmdom
are bound to be favorably impressed...."

"[M. Treville's] conception of Holmes will be of the
greatest interest, perhaps, to those who have followed the
detective through his many adventures. If the filmed inter-
pretations shall show more of animation and less of taciturn-
ity than was expected, allowance must be made for the absence of speech and the necessity for sufficient action ade-
quately to indicate the intentions as well as the observations
of the actor...."

The Bioscope trade magazine also praised The Speckled
Band and the series in general. "[The films] are played by
the same company and taken amidst the surroundings which
have been so graphically described by the author. The scen-
ery, which is very beautiful, is shown to the greatest advan-
tage by the most perfect photography, and the uniform excel-
lence of the cast adds greatly to the interest of the subjects
(September 18, 1913)...."

Besides The Speckled Band, the Franco-British Holmes
series also included Silver Blaze, with Holmes solving the
mystery of a prize race horse that vanished; The Mystery of
Boscombe Vale, where Holmes investigated the baffling murder of McCarthy in a country district near Herefordshire;
The Copper Beeches, in which Miss Violet Hunter, a governess, asked Sherlock Holmes to look into the very odd goings-
on at the home of Jephro Rucastle in Hampshire; The Stolen
Papers, which was based on the story "The Adventure of the

Opposite, left: Trade advertisement for The Speckled Band
and Silver Blaze, Eclair's first two titles in their 1912
Holmes adaptations. (From The Bioscope, September 18,
1913.) Right: Georges Treville as Holmes in The Speckled
Band (Eclair 1912). (From The Moving Picture World,
November 23, 1912.)

Naval Treaty," and saw Percy Phelps of the Foreign Office
begging Holmes to locate a secret British-Italian treaty that
had been entrusted to his care and then stolen from his office; The Musgrave Ritual, which had Holmes solving a remarkable case at Musgrave Manor in western Sussex; The
Beryl Coronet, in which banker Alexander Holder hired
Holmes to find a valuable coronet that disappeared; and The
Reigate Squires, in which Holmes tackled a series of inexplicable burglaries in Surrey.

All the films followed the original stories very closely,
although Watson didn't appear in some of the early titles.
There was also a slight deviation in adaptation with The
Beryl Coronet film, which now saw Professor Moriarty as the
mastermind behind the theft of the valuable coronet. Besides
playing Holmes in the series, however, Treville also directed
the films, which featured an all-English cast except for himself (he was French). The stories were taken from Conan
Doyle's books of The Adventures of Sherlock Holmes and The
Memoirs of Sherlock Holmes, and it is significant that beginning with these Franco-British (Eclair) films practically every
Sherlock Holmes film, television show or radio program made
in England since 1912 has been based--and rather faithfully--
on one of the Conan Doyle stories. There has really been
very little Sherlock Holmes screen-originality coming from
England. One reason for this is the tight control usually
exercised by the Conan Doyle Estate over all British Holmes
productions. The Estate seems to be primarily concerned
with the idea that Sherlock Holmes should, and should only,
be portrayed in exploits taken directly from the original
stories. When leasing screen rights to other countries, however, the Estate's control or concern seems to lessen a bit.
A case in point here would be the series of Universal films
made in America in the 1940s starring Basil Rathbone and
Nigel Bruce. Although the Estate granted Holmesian screen
rights to Universal, the films were hardly faithful adaptations
of any of the stories, even though the original contract had
called for a certain number of the Universal films to be
taken directly from Conan Doyle's works. The Universal
films were nearly entirely original screenplays from start to
finish, although certain incidents or characters in these
scripts did come from the stories themselves.

For the most part, this kind of Holmes film production
could never have happened had these films been made in England. (The Arthur Wontner films of Sherlock Holmes made
in England in the 1930s are virtually the only exception. See
Chapter Six.)

The Franco-British Sherlock Holmes series, though,
was actually Conan Doyle's first contact with the world of
movie making, and the success of these films in America,
England and elsewhere soon enough opened up yet more film
prospects for Conan Doyle's books and stories. The very
next year, in fact, Doyle signed contracts for another adaptation, this time with the London Film Company for the production of The House of Temperley, produced and directed
by Harold Shaw, and starring Charles Maude as Captain Jack
Temperley. The House of Temperley was based on the author's novel Rodney Stone, and in 1915 he signed more contracts for more films: with Barker Films Ltd. for Brigadier
Gerard, directed by Bert Haldane and starring Lewis Waller
as Gerard, and then again with the London Film Company
for a second Harold Shaw production, The Firm of Girdlestone, starring Fred Graves as Ezra Girdlestone, and
Charles Rock as John Girdlestone.

Later years would see even more non-Holmes books
and stories by Conan Doyle being turned into pictures; including, even, a one-time talking screen appearance by Doyle
himself, in which he would talk openly about Sherlock Holmes
and his then favorite subject, spiritualism.

It was the critical and financial success of the Franco-
British Sherlock Holmes series that urged other studios and
producers also to start thinking along the lines of adapting
Holmes stories to the screen, rather than developing completely original screen stories about the detective. Before
the decade was out, in fact, all four of Doyle's Sherlock
Holmes novels became motion pictures too.

The year of the Franco-British series also saw the
release of Diabolical, More Diabolical, and The Most Diabol-
ical, an Eclipse film made in France that teamed Sherlock
Holmes up with Nick Carter, Nat Pinkerton of America's
Pinkerton Detective Agency, and Nick Winter, a popular
French hero. The half-hour exploit had the four sleuths
tracking down and then capturing a jewel thief aboard a train.
There was also a new Sexton Blake thriller that year; produced by England's Humanity Story Films, Sexton Blake vs
Baron Kettler was directed by Hugh Moss and starred C.
Douglas Carlile in his final bow as Baker Street's second
most favorite detective. The adventure saw Blake rescuing
a set of top-secret government plans from that master criminal and enemy of England, Baron Kettler.

The first of the "new wave" Holmes films (those adapted from Conan Doyle stories) after the 1912 Franco-British series was Sherlock Holmes Solves "The Sign of the Four" in 1913.   Produced by Thanhouser in America, the two-reeler was based on the novel The Sign of the Four, and "gives us a new kind of Sherlock Holmes, a younger and heavier built man [Harry Benham] than we usually see in the part.   But once the story gets into action, with its weird, Oriental atmosphere, we forget everything else" (The Moving Picture World, March 8, 1913).

A faithful version of the novel, "the story of the Agra treasure is pictured for us in an intensely fascinating manner. The one-legged man, the East Indian with his blowpipe, the Sholtos, the Baker Street lodgings, the scenes in India, and the various exciting episodes combine to make this a success-ful offering.   The treasure never comes into the hands of the rightful owner, Mary, as it was cast into the river.   A strong production of a famous narrative...."

Dr. Watson was also in the film, but at the end of the story he didn't marry Miss Mary Morstan, as he had in the novel.   When Sherlock Holmes Solves "The Sign of the Four" was released in England, however, it was played in theatres as the ninth adventure in the Franco-British Sherlock Holmes series of two-reelers.

Griffard's Claw and Sherlock Holmes vs the Black Hood were also made in 1913.   Original screen stories both, Griffard's Claw [also called In the Grip of the Eagle's Claw] was produced by the Ambrosia Film Company of Italy, and had Holmes in one sequence flying an airplane to catch a criminal, while Sherlock Holmes Vs the Black Hood was an-other Holmes film made in Germany.   There was also a Sexton Blake comedy that year, Sun's The Would-Be Detective, a spoof with a character named Bexton Slake chasing kidnap-pers who had stolen a baby.

Then came Vitascope's film of The Hound of the Bas-kervilles.

THE YEAR VITASCOPE put the infamous Hound on film was a particularly active year for Sherlock Holmes: 1914 also saw the publication in The Strand Magazine of Conan Doyle's brand new Holmes novel, The Valley of Fear, and besides Vitascope's The Hound of the Baskervilles and

its opening sequel films, there were as many as five other
Holmes movies, two of them based on the very same story.
On the comedic side of Baker Street there were also many
new parodies of the Great Detective.

Besides Vitascope's Hound picture, the most outstanding of all the other 1914 Holmes films was G. B. Samuelson's
A Study in Scarlet. Made in England and directed by George
Pearson, A Study in Scarlet was a 64-minute adaptation of
the first of all Holmes stories, and featured James Braginton
as the sleuth. The script was written by Harry Engholm,
and the picture was very favorably received at the time. It
is a faithful screen version of Conan Doyle's story about murderous revenge taken in England for a crime previously committed in Utah in the United States. But while the others in
the cast of characters included Fred Paul as Jefferson Hope,
Agnes Glynne as Lucy Ferrier, Harry Paulo as John Ferrier,
and Winifred Pearson, the director's daughter, as Lucy as a
child, Samuelson's production of A Study in Scarlet was, oddly
enough, without the august presence of Dr. Watson. There
was, therefore, no scene (as in the original novel) where
Holmes and Watson meet for the first time. (The only time
this first meeting between Holmes and Watson has ever been
filmed was in The New Adventures of Sherlock Holmes television series. See Chapter Eleven.) For that matter, Sherlock Holmes himself was hardly in the film. Capably played
by a properly lean-faced, hawk-nosed James Braginton,
Holmes didn't arrive on screen until late in the film, and
then only to solve the crime.

Despite the brevity of Sherlock Holmes' appearance in
the film and the total absence of Watson, Samuelson's film of
A Study in Scarlet was nevertheless both a critical and financial success, though it is anybody's guess why the producer
should have chosen to take that course in adaptation. Regardless of the success of the film, though, when two years later
Samuelson again turned to Conan Doyle stories for movie material and filmed The Valley of Fear, he prominently featured
both Holmes and Watson in the center of all the mysterious
activities.

Actually there were two films of A Study in Scarlet
released in 1914. The second version was produced by Universal Pictures in Hollywood, but unlike Samuelson's feature
length, Universal's film was only a brief twenty minutes.
But also unlike the Samuelson film, Universal's A Study in
Scarlet had both Holmes and Watson very much in the picture.

A Study in Scarlet (G. B. Samuelson 1914) starred James
Braginton as Holmes in the first film version of the first
Sherlock Holmes story Conan Doyle ever wrote.

This second version of the novel was directed by Francis Ford,
who also starred as Holmes in the film, and Watson was played
by Jack Francis. In later years, Jack Francis became more
famous as a film director, under the name John Ford.

The other Sherlock Holmes films released in 1914
were Night of Terror, a Danish production starring Emilie
Sannom; Where Is She?, another lost Danish film, this one
starring M. Gregers as Holmes; and Sherlock Holmes vs
Dr. Mors, a Vitascope film starring Ferdinand Bonn as

Holmes and Friedrich Kuhne as the villainous Dr. Mors.
The picture was based on Sherlock Holmes, a stageplay writ-
ten by Ferdinand Bonn and first performed (with Bonn as
Holmes) in Berlin in 1906.

The Holmesian comedies that year included Kalem's
Sherlock Bonehead, starring Marshal Neilan, Ruth Roland (the
serial queen), Lloyd Hamilton and Dick Rossen; Superba's
The Champeen Detective, starring Charles De Forrest; Thanhouser's The Amateur Detective, starring Carey Hastings
and Ernest C. Ward; Solax's Padlock Bones; and Captain Ket-
tle's Jawlock Jones, directed by C. J. Cutcliffe-Hyne, about
detective Jawlock Jones who goes after kidnappers who have
snatched a baby.   There was also a trio of new Sexton Blake
films.

Kinematograph Trading Company's The Mystery of the
Diamond Belt was written and directed by Charles Raymond
and introduced Phillip Kay to the role of Sexton Blake, with
Lewis Carlton as assistant Tinker.   The 39-minute exploit
featured Douglas Payne as George Marsden Plummer and Eve
Balfour as Kitty the Moth, and had Blake capturing the notorious thief Plummer after Plummer had impersonated a man
of distinction so he could steal a priceless set of diamonds
from a London jeweler.   Kinematograph's Britain's Secret
Treaty and The Kaiser's Spies followed shortly thereafter.
These other two Blake films were also written and directed
by Charles Raymond, and again starred Phillip Kay as Blake
and Lewis Carlton as Tinker.   Britain's Secret Treaty had
Blake battling the Count (Thomas Canning), a German enemy
mastermind who had stolen a secret treaty.   To catch him,
Blake assumed the disguise of a foreign war minister, but
the Count captured the sleuth nevertheless and designed a
most unusual death for him: he lashed a time bomb to Blake
and then suspended him by his wrists from the top of a cliff.
The Kaiser's Spies, on the other hand, saw Blake tracking
down the leader of a German spy ring who was operating in
England from a remote tower located in Epping Forest.

The next year, 1915, actually saw more Sexton Blake
films released than Holmes exploits.   On the lighter side,
however, there were more Holmes comedies than Blake comedies.

The only two Sherlock Holmes pictures released in
1915 both starred Alwin Neuss.   The first was A Scream in
the Night, produced by Decla in Germany, a 30-minute

Lady Jean Conan Doyle and Sir Arthur visit Mary Pickford
and Douglas Fairbanks in Hollywood (circa 1924).   (Courtesy
Eddie Brandt's Saturday Matinee.)

---

adventure costarring Edward Seefelu as Watson.   The other
film was William Voss, produced by Meinert Pictures, also
in Germany.   Theodore Burgardt played Voss, the villain.
The year's comedies were The Mystery of the Leaping Fish,
starring Douglas Fairbanks as master sleuth Coke Anaday
(Cocaine-A-Day); Sherlock Boob, Detective, with Allen Fea-
lick and Rena Rogers; Bloomer Tricks Sherlock Holmes, an
Italian film; The Flea of the Baskervilles, another Italian
travesty; The Great Detective, an Edwin McKim production
for Lubin Films in America; and no less than four "Pimple"
films from England.

The Sexton Blake adventures in 1915 were The Stolen
Heirlooms, The Counterfeiters, and The Thornton Jewel Mystery.   Produced by Walturdaw, The Stolen Heirlooms was
directed by Charles Raymond and starred a new Sexton Blake
and a new Tinker: Harry Lorraine and Bert Rex.   The

adventure had them coming to the defense of an ex-gambler
accused of stealing some jewels. But in tracking down the
real thieves, Blake was captured and taken to an old sawmill
where the villains lashed him up to a log and then got ready
to send the Baker Street sleuth into the screaming blades of
a buzzsaw. But fortunately Tinker showed up in time to rescue Blake, and then they speedily collared the crooks. The
next Blake film, The Counterfeiters, was also directed by
Charles Raymond, starred Harry Lorraine and Bert Rex, and
again took place at the same sawmill location. This time
out, however, Blake and Tinker were both captured--by counterfeiters they were chasing. The villains tied Blake to the
waterwheel, and Tinker to the lock gates. But they both
managed to escape in the nick of time and capture the bad
guys.

The last of the three 1915 Blake films was The Thornton Jewel Mystery, a Serra release again directed by Charles
Raymond, and starring Harry Lorraine and Bert Rex. In
this twenty-minute exploit, Blake rescued a girl from criminals who had stolen jewels, a crime which the girl had
blamed on an innocent man. The climax took place aboard
the criminal's boat. In between these Sexton Blake films,
though, Lorraine and Rex made a similar type adventure,
The Great Spy Raid, which saw them battling a ring of German spies operating in London.

There was also a Sexton Blake comedy that year--a
"Pimple" film.

Produced in England, the enormously popular "Pimple"
films were all about the misadventures of a bungling chap
named Pimple, and the comedies were the workings of the
Evans brothers, Fred and Joe, who not only created and directed the screwball pictures but also starred in them. In
all, they made more than a hundred Pimple films and many
times in their films they took on and satirized famous characters like Raffles the Cracksman, [1] and in 1915 they tried
their hand at both Sherlock Holmes and Sexton Blake.

The Evans' Pimple-Holmes comedies were Pimple's
Million Dollar Mystery, [2] Pimple's the Case of Johnny
Walker, and Pimple's Boy Scout. The satires starred Fred
Evans as Sherlock Pimple, who tracked down bank robbers
in Pimple's Million Dollar Mystery, chased after whiskey
thieves in Pimple's the Case of Johnny Walker, and disguised
himself as a Boy Scout to bring kidnappers to justice in
Pimple's Boy Scout.

Not quite satisfied with what they'd already done to the reputation of Sherlock Holmes in their Pimple comedies, however, Fred and Joe Evans got together later in 1915 for a fourth Holmesian massacre. This wasn't a Pimple exploit but an all-out Baker Street burlesque called A Study in Skarlit, in which Fred Evans took on the biting role of Sherlokz Holmz, while brother Joe snickered menacingly and plotted evil as Sherlokz Holmz' archenemy, Professor Moratorium.[3]

The Sexton Blake comedy they made was called Sexton Pimple. With Fred Evans as the bumbling sleuth Sexton Pimple, the film satirized the then-current trend of the real Blake films (which saw Blake fighting German master spies) and had Sexton Pimple also routing German spies, here to rescue the King of Cork from their evil clutches.

The first two Craig Kennedy films were also released in 1915. Created by Arthur B. Reeve for Cosmopolitan Magazine stories in 1910, the Craig Kennedy character was a scientific Sherlock Holmes living in New York City. His Watson was a newspaper reporter named Walter Jameson, and any Craig Kennedy story was very likely to find the master sleuth either inventing, using or coming up against such gadgets and devices as death rays, death germs, invisible rays, television projectors, or even life-reviving machines. Kennedy's adventures were always of a more fantastic nature than any Holmes exploit, more on the order of the later Doc Savage thrillers by Kenneth Robeson than any Baker Street tale by Conan Doyle, but Kennedy's methods of deduction were nevertheless very much Holmesian. After awhile, Kennedy even became known as "the American Sherlock Holmes," and Arthur B. Reeve's many stories and books about Craig Kennedy were very popular during the first quarter century.

Because of all the fantastic marvels and devices on hand in his world, Craig Kennedy was a rather ideal choice for movie serials and, in fact, all the films ever made about the character were serials,[4] the first of which was The Exploits of Elaine, produced by Hearst-Pathé, and starring Arnold Daly as Kennedy, and Creighton Hale as Jameson. The Exploits of Elaine was written by Arthur B. Reeve, and costarred Pearl White as the put-upon heroine. The 14 chapters saw Kennedy and Elaine battling a mysterious criminal mastermind called the Clutching Hand, who was equally as scientific as Craig Kennedy. The fiend had diabolical death ray projectors, gas-filled murder rooms, hypnotic mind drugs, and, among other deaths, an electrifying one by telephone.

The serial was a fast success, and immediately that
year spawned a sequel that was appropriately enough entitled
The New Exploits of Elaine, again with Arnold Daly as Kennedy, Pearl White as Elaine, and Creighton Hale as Jameson.
The ten chapters featured a new villain, the Frog, and more
scientific horror and heroism.

NOTES

[1]What Happened to Pimple--The Gentleman Burglar (1914),
     Pimple and the Stolen Plans (1914), The Adventures
     of Pimple--The Spiritualist (1914), Mrs. Raffles Nee
     Pimple (1915), Judge Pimple (1915), Pimple Copped
     (1915), Pimple's a Woman in the Case (1916), Pimple's
     Monkey Business (1916), and Saving Raffles (1917).
     In all these films, Fred Evans played Pimple, and
     Joe Evans played cracksman Raffles.

[2]In America the film was called Flivver's Famous Cheese
     Hound. "Flivver" became, in fact, the name generally
     given the Pimple character whenever the films were
     released in the United States.

[3]A year earlier, in 1914, the Evans brothers lampooned an-
     other Conan Doyle story: taking off on 1913's The
     House of Temperley film, they filmed a comedy called
     The House of Distemperley.

[4]The single possible exception to this was a Craig Kennedy
     television series in 1952. But again, these films
     were short, 30-minute exploits and not feature-length
     dramas.

Three

THE VALLEY OF FEAR
AND WILLIAM GILLETTE

While my first introduction to Holmes, Watson and
Baker Street adventuring was through films like Universal's
The Scarlet Claw and Terror by Night with Basil Rathbone
and Nigel Bruce, the first Sherlock Holmes story I ever read
was The Valley of Fear. The edition featured a special introduction by John Dickson Carr, who called it "a roaring
story," and having read the book a number of times since
then, I still think of it as one of the better Holmes stories.
It has a great puzzle, the spectre of Professor Moriarty
falls ominously over the events, and I remember I particularly liked the second part of the book, "The Scowrers,"
which was a long flashback chronicling all the circumstances
that had led up to murder in Sherlock Holmes' day.

Like the earlier A Study in Scarlet novel, The Valley
of Fear was also a tale about avenging death in England for
a heinous crime previously committed in the United States,
this time in the coal fields of Pennsylvania, and in the story
Sherlock Holmes had some of his finest moments. The Valley of Fear was also the last Holmes novel Conan Doyle ever
wrote, and coincidentally the last of the Conan Doyle novels
about Holmes to be brought to the screen, in 1916. This
first film version of The Valley of Fear was produced, in
fact, by the man who had two years earlier produced the
first screen version of A Study in Scarlet: G. B. Samuelson,
in England.

Samuelson's film of The Valley of Fear was directed
by Alexander Butler and scripted by Harry Engholm, who had
also adapted A Study in Scarlet to the screen. The Valley
of Fear starred H. A. Saintsbury as Sherlock Holmes, Arthur M. Cullin as Dr. Watson, Booth Conway as Professor
Moriarty, Cecil Mannering as John McMurdo, Daisy Burrell

H. A. Saintsbury as Holmes in The Valley of Fear (Samuelson 1916).

as Ettie Douglas, Lionel D'Aragon as Captain Marvin, Bernard Vaughn as Shafter, and Jack Macauley as McGinty; and except for the fact that in the film Moriarty was plotting on screen, rather than only working behind the scenes as he had in the novel, Samuelson's The Valley of Fear was a very faithful adaptation of the original story.   The picture was also well received, and certainly added to H. A. Saintsbury's fame as Sherlock Holmes.

Saintsbury had originally portrayed Holmes on stage in 1910, at the Adelphi Theatre in London, in The Speckled Band: An Adventure of Sherlock Holmes, a play written expressly for the theatre by Sir Arthur Conan Doyle himself, based on his "Speckled Band" short story.   Later productions of this stageplay saw such actors as Charles Millward, A. Corney Grain and H. Cooper-Cliffe playing Holmes, but Saintsbury was the first and stayed with the production for four months before going on to other theatrical work.   Nor was Saintsbury through with either Sherlock Holmes or the Conan

Doyle play after starring in Samuelson's The Valley of Fear
film: in 1921 Saintsbury returned to The Speckled Band for
an additional 112 performances in London. Then in 1929
Saintsbury starred as the sleuth in a London version of the
William Gillette play. It is interesting to note that Saintsbury's Watson in the 1929 Gillette Sherlock Holmes play was
George Pearson, who had directed 1914's A Study in Scarlet
film for G. B. Samuelson.

Besides Saintsbury, however, the original 1910 cast
of The Speckled Band play had, prophetically enough, also included Claude King as Watson, and Lyn Harding as Dr. Grimsby
Rylott [sic]. Like H. A. Saintsbury himself, both Claude King
and Lyn Harding also went on to later appear in Sherlock Holmes
movies. Harding, in fact, not only recreated his Rylott character for a 1931 talking screen version of The Speckled Band play,
but also went on to become one of the most famous Moriartys of
that decade.

Despite G. B. Samuelson's success with The Valley
of Fear and the earlier A Study in Scarlet, he never did film
any more adventures of the Great Detective. That year 1916
did see a trio of other Holmes pictures, however: William
Gillette's Sherlock Holmes; and Sherlock Holmes and the Midnight Meeting and Sherlock Holmes on Leave. The last two
were produced by Vitascope Pictures in Germany, and both
starred Alwin Neuss as Holmes. There were also a number
of 1916 comedies: Victor's A Society Sherlock, produced,
directed by, and starring William Garwood, with Irma Daw-
kins; Eiko Pictures' The Hand, made in Germany; Vitagraph's
A Villainous Villain, starring Larry Semon as Sherlock, and
featuring Joe Rock; and Globe's The Terrible 'Tec, which
was made in England and was actually a takeoff on both Sherlock Holmes and Sexton Blake at the same time. Directed
by W. P. Kellino and written by Reuben Gillmer, The Terrible 'Tec starred Billy Merson as Sherlock Blake, and Winifred Delevanti as his secretary and companion. The story
had Sherlock Blake using various comical disguises to track
down a diamond thief, played by Fred Dunning.

The year also saw a new Craig Kennedy serial, and two
different comedy films about this American Sherlock Holmes,
one of them made by the highly irreverent Evans brothers.

Produced by Pathé, the Kennedy serial was The Romance of Elaine, starring Arnold Daly as Craig Kennedy,
Pearl White as Elaine, and Creighton Hale again as Jameson.

The villain this time around was Marcus Del Mar, played by
Lionel Barrymore (brother of John Barrymore). Marcus Del
Mar was one of wartime Germany's ace saboteurs who for 12
chapters sought to destroy America.

The two Kennedy comedies were Pimple's Clutching
Hand and Tubby's Clutching Hand. Released by Browne Films,
the Pimple comedy had Fred Evans as Pimple betting a group
of friends that he could capture Craig Kennedy's archenemy,
the Clutching Hand (first seen in 1915's Kennedy serial The
Exploits of Elaine). Pimple's friends took the bet and to
make sure they won, they each took turns dressing themselves
up as the Clutching Hand. When Pimple thought he caught
the Clutching Hand, another Clutching Hand showed up, and
when he caught that Clutching Hand, yet another Clutching
Hand popped up. Before it was all over, though, Pimple outsmarted them all and captured all six Clutching Hands. Thanhouser's Tubby's Clutching Hand, however, only featured one
Clutching Hand. Directed by Frank Wilson, the story had
Tubby (Johnny Butt) trying to rescue his wife after the villain
kidnapped her.

But no matter all the Holmesian (and near-Holmesian)
movie activities that year, the highlight of 1916 remains the
filming of William Gillette's play of Sherlock Holmes.

THE MOST FAMOUS and celebrated of all Holmes
stageplays, William Gillette's Sherlock Holmes: A Drama in
Four Acts was brought to the screen as Sherlock Holmes,
starring William Gillette himself as Holmes, Edward Fielding
as Dr. Watson, Marjorie Kay as Miss Alice Faulkner, Ernest Maupin as Professor Moriarty, Stewart Robbins as Ben-
jamin Foreman, Mario Majeroni as James Larrabee, Grace
Reals as Madge Larrabee, and Buford Hampden as young
Billy, the Baker Street pageboy. The year before, Edward
Fielding, Stewart Robbins and Buford Hampden had all been
playing their screen roles of Watson, Foreman and Billy with
Gillette on stage at the Empire Theatre in New York City.

William Gillette's play of Sherlock Holmes was actually
a kind of collaboration with Conan Doyle, and writing credits
for the play have properly credited them both as the authors,
although they never literally worked together on the writing.

What happened was that Conan Doyle had in 1897 written a play titled Sherlock Holmes, basing it on various

elements from his Holmes stories. He had great hopes the
play would be successful enough to gain him considerable
fame as a playwright as well as an author. But his play
about Holmes, oddly enough, wasn't received well and never
found a production home in England. When later his agent
sent the script to America, to Charles Frohman, the well-
known New York producer, Frohman, in turn, handed it over
to William Gillette, equally renowned as an actor.

Gillette read the script, liked the idea, and said that
he was even interested in starring in the play himself. But
first, he said, he wanted to make some changes in both dialogue and story. As with any play he decided on doing, Gillette wanted also to tailor-make Sherlock Holmes to his own
individual acting style. When told of Gillette's requirements
for production, however, Conan Doyle did not object in the
least and said that Gillette could do anything at all he wanted
with the script. So after considerable rewriting of Conan
Doyle's original manuscript, Gillette came up with a script
that satisfied him, and went ahead with the venture.

Giving the production the full theatrical title of Sherlock Holmes: A Drama in Four Acts, Gillette opened the
play at the Star Theatre in Buffalo, New York. That was on
October 23, 1899, and it marked the beginning of a very long
and very rewarding Sherlock Holmes career for Gillette that carried well into the thirties. Gillette appeared in thousands of performances of the play and even did a one-hour radio version of
it over the ABC Radio Network on November 18, 1935; the next
year he also recorded a portion of the play on a record album
that appropriately enough featured Gillette as Holmes on one
side, and Conan Doyle talking about Holmes on the other. [1]

William Gillette was the first actor to gain an enormous
international reputation and acclaim for playing Sherlock Holmes
in drama of any kind--a reputation and strong, lasting identification with the role that continues healthily even through today--
and in 1916 he took some members of his New York City Sherlock Holmes stageplay company to Chicago where, with other
actors and actresses, they put the legendary play on film.

Opposite: William Gillette (left) recreates his most famous
stage role for the movie camera. This scene is from Sherlock Holmes (Essanay 1916) and shows Ernest Maupin as
Professor Moriarty, confronting Holmes at Baker Street.
(Courtesy Eddie Brandt's Saturday Matinee.)

Produced by the Essanay Film Company under the direction of Arthur Bethelet, the film of Gillette's Sherlock Holmes was a 64-minute screen version of his famous melodramatic stage thriller about Professor Moriarty, Holmes, and the criminal team of Madge and James Larrabee all trying to obtain a packet of compromising letters that once in the wrong hands would spell certain disaster to the forthcoming marriage of a scion of a family of nobility.

"William Gillette as Sherlock Holmes, in moving pictures, even at the ripe age of 63 years, was 'a consummation devoutly to be wished,'" reviewer James S. McQuade said at the time (The Moving Picture World, May 27, 1916). "A few more years," he continued, "and it would have become impossible for Mr. Gillette to take the part with the physical vigor that would recall his best efforts of the old days to his international-wide admirers, and at the same time would leave in comparatively permanent form, his Sherlock Holmes for the delight of future generations...." McQuade did not know, but he hoped that "Essanay took two good negatives of this subject, so that the period of future time during which positive reproductions can be successfully made, shall be prolonged to the classic limit...."

Acting like a seasoned veteran in front of the camera, William Gillette looked just as natural and forceful as anybody had ever seen him on stage, and reviewer McQuade thought the sequence taking place in Edelweiss Cottage, where the villainous Larrabees were holding Miss Alice Faulkner their prisoner, certainly showed Gillette as the Holmes of years gone by. The entire cast, he said, was in fact commendable, and added that the greatest scene in the whole film, just as it had been on stage, was that sequence at Baker Street "showing the test of wit and cunning and masterful resourceful ability between the detective and Professor Moriarty.... Mr. Gillette never had a stronger opposite than Ernest Maupin in this great scene ..." and as far as he was concerned, Ernest Maupin also well deserved "the distinction of being entombed in films for coming years with the master of all detective impersonators ..." (Moving Picture World, May 27, 1916).

Marjorie Kay played Alice Faulkner and Edward Fielding, Dr. Watson. The part of "Billy" was taken by Burford Hampden, the "Buttons" in Sherlock's home; William Postance played Prince; Mario Marjeroni and Grace Reals appeared as James and Madge Larrabee; the Sir Edward Leighton character was played by Hugh Thompson, and Ludwig Kreiss appeared as Count von Stalburg. "All stood out prominently ..."

Despite McQuade's glowing tribute, other reviews have come to light that were not entirely so favorable towards the picture.   The consensus was that the film version had been a bit too faithful to the original play.   Being a stage play it was of course necessarily a very talkative adventure, but for movies that were still very much silent and largely dependent on action to carry the story along, a too-literal adaptation of the play from stage to screen seemed a rather ill-advised concept.   Regardless, Mr. McQuade really should have asked Essanay about whether or not they "took two good negatives of this subject ..." because today the film is lost.   No prints are known to exist anywhere in the world.   Modern audiences, it appears, will never have the opportunity to see and judge the picture for themselves.   The legend of William Gillette survives very well, but aside from the recording he made in 1936 and various photographs of Gillette in the role of Sherlock Holmes, today's audiences and historians have absolutely no way, now, of ever seeing the most famous portrayer of Holmes in living film action.   Conan Doyle himself perhaps provides some additional insight into Gillette's legendary portrayals of Sherlock Holmes when he says:

"It is not given to every man to see the child of his brain endowed with life through the genius of a great sympathetic artist, but that was my good fortune when Mr. Gillette turned his mind and his great talents to putting Holmes upon the stage.   I cannot end my remarks more fittingly than by my thanks to the man who changed a creature of thin air into an absolutely convincing human being" ("Some Personalia about Sherlock Holmes," The Strand Magazine, December, 1917).

Over the past few decades there's been a rumor that Gillette not only put his Holmes play on film, but also at one time filmed The Painful Predicament of Sherlock Holmes, which he wrote and starred in on stage at New York City's Metropolitan Opera House on March 24, 1905. [2]   A curtain-raiser, it was a very short skit which saw the flighty Gwendolyn Cobb coming to Holmes and talking her head off, without letting Holmes get in a word edgewise.   It was meant to be taken very lightly, and Gillette used it for awhile as a curtain-raiser to the main play he'd be performing that evening, a non-Holmes play, like Clarice, for example.   But if a film of The Painful Predicament of Sherlock Holmes was ever made, it too seems everlastingly gone.

After Gillette's film of <u>Sherlock Holmes</u> there weren't
any major Holmes pictures produced until 1921, when Stoll
Films in England started making a long and highly successful
series of Sherlock Holmes movies starring Eille Norwood
and Hubert Willis.   But in 1918 there was still Germany's
Meinert Films' <u>Rotterdam-Amsterdam</u> starring Viggo Larsen,
the first actor ever to gain fame as a Sherlock Holmes of the
screen.   That same year there was also a rather unusual
film called <u>A Black Sherlock Holmes</u>.   Produced by Ebony
Films in Hollywood, <u>A Black Sherlock Holmes</u> featured an
all-black cast of players, and the film is actually believed
to be one of the very earliest, if not the very first of <u>all</u>
all-black films of any kind ever made.   The year also saw
the inevitable Holmesian comedy too, this one called <u>Sherlock
Ambrose</u>.   Produced by L-Ko Pictures in Hollywood, <u>Sher-
lock Ambrose</u> starred Mack Swain as the sleuth.

In 1919 Viggo Larsen returned to the screen for his
fourteenth and final performance as Sherlock Holmes.   Larsen made his last bow in the role in Bioscop's <u>Three Days
Dead</u>, another German film.   And there were more Sexton
Blake and Craig Kennedy films that year too.

Produced and directed by Harry Lorraine, who him-
self had played Sexton Blake in 1915 films, Gaumont's <u>The
Further Adventures of Sexton Blake--The Mystery of the S.S.
Olympic</u> starred Douglas Payne as Blake.   In the Blake film
of 1914, <u>The Mystery of the Diamond Belt</u>, Douglas Payne
had been featured as the villain of the piece, but now he was
reformed and starred as Blake himself.   Playing opposite
Payne's Blake in the new exploit about the S.S. Olympic was
Neil Warrington as Tinker, Jeff Barlow as Reese, Marjorie
Willis as Gwenda Howard, and Frank Dane as Hamilton.   The
50-minute thriller saw Blake rescue Gwenda, a scientist's
daughter, from murderers and kidnappers who were after her
father's important secret formula.

The Craig Kennedy serial that year was <u>The Carter
Case</u>, a 15-chapter cliffhanger featuring Herbert Rawlinson
as the American Sherlock Holmes.   The cast included Ethel
Terry, Louis Wollheim, and Marguerite Marsh, and was produced by Olive Pictures.   The story had Craig Kennedy brav-
ing life-and-death predicaments involving phosgene bullets,
nerve-graphs, lethal vacuum rooms, and even an invisible airplane.

There was also a new Sherlock Holmes-Sexton Blake

comedy in 1919.   Released by Ideal Films in England, I Will,
I Will, I Will was directed by Hubert Herrick and Kenneth
Foss, and starred Guy Newall as Eustace Dorsingham, a lazy
young man who is helped by Sherlock Blake (Wally Bosco) to
win the hand of a socialite's daughter.   One of the others in
the cast was Philip Hewland, playing a landlord.   In the
1930s, Hewland became a regular in the Sherlock Holmes
films starring Arthur Wontner; a well-remembered series of
adventures in which Hewland had the choice role of Inspector
Lestrade of Scotland Yard.

There weren't any new Holmes films in 1920, but
there was another Conan Doyle picture: Screen Plays' Rodney Stone, based on Doyle's novel and directed by Percy
Nash.   The boxing story featured Robertson Braine as Rodney Stone, and Douglas Payne as James Harrington.

SET IN CONTEMPORARY LONDON, Stoll Films of
England's Adventures of Sherlock Holmes was a 1921 series
of 15 two-reelers all based on Conan Doyle's original Holmes
stories.   The adventures starred Eille Norwood as Holmes,
Hubert Willis as Watson, and Mme. d'Esterre as Mrs. Hudson.   The series was well received wherever it played, and
was such a success, in fact, that over the next two years
Stoll produced another 32 films about the best and wisest man
Dr. Watson had ever known.

In effect, Photoplay Magazine summed up all 47 of the
Eille Norwood films when they said, "The real Sherlock
Holmes, this time, done into a number of two reel pictures
that each tell, as a separate story, one of the world famous
mysteries.   There is no sticky love interest to be upheld--
this is the cool detective of the test tubes and the many clues
--who works, step by step, towards a solution.   The cast is
well chosen of English players.   Worth while ..." (August,
1922).

Eille Norwood was already a famous British West End
theatre player before he ever took up residence at Stoll's
Baker Street for the initial adventure, The Dying Detective,
which featured Cecil Humphreys as villainous Culverton
Smith, the "well-known resident of Sumatra, now visiting
London."   By eventually playing Sherlock Holmes in 47 films
that were very popular everywhere, and then also playing
Holmes once on the stage afterwards, Norwood gained an
even greater fame, and there are still aficionados who contend

he remains the best Holmes of all.   Certainly his performances as Sherlock Holmes are as important to the drama-
tized canon as those later given the sleuth by Basil Rathbone,
Peter Cushing, and Arthur Wontner (who, however, more
closely resembled Doyle's own conception of Holmes than any
other actor who ever played the part), but Norwood did not
really present a very forceful Holmes, particularly by comparison to some of the later actors.   Norwood's detective
seemed more retiring, not unlike Wontner's Holmes, except
that Norwood didn't really look very much like Holmes.   Regardless, he was an extremely capable and professional actor, and his Sherlock Holmes is never to be taken lightly.
Conan Doyle himself, having seen Norwood in the role,
seemed as equally impressed with him as were Norwood's
general movie audiences.

"He has that rare quality which can only be described
as glamour, which compels you to watch an actor eagerly,"
Conan Doyle said.   "He has the brooding eye which excites
expectation and he has also a quite unrivalled power of disguise."

Norwood was in fact a great stickler for sticking to
the type of Holmesian disguises described by Conan Doyle in
the published stories, and even created many of the makeups
for the films himself.

Directed by Maurice Elvey, Stoll's Adventures of
Sherlock Holmes series was faithfully adapted (except for the
modern 1920s setting) from the Conan Doyle stories by William J. Elliott, and besides Eille Norwood, Hubert Willis[3]
and Mme. d'Esterre, the cast featured Arthur Bell as Inspector Lestrade of Scotland Yard.   The 15 adventures were
released to theatres at the rate of about one new episode
every week, and actual movie serials notwithstanding, the
Stoll pictures were scheduled rather like today's weekly television series are shown.   Each week there was a new exploit.

Debuting with The Dying Detective, the series contin-
ued with The Devil's Foot with Hugh Buckler as Dr. Stern-
dale, and Harvey Braban as Mortimer Tregennis; A Case of
Identity with Nelson Ramsey as Hosmer Angel, and Edna
Flugrath as Mary Sutherland; The Yellow Face with Clifford
Heatherley as Grant Munro, and Norma Whalley as Effie
Munro; The Red-Headed League with Edward Arundell as
Jabez Wilson, and H. Townsend as Spaulding; A Scandal in
Bohemia with Joan Beverley as Irene Adler, and Alfred

Drayton as the King of Bohemia (and Holmes baffling Miss
Adler in the disguise of a bald-headed, bushy-browed clergy-
man wearing glasses); and The Resident Patient with C. Pitt-
Chatham as Dr. Percy Trevelyan, Judd Green as Blessington,
and Wally Bosco as Moffat.

   Other entries in the series included The Man with the
Twisted Lip with Robert Vallis as Neville St. Clair, and
Paulette Del Baye as his dreadfully concerned wife; The Cop-
per Beeches with Lyle Johnson as Jephro Rucastle, and
Madge White as Violet Hunter; The Tiger of San Pedro (from
"The Adventure of Wisteria Lodge") with George Harrington
as Scott Eccles, Lewis Gilbert as Murillo, and Arthur Wal-
cott as Garcia; The Empty House with Sidney Seward as Col-
onel Sebastian Moran, Austin Fairman as Ronald Adair, and
Cecil Kerr as Sir Charles Ridge; The Beryl Coronet with
Henry Vibart as Alexander Holder, and Molly Adair as Mary;
The Noble Bachelor with Fred Earle as Moulton, Hetty Doran
as Temple Bell, and Cyril Percival as Simon; The Solitary
Cyclist with Violet Hewitt as Violet Relph, and R. D. Sylvester as Carruthers; and The Priory School with C. H. Croker-
King as the Duke of Holderness, Irene Rooke as the Duchess,
and Patrick Kay as Lord Saltaire.

   No sooner had Stoll completed the final Adventure,
however, than they started work on a full-length Sherlock
Holmes film. The Hound of the Baskervilles was directed
by Maurice Elvey, written by William J. Elliott, and starred
Norwood, Willis and Mme. d'Esterre again as Holmes, Watson and Mrs. Hudson. Others in the cast of the 61-minute
film were Rex McDougall as Sir Henry Baskerville, Robert
English as Dr. Mortimer, Lewis Gilbert as Stapleton, Catina
Campbell as Beryl Stapleton, Fred Raynham as Barrymore
the butler, Miss Walker as Barrymore's wife, and Robert
Vallis as Selden, the escaped convict living on the moors.

   "All things considered they have turned out a film calculated to make anyone sit up and take notice," Laurence
Reid said in his review at the time (The Moving Picture
News; September 22, 1922). "If they have faltered," he continued, "it is in allowing too many captions to interrupt the
sequences--captions which explain facts which are immediately
followed by the illustrations. This is contrary to good con-
struction.... Eliminate many of these subtitles," Reid suggested, "and the picture would carry more mystery. Yet it
carries suspense. It couldn't help but carry it--seeing that
it is an adaptation of a masterpiece of its kind...."

In The Hound of the Baskervilles (Stoll 1921), Eille Norwood as Holmes points an inquisitive finger at Fred Raynham, playing Barrymore the butler. Hubert Willis (center) as Watson and Rex McDougall (seated) as Sir Henry await the butler's reply. (Courtesy Ronnie James Collection.)

The photography of W. Germain Burger effectively brought out the misty, bleak moors of the English countryside, and it was thrilling, Reid said, to see Sir Charles Baskerville frightened about the next reappearance of the ghostly hound. Then when Sir Charles died, Holmes and Watson stepped into the picture with an intensity "to thrill everyone" and it was a neat touch when Barrymore, the butler, was shown flashing a signal to someone out there on the misty moors. Another good incident "discloses the Druid stones silhouetted against the darkened sky. What about that scene when Holmes is horror-stricken in watching the criminal sink in the quagmire? There is imagination there."

Besides the film itself, he praised as so many others did, the work of Eille Norwood, who "makes a good Holmes.

He seems to step right out of the pages of the story. The
book is more exciting, but the film," he concluded, "will
give you a thrill...."

     The Hound itself was a large police dog and also fared
well on screen. According to historian William K. Everson,
it appeared in all its properly shocking horror thanks to the
clever special effects touch of hand-painting each frame of
film in which it appeared with a phosphorescent glow.

     These initial Stoll films, The Adventures of Sherlock
Holmes series and The Hound of the Baskervilles feature
film, were very popular at the time, and remain entertaining
today, but even so, like Reid said in his review, one can't
help but think how "talkative" are these silent movies. Of
course good detective stories are always talkative because
they're basically verbal exercises in question-and-answer,
question-and-answer, over and over again until the final solution to the mystery is realized, and faithfully adapted from
the Conan Doyle stories, the Stoll-Holmes films remain
largely just this type of detective story. The studio did not
take any particular screen license with the adaptations just
because the stories were now being made into movies.
There are many sequences in the various Stoll films where
Holmes, Watson or other characters stand around, or walk
together, discussing the various aspects of the particular
problem at hand, with the dialogue cards only offering the
most essential bits of the conversation so the viewer will
know what is going on.

     Nevertheless, whether the Stoll films are more typi-
cally silent-movie, action-oriented stories or not, the films
remain enjoyable and interesting, and The Hound of the Baskervilles was released in 1921 as a sort of grand, full-length
climax to all the studio's Holmes movie activities that year.

     Shortly after The Hound of the Baskervilles was re-
leased, a new series of Holmes two-reelers produced by
Kowo Films in Germany was also released. This other
Sherlock Holmes series comprised nine films that were, according to scholar Michael Pointer, actually filmed in 1917-
18 though not released until 1921.

     Directed by Karl Heinz Rolf, Kowo's "Sherlock Holmes"
series led off with The Earthquake Motor, The Mysterious
Casket, The Snake Ring, and The Indian Spider, all starring
Hugo Flink as Holmes. Then came The Mirror of Death,

The Poisoned Seal, The Fate of Renate Yongk, and The Cardinal's Snuffbox, all starring Ferdinand Bonn, who had first
played Holmes on screen in the 1914 Sherlock Holmes vs
Dr. Mors.

The final title was The Murder in the Hotel Splendid,
with a third Holmes, Kurt Brekendorff, who had first played
Holmes in 1902, on stage in Stockholm in William Gillette's
play.

The Kowo series is practically unknown nowadays,
having generally been distributed only in Germany during the
twenties and even then soon disappearing from view. Judging
by the titles alone, however, it would seem Kowo's films
were all much more action-oriented than the Stoll series--
the kind of rousing Holmesian exploits Germany and other
countries had, in fact, been producing all along through the
silent movie era.

There was also a Holmesian comedy in 1921. Released by Metro pictures in America, Sherlock Brown was
produced and directed by Bayard Veiller, written by Veiller
and Lenore Coffee, who was quite a prolific silent screen
writer, and starred Bert Lytell as a dapper though humor-
inclined detective.

Bert Lytell was also the movies' first "Lone Wolf"
and "Boston Blackie." In 1917 he had starred for Selznick
Pictures in The Lone Wolf, directed by Herbert Brendon.
He continued as Louis Joseph Vance's debonair jewel thief-
turned-sleuth in The Lone Wolf Returns (1926), Alias the
Lone Wolf (1927), The Lone Wolf's Daughter (1929), and The
Last of the Lone Wolf (1930), all made by Columbia--who
also produced the original Boston Blackie films: Boston
Blackie's Little Pal (1918) and Blackie's Redemption (1919),
both starring Lytell as Jack Boyle's professional crook-
turned-sleuth.

There was also a Conan Doyle film in 1921: Screen
Plays' The Croxley Master, directed by Percy Nash, and
written from Conan Doyle's book by Harry Engholm, who had
scripted both the 1914 A Study in Scarlet and the 1916 The
Valley of Fear films. The Croxley Master starred Dick
Webb as Robert Montgomery, a young doctor who became a
boxer so he could win enough money to start his own practice and win the hand of Dorothy Oldacre (Dora Lennox), the
pretty daughter of his employer, Dr. Oldacre (Cecil Morton
York).

NOTES

[1]Sherlock Holmes Explained by His Creator, Sir Arthur
      Conan Doyle, and Presented in Action by William
      Gillette was released in 1939 by the National Vocar-
      ium. The Conan Doyle part of the record came from
      the soundtrack of Fox-Case Movietone's Sir Arthur
      Conan Doyle. See Chapter Four.

[2]The first actress to play the part of the talkative Miss Cobb
      was Ethel Barrymore, soon to become one of the
      great ladies of the stage, and later the screen. When
      Gillette performed the skit at London's Duke of York's
      Theatre on October 3, 1905, playing the part of Billy
      the pageboy was another name shortly destined for im-
      mortality, Charles Spencer Chaplin.

[3]A rather stocky, no-nonsense looking Watson, Hubert Willis
      began his association with Conan Doyle films in 1913's
      The House of Temperley, in which he had the role of
      Shelton.

Four

THE FURTHER ADVENTURES
OF SHERLOCK HOLMES

During the 1920s silent movie years, Stoll's Sherlock Holmes films dominated the screen. With the exception of Kowo's elusive Holmes series in 1921, Samuel Goldwyn's major production of Sherlock Holmes in 1922, and then Vitascope's later remake of The Hound of the Baskervilles in 1929, there were no other silent film exploits of Holmes and Watson but those made by Stoll Films in England. Eille Norwood and Hubert Willis, the Basil Rathbone and Nigel Bruce of their day, virtually had the decade to themselves.

Under the direction of George Ridgwell, Stoll Films returned Eille Norwood, Hubert Willis, and Mme. d'Esterre to Baker Street film life in 1922 for The Further Adventures of Sherlock Holmes. This second series of 15 twenty-minute mysteries was written by Patrick L. Mannock and Geoffrey H. Malins from other of the Conan Doyle stories, but this time Stoll left Inspector Lestrade out of the scripts. Instead, they cast Teddy Arundell as Inspector Hopkins for the resident Scotland Yard man of the new series.

The series opened with Charles Augustus Milverton costarring George Foley as "the worst man in London" and The Norwood Builder with Cyril Raymond as the unhappy John Hector McFarlane. The Further Adventures ... gave Eille Norwood full reign again in the matter of Holmesian disguises. The twelfth adventure, Black Peter, for example, with Fred Paul as Peter Carey, saw Norwood effectively donning makeup and wardrobe for the guise of a crusty ship's captain, while two adventures later, in The Greek Interpreter, with Cecil Dane as Melas, the interpreter, Norwood managed to outdo even his own usually fine work as a master of disguise by fooling one and all with the disguise of an old woman. The Further Adventures of Sherlock Holmes is more

particularly noteworthy, however, because it is in this series
that Holmes' brother Mycroft makes his one and only appearance in a Stoll film.

In The Bruce-Partington Plans, the series' last adventure, with Malcolm Todd as Cadogan West and Ronald
Power as Colonel Valentine Walter, Mycroft Holmes came to
life as played by Lewis Gilbert, who had had the role of
Murillo in the first Stoll series' The Tiger of San Pedro episode.

The other ten adventures of this second Stoll series
included The Reigate Squires with Arthur Lumley as Colonel
Hayter and Richard Atwood as Alec Cunningham; The Abbey
Grange with Lawford Davidson as Sir Eustace Brackenstall,
Madeline Seymour as Lady Brackenstall, and Leslie Stiles as
Captain Croker; The Red Circle with Bertram Burleigh as
Gennaro Lucca and Sybil Archdale as Amelia; The Six Napo-
leons with Jack Raymond as Pietro Venucci, Alice Moffat as
Lucretia, and George Bellamy as Beppo; The Naval Treaty,
"a case of national importance ... marked by several inci-
dents which gave it a unique character," with Jack Hobbs as
Percy Phelps, and Nancy May as Annie Harrison; The Bos-
combe Valley Mystery with Hal Martin as Charles McCarthy
and Fred Raynham as John Turner; The Second Stain with
Cecil Ward as Lord Bellinger and Dorothy Fane as Miss
Hope; The Stock-Broker's Clerk with Olaf Hytten as Hall
Pycroft, Aubrey Fitzgerlad as Pinner, and director George
Ridgewell himself as Beddington; The Musgrave Ritual with
Geoffrey Wilmer as Musgrave, Betty Chester as Rachel
Howells, and Clifton Boyne as Brunton; and The Golden
Pince-Nez with Cecil Morton York as Professor Coram, and
Norma Whalley as Anna.

Unlike the previous year, however, Stoll did not film
a full-length adventure of Sherlock Holmes after completing
the final short adventure. The major release of Samuel Goldwyn's Sherlock Holmes feature, produced in America with location filming in London, and released around the world right
in the midst of Stoll's Further Adventures series, may have
been the deciding factor in the studio's foregoing their own
Holmes feature that year.

SAMUEL GOLDWYN'S Sherlock Holmes was based on
William Gillette's stageplay of Sherlock Holmes, and starred
a rather ideal choice for Holmes: John Barrymore, the

"Great Profile," playing the sleuth who more often than not
is himself shown in profile in book illustrations and magazine
art.   Directed by Albert Parker, Goldwyn's big A production
was adapted to the screen by Earl Brown and Marian Fairfax,
and costarred Roland Young as Watson, Gustav Von Seyffertitz as Professor Moriarty, and Carol Dempster as Miss
Alice Faulkner.   Later, Roland Young was to become more
famous as Topper in a series of films produced by Paramount
in the late 1930s.   Two other members of the Goldwyn-Holmes
picture were also destined for particular fame in Hollywood:
William Powell, playing Forman Wells here, went on to become one of the greats and even had two of his own mystery
movie series, Philo Vance and the Thin Man; Hedda Hopper,
playing the villainous Madge Larrabee in Goldwyn's film,
went on to international fame as one of Hollywood's top gossip columnists. [1]

Others in the cast included John Willard as Inspector
Gregson of Scotland Yard, Anders Randolf as James Larrabee, David Torrence as Count Von Stalburg, Reginald Denny
as Prince Alexis, Robert Schable as Bassick, Moriarty's
chief lieutenant; Louis Wolheim as Craigin, Lumsden Hare
as Dr. Leighton, Margaret Kemp as Terese, and Jerry Devine as Billy, the Baker Street pageboy.

Always a fine actor, particularly in his younger days
before he started aping himself in films, John Barrymore
actually played two Sherlock Holmeses in the Goldwyn film.
The first Holmes was a young man at college--a specially
written prologue sequence saw Holmes' first meeting with
Moriarty, one of his professors at school--while Barrymore's
second Holmes was the older, more familiar-looking sleuth
of Baker Street.   As the older Holmes, Barrymore's makeup was extremely effective (Barrymore was a comparatively
young man himself in those days), and looking over some
photos of Barrymore as Holmes, Christopher Lee, who later
himself played Holmes in Sherlock Holmes and the Deadly
Necklace (1962), said in fact that "Something makes me think
he might well have been the greatest one of them all, even
though I would probably agree with most people in regarding
Basil Rathbone as the definitive Holmes ("Letters," E-Go
Collectors Series 4 [John Wayne], September, 1976).

Gustav Von Seyffertitz' makeup as the bald-domed
Moriarty was also convincing, and even frightening: showing
an extremely melodramatically sinister Moriarty, who looked
incomparably evil and corrupt with a boldly leering face and

skull. A Moriarty who might easily have doubled for Dr.
Jekyll's Mr. Hyde anytime.

The film itself was "one of the most artistic and unusual films ever made," Photoplay Magazine said (July, 1922).
"Its settings and photography are amazingly fine. Its cast is
one of the few real all-star affairs...." But reviewer Laurence Reid's critique of the film was more detailed.

Writing in Motion Picture News (May 27, 1922), Reid
said that quite obviously the producers of Sherlock Holmes
had spared no expense in making their film distinct from the
general run of movies because other than assembling a large
cast with names familiar on Broadway, the producers had
taken the players "to London to catch the exact local color
and atmosphere...." With exterior scenes filmed on location, Sherlock Holmes was technically "almost perfect. The
settings of Holmes' Baker Street home, the street scenes,
the brief interlude in the Alps--these are richly suggestive
of the background against which revolved the thrilling episodes
which concerned the detective.... Here [Sherlock Holmes] is
shown using his powers of deduction at an early age--almost
upon graduation from college. He has a big job on his hands
attempting to capture London's boldest and yet most cunning
criminal--a crook and murderer extraordinary."

One thing Reid couldn't understand, however, was why,
after their battle of wits, Holmes let Moriarty escape even
though he had the professor in his net then? "This is most
perplexing," Reid said, "considering [Moriarty's] murderous
activities. The reason must be found in piling on the suspense so as to give the spectator a terrifying climax--with
lights and shadows, secret panels, dungeons, dark stairways,
various disguises, stealthy sleuthing in cabs, and what not
being employed...." But while he thought John Barrymore
succeeded in carrying out the demands of the Sherlock
Holmes role, he did not think Barrymore's appearance suggested the Holmes of the stories. Nevertheless, "it is a
finely imaginative performance. He added, "Roland Young
does not suggest Watson at all, though his work is satisfac-
tory...."

Nearly everybody who has ever seen a photograph of
Barrymore as Holmes thought the actor indeed looked the
part, but obviously reviewer Reid, for one, did not. Regardless, for many years the film was thought to be yet another
of the many lost, but not forgotten Holmes movies. In 1975

John Barrymore as the Great Detective in Sherlock Holmes (Goldwyn 1922). (Courtesy Eddie Brandt's Saturday Matinee.)

---

however, a viewable print was finally reconstructed by the Eastman Kodak Company from various amounts of footage and negative located over the years in Hollywood, Europe, and also at Eastman's own laboratories on the East Coast. But if the company has any intentions of ever reissuing Goldwyn's Sherlock Holmes to theatres or television for general viewing again, perhaps with an added musical score, they haven't publicly disclosed such intent. One or two of the eastern Sherlock Holmes societies have been allowed to screen the reconstructed picture, but afterwards the print went directly back into the Eastman vaults. Which is unfor-

tunate, of course. A Barrymore film like this one is important not only because it has the legendary Barrymore in a
one-time screen appearance as the legendary Holmes, but
also because Samuel Goldwyn's production of Sherlock Holmes
was filmed during those years when Barrymore was still very
much at the height of his theatrical powers. Alcohol and despair had not yet had the opportunity to consume him.

The year 1922 also saw the release of two Holmesian
comedies, and a new Sexton Blake film. Produced by Revue
in England, The Affected Detective was directed by Bert Haldane, who had directed the 1915 Conan Doyle film of Brigadier Gerard, and it starred Cecil Mannering of the Stoll-
Sherlock Holmes films as a famous sleuth who liked cocaine.
The story by Susan Schofield had this detective taking his cocaine, becoming affected by it, and then taking off into a
dream world where he imagined he was tracking down criminals in the far-away Orient.

The other comedy, Jazz Hounds, was produced by
Reol Pictures in America, and like the earlier A Black Sherlock Holmes (1918) was also an all-black, two-reel short.
In Jazz Hounds the star playing Sherlock Holmes dressed up
exactly like the famous caricatures of Holmes, complete with
deerstalker, cape and pipe, and tracked down a crime against
the film's musical-mystery background.

Jazz Hounds was a silent film, but theatres running
the comedy no doubt made sure their pianist, or organist
played appropriate, hot jazzy licks in time to Holmes' sleuthing on the screen.

The Sexton Blake adventure was The Dorrington Diamonds, from Screen Plays in England. Produced by Percy
Nash, and written and directed by Jack Denton, The Dorrington Diamonds featured Douglas Payne in his second portrayal
as a Blake of the movies, and costarred George Bellamy as
Tinker. The others in the cast included Jeff Barlow, Mildred Evelyn, and Cecil Burke, and the story had the sleuth
from Baker Street rounding up another gang of unscrupulous
jewel thieves.

STOLL FILMS of England returned in 1923 with The
Last Adventures of Sherlock Holmes, their third and final
series of 15 twenty-minute mysteries taken from the Conan
Doyle stories. George Ridgewell was again the director,

Patrick L. Mannock and Geoffrey H. Malins the screenwriters, and Eille Norwood, Hubert Willis, and Mme. d'Esterre
the stars.   In The Last Adventures of Sherlock Holmes Stoll
also returned Inspector Lestrade to their films.   G. Lestrade
wasn't, however, the only representative of Scotland Yard on
hand here.   Inspectors Gregory and Taylor were also featured in various episodes, and interestingly enough they were
all three played in their respective films by the very same
actor, Tom Beaumont.

Besides including quite a few of the more famous
Holmes stories, The Last Adventures of Sherlock Holmes
also climaxed with an appropriate (for the title of the series,
anyway) closing adaptation of the story "The Final Problem,"
which marked Professor Moriarty's one and only appearance
in any of the 47 Stoll films of Sherlock Holmes.

In The Final Problem, the criminal Professor was
played by Percy Darrell Standing, who had come to the role
with some very good credentials.   In 1915 Standing had starred as the Frankenstein Monster in Ocean Films' Life Without Soul, directed by Joseph Smiley from Mary Shelley's
classic novel Frankenstein.

The Last Adventures of Sherlock Holmes also included
Silver Blaze with Knighton Small as Colonel Ross, Sam Austin as Silas Brown, and Sam Marsh as Straker; The Speckled
Band with Lewis Gilbert as Dr. Grimesby Roylott [sic], Cynthia Murtagh as Helen Stoner, and Henry Wilson as a baboon
on the grounds of Roylott's infamous estate; The Gloria Scott
with Reginald Fox as Victor Trevor, Roy Raymond as Pren-
dergast, and Laurie Leslie as Miss Hudson; The Engineer's
Thumb with Bertram Burleigh as Hatherley, and Ward McAllister as Ferguson; The Blue Carbuncle with Douglas Payne
(1922's Sexton Blake of movies) as Petersen, Sebastian Smith
as Henry Barker, and Mary Mackintosh as Mrs. Oakshot;
His Last Bow with Nelson Ramsey as Von Bork and Van
Courtland as Baron Herling; The Disappearance of Lady
Frances Carfax with Evelyn Cecil as Lady Frances, Cecil
Morton York as Holy Peters, "one of the most unscrupulous
rascals that Australia has ever evolved," Madge Tree as
Mrs. Peters, "his so-called wife," and David Hawthorne as

Opposite: The Jazz Hounds was an all-black Holmes comedy
(Reol Productions 1924).   (Courtesy Eddie Brandt's Saturday
Matinee.)

the Honorable Phillip Green; The Three Students with William
Lugg as Soames, A. Harding Steerman as Bannister, and L.
Verne as Gilchrist; The Cardboard Box with Maud Wolff as
Miss Cushing and Hilda Anthony as Mary Browner; The Stone
of Mazarin (from "The Adventure of the Mazarin Stone") with
Lionel D'Aragon as Count Sylvius and Laura Leslie as Miss
Merton; and The Missing Three-Quarter with Cliff Davies as
Lord Mount James, Albert Rayner as Dr. Leslie Armstrong,
Hal Martin as Overton, and Leigh Gabell as Staunton.

The last three exploits were The Mystery of the Danc-
ing Men (from "The Adventure of the Dancing Men") with
Frank Goldsmith as Hilton Cubitt, Dezma du May as Mrs.
Cubitt, and Wally Bosco as Slaney; The Mystery of Thor
Bridge (from "The Problem of Thor Bridge") with Violet
Graham as Miss Dunbar, A. B. Imeson as Mr. Gibson, and
Noel Grahame as his wife; and The Crooked Man with Jack
Hobbs as Henry Wood, Gladys Jennings as Mrs. Barclay,
Richard Lindsay as Major Murphy, and Dora De Winton as
Miss Morrison.

After filming Holmes and Moriarty in The Final Problem episode, Stoll did not, however, entirely forsake Holmes
for other kinds of films.   They brought the detective back in
The Sign of the Four, a full-length feature film released later
in 1923.   Directed by Maurice Elvey, who had directed the
first Stoll-Holmes series and also their first Holmes feature,
The Hound of the Baskervilles in 1921, The Sign of the Four*
was adapted from Conan Doyle's novel by Patrick L. Mannock
and Geoffrey H. Malins, and starred Eille Norwood as Holmes,
and Mme. d'Esterre as Mrs. Hudson.   This final Stoll-
Holmes film, though, featured a new Dr. Watson: Arthur M.
Cullin, who had originally played that role in the 1916 The
Valley of Fear with H. A. Saintsbury.   A younger looking
man than Hubert Willis, Cullin more closely fitted the Watson
of The Sign of the Four, who in that novel met and married
Miss Mary Morstan.

*For the most part film producers, publishers, reviewers,
writers and the world in general have always insisted on calling the story by the title The Sign of the Four although Conan
Doyle himself always preferred The Sign of Four.   It was
originally published simultaneously in both America and England as The Sign of the Four in Lippincott's Monthly Magazine in February 1890, while its first appearance under Conan
Doyle's personally preferred title was three months later, in
The Bristol Observer for May 17, 1890.

Eille Norwood as Holmes and Isobel Elsom as Mary Morstan in The Sign of the Four (Stoll 1923). (Courtesy George Morgan Collection.)

A faithful, entertaining version of the novel, Stoll's The Sign of the Four costarred Norman Page as Jonathan Small, Isobel Elsom as Mary Morstan, Fred Raynham as Prince Abdullah Khan, and Henry Wilson as Tonga, Small's fierce pygmy companion. Arthur Bell, the Lestrade of the first Stoll-Holmes series, returned to Baker Street here in the role of Scotland Yard's Athelney Jones, and Humbertson Wright had the part of Dr. Thaddeus Sholto. Later that same year Humbertson Wright became more famous in movies as Dr. Petrie, in Stoll's new series of shorts, The Mystery of Fu Manchu, [2] based on Sax Rohmer's Fu Manchu stories and

starring H. Agar Lyons as the Yellow Peril and Fred Paul
as Sir Dennis Nayland Smith. [3]

After starring in The Sign of the Four at Stoll, Eille
Norwood took on the role of Sherlock Holmes one final time.
As a sort of grand last bow, Norwood appeared as the detec-
tive that fall, 1923, on stage at the Prince's Theatre in Lon-
don in a play called The Return of Sherlock Holmes. Written
by J. E. Harold Terry and Arthur Rose from various Conan
Doyle stories, The Return of Sherlock Holmes costarred H.
G. Stoker as Dr. Watson, Lauderdale Maitland as Colonel
Sebastian Moran, Eric Stanley as Charles Augustus Milverton,
and Molly Kerr as Lady Frances Carfax, and had Holmes
battling Moran's gang to rescue the much put-upon Lady
Frances from various terrifying predicaments.

The next Sherlock Holmes film was not produced until
1929. Meanwhile, however, there were other related film
activities. Released the very month in 1923 that Stoll released The Final Problem episode, Gaumont's Fires of Fate
(called in America The Desert Sheik) was, for example, a
54-minute adaptation of Conan Doyle's novel The Tragedy of
the Korosko. The film was directed by Tom Terriss and
told the story of Colonel Egerton (Nigel Barrie) who went to
Egypt with only one year to live. During this time, though,
he found hair-raising adventure when he rescued Dorinne
Adams (Wanda Hawley) from the Arabian Prince Ibrahim
(Pedro De Cordoba). Featured in the cast were Arthur M.
Cullin (Watson in Stoll's The Sign of the Four) and also
Percy Darrell Standing (Moriarty in Stoll's The Final Prob-
lem).

Pathé's Is Conan Doyle Right? was also released in
1923, only a few months after The Sign of the Four. Directed by John J. Harvey, Is Conan Doyle Right? was a 20-
minute documentary film about spiritualism, a cause that had
come practically to dominate all of Conan Doyle's energies
during his later years. Pathé's film offered the author's
personal views about his belief in spiritualism, asked the
audience if perhaps Conan Doyle's faith in spiritualism was
not so unfounded, and also showed various methods by which
fake mediums and occult opportunists can and have hoodwinked
the public. This documentary was followed in 1924 by a
Holmesian comedy, Metro's Sherlock Jr., which saw the
famous silent screen comedian Buster Keaton playing a movie
theatre projectionist who leads a dull life but imagines himself leading an exciting life as a great investigator.

Conan Doyle's <u>The Lost World</u>, <u>How It Happened</u>, and another Holmesian comedy, <u>Sherlock Sleuth</u>, were released the following year.

Produced by First National Pictures, the 1925 <u>The Lost World</u> starred Wallace Beery as Professor George Edward Challenger, Lewis Stone as Sir John Roxton, Arthur Hoyt as Professor Summerlee, Lloyd Hughes as reporter Edward Malone, and Bessie Love as Paula White. Directed by Harry Hoyt, the film was a grand, thrilling production which author-biographer John Dickson Carr aptly called "one of the best of all motion pictures." The amazing prehistoric world's special effects were all created by Willis O'Brien, who in 1933 was to father that mighty film ape King Kong, the Eighth Wonder of the World.

Conan Doyle's <u>How It Happened</u> motoring story was one episode of Reciprocity Films' series of <u>Twisted Tales</u>. Produced by G. B. Samuelson and directed by Alexander Butler, the same team who had filmed the 1916 <u>The Valley of Fear</u> Sherlock Holmes adventure, <u>Twisted Tales</u> comprised 12 one-reelers featuring stories with surprise endings. <u>How It Happened</u> starred Sydney Seward as the wayward motorist, while other titles in the <u>Twisted Tales</u> film included the likes of <u>The Skeleton Keys</u>, <u>The Death of Agnes</u>, <u>The Eternal Triangle</u>, and <u>Her Great Mistake</u>, written by other authors. Pathe's <u>Sherlock Sleuth</u> was also a short--a comedy starring Stan Laurel (without Oliver Hardy) as yet one more Holmes-inspired fumbling detective.

Another Conan Doyle story was used in another silent movie series the next year. Produced by H. B. Parkinson and Geoffrey H. Malins (who had written so many of the Stoll-Holmes films), <u>Romances of the Prize Ring</u> was a series of eight films all about the sport of boxing. One episode, <u>When Giants Fought</u>, was based on an incident in Conan Doyle's novel <u>Rodney Stone</u> and featured Joe Beckett as Tom Crabbe stepping into the prize ring to fight Frank Craig as Tom Molyneux. The series was particularly unique in that all the stories had a host, played by Wyndham Guise, who then proceeded to "tell" you a new romance of the prize ring.

Craig Kennedy, the American Sherlock Holmes, also returned to the screen in 1926. Directed by William Cringley and William Craft, Universal's <u>The Radio Detective</u> was a ten-chapter serial starring Jack Mower as Kennedy, who battled villains out to get hold of an invention called Evansite,

The short sound film Sir Arthur Conan Doyle (Fox-Case Movietone 1927) presented Holmes' creator talking about writing
the Sherlock Holmes stories and about his interest in spiritualism. (Courtesy Blackhawk Films.)

---

named for its inventor Evans (played by Jack Dougherty).
The Gadget was going to revolutionize that new wonder medium, radio. The year also saw Pathé filming the first of
all Charlie Chan pictures, The House Without a Key, based
on the novel by Earl Derr Biggers. Like the Craig Kennedy
serial, The House Without a Key was also a ten-chapter cliffhanger, faithfully adapted from the original story, and featured Walter Miller and Allene Ray, the famous serial team
of the time. Chan of the Honolulu Police Department was
played by George Kuwa.

        In 1927 a very special Conan Doyle film was released.
Produced and directed by Jack Connoly, Fox-Case Movietone's
Sir Arthur Conan Doyle starred Conan Doyle himself in the
only sound film he ever made. Released, in fact, the very
year in which his last Sherlock Holmes book of all was published, The Casebook of Sherlock Holmes, the 13-minute film
opened with Conan Doyle and his dog walking through the garden

of his home at Tunbridge Wells and steadily approaching the
camera.   Then making himself comfortable in a chair posi-
tioned in front of the camera, Conan Doyle began his talk to
the audience with, "I've got to say a word or two just to try
my voice." For the rest of this truly historically important
film, and also very warm-hearted meeting with the author,
Conan Doyle talked first about how he came to write the Sherlock Holmes stories, and then he talked about his keen personal interest and belief in spiritualism.

In 1975, Sir Arthur Conan Doyle was wisely reissued
to theatres in America for a special "Evening with Sherlock
Holmes" program.   Distributed by Specialty Films of Seattle,
the "Evening with Holmes" also included 1939's The Hound
of the Baskervilles with Basil Rathbone and Nigel Bruce, and
a showing of Buster Keaton's Sherlock Jr. comedy of 1924.[4]

The year Fox-Case Movietone released Sir Arthur
Conan Doyle, another Conan Doyle film was released.   This
was Pathé's The Fighting Eagle, produced, directed by and
starring the noted actor Donald Crisp in a long, 85-minute
screen adaptation of Conan Doyle's novel The Exploits of
Brigadier Gerard.   Then in 1928, while Pat Sullivan's cartoon hero Felix the Cat romped his way through the animated
Sure-Locked Homes in America, Harry Blyth's Sexton Blake
returned to films in England in a brand new series of action-
laden, deductive exploits.   Produced by British Filmcraft,
the six-picture series of 20-minute shorts starred Langhorne
Burton as Blake, Mrs. Fred Emney as Mrs. Bardell, and
Mickey Brantford as Tinker.

Directed by George J. Banfield, the 1928 Sexton Blake
series led off with Sexton Blake, Gambler featuring Frank
Atherley as Lord Fairfield, and Adeline Coffin as Lady Fair-
field, after which George A. Cooper took over the directorial
reins for the next three titles: Blake, the Lawbreaker with
Fred Raynham and Leslie Perrins; The Clue of the Second
Goblet with Fred Raynham as George Marsden Plummer, and
Gabrielle Morton as Helen; and The Great Office Mystery
with Fred Raynham as Gordon Wincliffe and Ronald Curtis as
Kestrel.   Raynham, who had appeared in quite a few of the
Stoll-Sherlock Holmes films, left the Sexton Blake series at
this point, and other actors took over the featured male spot.
A new director also came into the pictures, Leslie Eveleigh,
who directed the last two entires, The Mystery of the Silent
Death with Roy Travers as Mr. Reece, Thelma Murray as
Peggy, and Roy Raymond as Ross, and Silken Threads with

Charles Eaton and Helen Twelvetrees in The Ghost Talks
(Fox 1929).   (Courtesy Eddie Brandt's Saturday Matinee.)

Leslie Perrins as Stormcroft and Marjorie Hume as Nadia
Petrowski.

        In early 1929 Fox released The Ghost Talks.   Directed
by Lewis Seiler, this was a talking picture starring Charles
Eaton and Helen Twelvetrees, and various publicity photos
showed Eaton in a deerstalker, with pipe, looking very much
like Sherlock Holmes.   In the film, however, Eaton was only
an amateur detective who'd learned to be a sleuth through a
mail-order detective course.   The story concerned Eaton's
getting involved with a real crime case when he met Helen

Twelvetrees, whose uncle had stolen $1 million worth of
bonds.   The uncle was dead now, but there were still four
crooks searching for the bonds.   A comedy, The Ghost Talks
had Eaton at one point mistaking the gangsters for government men, but in the end he tumbled to what was really going on, captured all the bad guys, and won the favor of Miss
Twelvetrees.

The famous black comedian, Stepin Fetchit, was also
in the film (interestingly enough he played a character named
Christopher Lee).

THE LAST OF ALL silent movie Sherlock Holmes adventures was released six months later.   Produced by Vitascope in Germany, the 1929 The Hound of the Baskervilles
was the third film version of the famous Conan Doyle novel,
and starred Carlyle Blackwell as Sherlock Holmes, Georges
Seroff as Dr. Watson, Livio Pavenelli as Sir Henry Baskerville, Fritz Rasp as Stapleton, Alexander Mursky as Sir Hugo
Baskerville, Betty Byrd as Beryl Stapleton, and Alma Taylor
as Mrs. Barrymore.   The film was directed by Richard Oswald, who had written the first Hound film in 1914, [5] and
scripted by Herbert Jutke and George Klarens.

"A good idea to revive this old thriller, one of the
best of the Sherlock Holmes novels," Variety said.   "It suits
itself excellently to the pictures and should have a success
on the Continent.   The same might even put it across for
moderate returns in the States...

"Richard Oswald has turned in a better piece of work
than he has had to his credit for some time; it is workman-
like throughout.   The old American favorite, Carlyle Blackwell, does well as Sherlock Holmes.   Fritz Rasp, Betty Bird
and Alexander Mursky fit into the general scheme ..." (October 2, 1929).

Despite its being a decent film, however, the 1929 The
Hound of the Baskervilles was not very successful.   In the
first place, this new Hound adventure had been made as a
silent film, and talking pictures were already more than only
just around the corner.   Many studios producing silent films
around this crucial time in motion picture history were, in
fact, caught short by the sudden boom in talking pictures; a
demand for talkies actually mushroomed during that very year
1929.   New silent films either received very limited distribution

or were entirely shelved. Some studios even converted some of their new silent films to sound by adding music or sound effects, or both, but the 1929 Hound picture wasn't one of these. It disappeared rather swiftly.

Another though much less important reason the film was not much of a success was that while Variety, for one, thought Carlyle Blackwell did well as Sherlock Holmes, others did not think so. A very popular American player, Blackwell left America to live in England in 1922, where he starred in Bulldog Drummond, a film that was quite a hit. His Drummond was every bit the rough and ready adventurer painted in novels by H. C. "Sapper" McNeile. In later films with Ronald Colman, Ray Milland, John Howard and Tom Conway, Drummond was portrayed as a rather suave crime chaser not terribly unlike Sherlock Holmes, but McNeile's original Bulldog was more on the order of Mickey Spillane's Mike Hammer, and this was the Drummond Blackwell had played so well in the 1922 film. When he starred as Holmes, though, some felt he didn't adapt himself enough to the Holmesian character, and so came off actually more like his earlier Drummond, which didn't help the atmospheric Hound film much.

But the major reason for the new Hound's lack of reception was the fact it was a silent film. Talking pictures were all the rage now, and silent films were swiftly becoming only screen history. Ironically, it was only a little over six weeks after Vitascope's Hound film was released that Paramount Pictures in America released The Return of Sherlock Holmes, the first talking Holmes movie adventure. For the first time at the movies now, audiences were not only going to see Baker Street and its famous occupants and curious visitors, but also hear with their own ears all the sounds of mysterious activity emanating from that most distinguished address.

NOTES

[1] Coincidentally, Hedda Hopper, who already was a famous newspaper woman in the thirties, was also featured in Roland Young's very first Topper film, called Topper, in 1937.

[2] Like their three Sherlock Holmes series, Stoll Films' The Mystery of Fu Manchu series also comprised 15

twenty-minute episodes faithfully adapted from their
literary sources, in this case Sax Rohmer's books
The Mystery of Fu Manchu, The Return of Fu Manchu,
and The Hand of Fu Manchu. In 1924, Stoll filmed
an additional eight Fu Manchu two-reelers under the
series title of The Further Mysteries of Fu Manchu.
Frank Wilson, who wrote the first series' scripts with
director A. E. Coleby, played Inspector Weymouth in
all 23 films.

[3]In 1928 H. Agar Lyons and Fred Paul starred in another
Oriental mystery film series, Pioneer's Dr. Sin Fang
(a Fu Manchu-like character). The Dr. Sin Fang
series comprised six episodes that once again featured
Lyons as the menace and Paul as the hero (i. e., Lt.
John Byrne).

[4]Blackhawk Films, 2198 Eastin-Phelan Building, Davenport,
Iowa 52808 has now made the film Sir Arthur Conan
Doyle available to home movie collectors too.

[5]The Hound of the Baskervilles was not the only film Richard
Oswald ever remade. Taken with stories of dark
mood and mystery, Oswald filmed Five Tales of Horror in 1919 and then remade the picture as Extraordinary Tales in 1931. Both films featured adaptations
of Edgar Allan Poe's "The Black Cat" and "The System of Dr. Tarr and Professor Fether," Robert Louis
Stevenson's "The Suicide Club," Oswald's own story
"The Ghost," and an original tale by Robert Liebmann
and Anselma Heinz. The major difference between
Five Tales of Horror and the remake, Extraordinary
Tales, was that the former was a silent film while
the latter was a talkie.

Five

ENTER THE ALL-TALKING DETECTIVE

A British ocean liner bound for America. A frantic girl, murder and kidnapping. Professor Moriarty's gift to Sherlock Holmes of a cigarette case containing a poisoned needle; Dr. Watson rescuing the Great Detective from apparent death. These were the key ingredients in Paramount's The Return of Sherlock Holmes, released in October 1929 as the first all-talking Sherlock Holmes movie adventure.

Directed by Basil Dean, The Return of Sherlock Holmes was adapted by Dean and Garret Ford from "His Last Bow" and "The Dying Detective" and starred Clive Brook as Sherlock Holmes, H. Reeves Smith as Watson, and Harry T. Morey as Moriarty. Only vaguely based on those two Conan Doyle stories, however, Paramount's film was set in modern times and featured Donald Crisp as Colonel Sebastian Moran, Moriarty's righthand man, and Betty Lawford as (surprisingly) Watson's grownup daughter Mary. The story involved Holmes tracking down the mastermind behind the London murder of Mary Watson's fiancé, and then, aboard an ocean liner shipping out for the United States, discovering that the mastermind was none other than Professor Moriarty. Later in the film Moriarty gave Holmes a seemingly innocent cigarette case that secretly contained a poisoned needle that was activated when the case was opened, but in opening the cigarette case Holmes only pretended to become its victim, thereby fooling Moriarty (and Dr. Watson too).

Successful enough in its time, The Return of Sherlock Holmes is rarely seen today. For that matter, nearly all the Sherlock Holmes films made prior to the Basil Rathbone-Nigel Bruce films of 1939-1946 are seldom if ever seen anymore, except perhaps at private screenings. In the early 1950s, before the Rathbone films were released to television, stations in America might occasionally run one of the Clive

Brook Holmes films, or more often the series of Holmes
films starring Arthur Wontner from the thirties, but once the
Rathbone films were packaged for the home screen and distributed, television stations everywhere became very reluctant
to play any Holmes film but a Rathbone. Audiences preferred
the Rathbones over the others, and so the earlier Holmes
talking pictures like The Return of Sherlock Holmes, The
Missing Rembrandt, The Triumph of Sherlock Holmes, and
A Study in Scarlet among others were (and still are) consistently shelved by television programmers. The upshot is that
to this day most people still think the only Sherlock Holmes
films ever made--before the more recent pictures in color
with Peter Cushing, Nicol Williamson, Stewart Granger,
Roger Moore, Robert Stephens and others--are those starring
Rathbone and Bruce.

     As Sherlock Holmes, Clive Brook presented an inter-
esting enough sleuth and though his first Holmes film, The
Return of Sherlock Holmes, even earned him a healthy reputation as Sherlock Holmes, the picture does suffer by comparison to the later Rathbone films--by which practically
everybody in the general audience will invariably judge any
Holmes film, old or new. But so do the other early 1930s
Holmes films suffer by comparison to the Rathbone pictures.
For one thing, they lack (now) the electricity, the chemistry,
the pacing, and overall dynamic performances and concept of
the Rathbone films, and so have become of interest now
mainly to Sherlock Holmes devotees, or historians and film
students. The earlier Holmes pictures also lack a quality
that is today an accepted, famous and even anticipated ingre-
dient of all the Rathbone films: they lack the warmth brought
to the stories by Nigel Bruce's Watson. Even the newer
films have mostly failed in this Watsonian respect, no matter
the production values, fine scripting or admirable Holmesian
performances on view in the respective titles. The Watsons
in other films have generally been rather dull men, express-
ing as much cordiality or camaraderie with Holmes or other
characters as a block of wood. Sometimes too the Watsons
of other films have been portrayed as continually overly-sur-
prised individuals who tend to leap about in fits of amazement whenever Holmes might make another of his noted deductions. And some Watsons have come off rather loud-
mouthed, or even plain offensive.

     Although The Return of Sherlock Holmes was popular
in its day, the reviews of the time were anything but favorable. "There isn't a real thrill in the whole picture,"

Freddie Schader said. "It proves a slow draggy affair....
The greater part of the action takes place on a trans-Atlantic
liner, and there is one real moment of suspense just before
the finish ..." (Motion Picture News, October 19, 1929).
Variety said, "Doyle readers will find Paramount's Sherlock
Holmes too youthful to recite antiquated lines.... Clive
Brook gives a smooth performance. But the dialog he is
forced to elocute is obviously intended for an older man and
therefore makes this Sherlock register as a decidedly preco-
cious individual. The flat, almost embarrassed execution of
H. Reeves Smith as Dr. Watson at times almost make the
great dick look ridiculous. Too many 'marvelouses' and
'elementaries'. And Doc Watson's enforced stupidity is too
apparent.... The best casting is that of Donald Crisp as
Dr. Moran, poison specialist of the insidious inventor and
classical criminal, Moriarty ..." (October 23, 1929).

In that same year 1929, Paramount also brought another famous fictional sleuth to the talking movie screen:
S. S. Van Dine's Philo Vance, that debonair detective of New
York City whom many consider America's first really classic
investigator in the Holmesian mold. Philo Vance only took
cases that interested him, and then not even for fees but for
the sake of his own curiosity, and because he was often
amused by criminal wiles. Also, he felt somewhat obligated
to help straighten out his good friend District Attorney John
F. -X. Markham's thinking on any particular murder case,
and so always keep Markham proceeding along the proper in-
vestigative track.

Vance debuted on screen in the 1929 The "Canary"
Murder Case, and The Greene Murder Case. Both films
starred William Powell as Vance, E. H. Calvert as Markham, and Eugene Pallette as Sergeant Heath, and were
adapted from the original Van Dine novels. The "Canary"
Murder Case featured Louise Brooks as a famous Broadway
singer who was murdered in her locked-up apartment, and
also in the cast was Gustav Von Seyffertitz, who had starred
with Powell in Samuel Goldwyn's 1922 Sherlock Holmes.
There Von Seyffertitz had played Moriarty, and here in the
Vance film he played Dr. Ambrose Lindquist, a fashionable
neurologist and major murder suspect. The other Vance
film, The Greene Murder Case, featured Jean Arthur in an
old "dark-house"-type mystery about the Greene family, who
are being murdered off one by one for the sake of the family
wealth.

Clive Brook (right) as Sherlock Holmes and William Powell
as Philo Vance in Paramount on Parade (Paramount 1930).
(Courtesy Eddie Brandt's Saturday Matinee.)

Besides Sherlock Holmes and Philo Vance, however,
Paramount Pictures was also making films about Fu Manchu
then, and in 1930 they teamed Holmes and Vance against Fu
Manchu in Paramount on Parade, a studio musical showcase
film that was highlighted by the rather odd dramatic sequence
called "Murder Will Out." Directed by Frank Tuttle, who
had directed Philo Vance's The Greene Murder Case, the
short sequence featured Clive Brook as Holmes, William
Powell as Philo Vance, and Warner Oland as Fu Manchu. 1
Supposedly a kind of satire or burlesque of the three characters, "Murder Will Out" showed Holmes and Vance trying to
figure out whether or not it was really Fu Manchu or someone else who had murdered a man whose corpse was now
propped up in a chair in Fu Manchu's bizarre sanctum sanc-
torum. But before either Holmes or Vance could arrive at
any definite conclusion about the matter, Fu Manchu decided
to kill them both, and then laughingly made good his escape.

Sergeant Heath (Eugene Pallette) from the Philo Vance
films was also featured in "Murder Will Out," while the
corpse in the chair was played by Jack Oakie, who was actually the host for the entire film.

Between Clive Brook's The Return of Sherlock Holmes
and Paramount on Parade, however, there was another unusual Holmes film. Released in 1930, Associated Films'
Herlock Sholmes in "Be-a-Live Crook" was an eight-minute
comedy starring Ottorino Gorno's Marionettes. The film was
actually part of a series of British burlesques of famous
American movie stars, and in episodes variously directed by
J. Elder Wills, John Grierson and Jack Harrison, the Gorno
marionettes had lampooned Douglas Fairbanks in Don Dougio
Fairbania, western star Tom Mix in Tom Mixup, and comedian Buster Keaton in Kuster Beaton. The Gorno burlesque
of Sherlock Holmes featured a Holmes puppet that was a takeoff on Clive Brook' portrayal of the sleuth in The Return of
Sherlock Holmes.

But amidst all the Holmesian screen activity and fri-
volity, there was also sadness that year: less than two
months after the release of Paramount on Parade, Sir Arthur
Conan Doyle died, on July 7, 1930. The great romantic
writer and fearlessly outspoken crusader--who would forever
be known by the world at large as the creator of Holmes,
Watson, and all that much-beloved gaslit and fog-bound world
of Victorian London and 221B Baker Street--died at his home
in Crowborough, in Sussex, at the age of 71.

Arthur Wontner (left) as Holmes confronts a masked Moriarty
(Norman McKinnell) in The Sleeping Cardinal [Sherlock Holmes'
Fatal Hour] (Twickenham 1930).

OF ALL THE ACTORS to play Sherlock Holmes on
screen during the early and middle thirties, no one stands
more honorably tall in the role than Arthur Wontner. Wontner's five films as Sherlock Holmes have, in fact, brought
him a lasting fame that ranks his performances as the Great
Detective right along with those given Holmes by Basil Rathbone, William Gillette, and Peter Cushing.

Looking very much like the Sherlock Holmes described
by Conan Doyle in the original stories, and then illustrated
by Sidney Paget in The Strand Magazine, Arthur Wontner arrived at Baker Street in British Warner Bros. -Twickenham's
1930 The Sleeping Cardinal. Produced by Julius Hagen and
directed by Leslie Hiscott, who was a very prolific director
of mystery films in the thirties, the script was written by
Hiscott and Cyril Twyford and based on the stories, "The
Final Problem" and "The Adventure of the Empty House."
The cast included Ian Fleming (not the creator of James

Bond) as Dr. Watson, Minnie Rayner as Mrs. Hudson, Philip
Hewland as Lestrade, Norman McKinnell as Moriarty, Louis
Goodrich as Colonel Sebastian Moran, Leslie Perrins as Ronald Adair, and Jane Welsh as Kathleen Adair. The story had
Moriarty robbing banks with his gang and forcing Ronald
Adair to take part in smuggling some of the stolen money out
of the country. "The Sleeping Cardinal" of the title was actually a wall painting behind which the Napoleon of Crime
would hide (in a secret passageway between rooms) and give
instructions to Adair. That way the blackmailed Adair never
really knew who he was working for. The film also included
the famous Holmes-Moriarty confrontation scene at Baker
Street, taken from "The Final Problem."

When the entertaining thriller was released in America,
its title was changed to Sherlock Holmes' Fatal Hour and because
Warner Bros. obviously didn't think the film was up to its own
standards of production, they sold American distribution rights
to First Division, a much smaller company. But the film turned
out to be a hit and, writing in Variety (July 14, 1931) reviewer
Kauf even went so far as to say it was "one of the best programmers ever turned out in England. Maybe the best. ... Beyond
having the draw of the name [Sherlock Holmes], a well sustained
yarn and several good thrill sequences, film has a fine piece of
acting by Arthur Wontner in the title part. He not only looks like
a detective but handles the role beautifully throughout, and makes
him more human than the stories did.... Cast is up to par with
the exception of Ian Fleming as 'Dr. Watson' who doesn't seem
to fit."

Twickenham Studios had signed Wontner to play Holmes
after Wontner's acclaimed portrayal of sleuth Sexton Blake on
stage in 1930, at the Prince Edward Theatre in London. Sexton
Blake was, after all, directly patterned after Sherlock Holmes,
so what was more natural than to star the Blake stage player in
the Holmes movie? Wontner's wide acceptance, and continued
good success as a Sherlock Holmes of the screen was, however, something unforeseen. In actuality his Holmes became
for the 1930s what Eille Norwood's had been a decade before,
and what Basil Rathbone's was shortly to become for all time.
Interestingly enough, though, Wontner had at various times in
his acting career starred with both Norwood and Rathbone in
films and on the stage.

In 1916 Arthur Wontner and Eille Norwood starred in
British Renaissance Films' Temptation's Hour, a society
drama with Fanny Tittel-Brune, and then in 1927 Wontner

and Basil Rathbone starred in La Prisonnière, a New York City stageplay during the run of which Wontner and Rathbone (and the rest of the cast as well) were arrested by the police one evening and taken into custody. A daring play for its time, about lesbianism, Edward Bourdet's La Prisonnière was produced by Charles Frohman (of the William Gillette-Sherlock Holmes stageplay fame), and featured Wontner as Jacques Vieieu, a man of wealth who was on the verge of marrying Irene de Montcel (played by Helen Menken), a woman who was secretly in love with another woman. Rathbone had the role of M. d'Aiguines, Jacques Vieieu's best friend, who knows the truth about Irene and who at one extremely dramatic and emotional moment in the play, felt obligated to tell Vieieu what he knows about the girl, before Vieieu married her.

Rathbone himself thought the Bourdet play was brilliant, brave and tragic; an important contemporary work of art. Nevertheless, it was deemed an obscenity by a vote-seeking politician running for office in New York, and one night during the run the cast was arrested and hauled into night court. At that same night court session was the star of another New York play considered obscene: Mae West, who had been arrested for performing her play Sex. Everyone connected with both plays, however, escaped jail terms by promising the court to never again perform their respective plays, though for years Rathbone remained incensed over the injustice of it all; over "this most infamous example," he said (in his book, In and Out of Character, Doubleday, 1962), "of the imposition of political censorship on a democratic society ever known in the history of responsible creative theater."

Wontner's The Sleeping Cardinal and the other four Sherlock Holmes films he made during the thirties were all set in contemporary London, and in their way were rather the forerunners of the contemporary Holmes pictures Rathbone and Bruce were going to start making a dozen years later at Universal in Hollywood. The Wontner films featured the Baker Street "family" of Holmes, Watson, Lestrade and Mrs. Hudson, and Wontner's Holmes was a confident, mature and decisive sleuth; a seasoned investigator oftimes amused by those around him, though keeping that amusement to himself. Ian Fleming's Watson, however, was more in the general vein of Watsons who had proceeded him on screen: a rather ordinary Britisher without any really strong, or particularly ingratiating personality of his own. More or less, Fleming's Watson only seemed to be there in the films.

Much of Holmes' repartee, then, was developed with Lestrade.
Mrs. Hudson wasn't very much of a personality in the films
either, but still this basic unit of the four had its appeal.

That year 1930 also saw two other significant Holmesian happenings. The first was Sherlock Holmes' debut as a
radio star, in an adaptation of "The Speckled Band." Broadcast over the NBC Radio Network on October 20, 1930, this
first of all Sherlock Holmes radio shows was a half hour adventure starring none other than William Gillette, who was at
that time touring the country on a farewell tour with his
Holmes stageplay. Gillette's Watson on The Speckled Band
radio show was Leigh Lovell, and it was actually the first
program in a continuing series of Sherlock Holmes radio exploits. The next week Holmes came back on the air with A
Scandal in Bohemia, and then in following weeks The Red-
Headed League, The Copper Beeches, The Boscombe Valley
Mystery, The Man With the Twisted Lip, and many more.
William Gillette, however, only appeared in the first show.
It was Richard Gordon who continued the radio series and
throughout, his Watson remained Leigh Lovell.[2]

The other event was Basil Rathbone's debut as a
screen sleuth. In MGM's The Bishop Murder Case, based
on the novel by S. S. Van Dine, Rathbone starred as the
debonair Philo Vance, with Clarence Geldert as District Attorney Markham, and James Donlan as Sergeant Heath. Roland Young (Watson in John Barrymore's 1922 Sherlock
Holmes) was also in the film, along with Alex B. Francis
and Lelia Hyams; but perhaps the most fascinating aspect of
The Bishop Murder Case--besides the fact it was Rathbone's
first screen role as a famous detective--was the studio's
original trade advertising for the film.

In MGM's Campaign Book for the year, in which the
studio advertised all their forthcoming releases, The Bishop
Murder Case was announced to movie exhibitors with a full-
page, full-color ad as a film that was shortly going into production; a film, MGM said, that would be much anticipated
by audiences everywhere. At that time, however, the cast
had not yet been set, so there were no photographs or names
of the players in the ad. But there was a nice little drawing
of Sherlock Holmes himself in the ad; in deerstalker and Inverness, and with his magnifying glass, Holmes was busily
inspecting some lines of the copy.

This artwork of Sherlock Holmes appearing in an ad

Raymond Massey (right) as Holmes and Lyn Harding as the villainous Dr. Grimesby Rylott in The Speckled Band (British & Dominion 1931). (Courtesy Ronnie James Collection.)

---

for a Philo Vance movie that was ultimately going to star Basil Rathbone is prophetically interesting; however, there was more: on the opposite page in the Campaign Book was another full-color ad, this one promoting a new MGM film that had been completed. The film was A Notorious Affair, and it starred Basil Rathbone (but not as a detective) and Billie Dove.

In 1931 RAYMOND MASSEY played Sherlock Holmes. Produced by British & Dominion Pictures in England, Massey's The Speckled Band costarred Athole Stewart as Watson, Lyn Harding as Dr. Grimesby Rylott, Marie Ault as Mrs. Hudson, Angela Baddeley as the frightened Helen Stoner, and

Joyce Moore as Helen's sister Violet.   The film was directed
by Jack Raymond, and written by W. P. Lipscomb from Conan
Doyle's 1910 stageplay of The Speckled Band: An Adventure
of Sherlock Holmes (which had also featured Lyn Harding as
Grimesby Rylott).   Massey's film version, though, was not
quite as successful as the stageplay.

        Although in general The Speckled Band was a better
than average British film, it had little mystery to it and exception was taken to the fact that British & Dominion had
tried modernizing Sherlock Holmes here by "turning his quarters in Baker Street into an ultra-modern office, complete
with stenogs and dictaphones ..." as reviewer Chap pointed
out (in Variety, March 25, 1931).   "Heaviest acting part goes
to Lyn Harding, as the murderer, who turns melodramatic
force into every action, giving an over-emphasized performance in keeping with the general hokum standard of the picture...."   Massey's Holmes was a rakish, cynical young fellow "but looked anything but the popular conception of the detective...."   Athole Stewart fared better as Watson, but Angela Baddeley as the put-upon heroine, Helen Stoner, didn't
"seem at ease," although she did well enough in the part.

        But whether Raymond Massey's Holmes film was a
classic or not, the fact remains that the picture is very
nearly a lost film today.   Prints do exist, and were even
shown on early American television, but because the film is
a rather slow-moving and ponderous one, even early television programmers did not schedule it for broadcast very often.   At that time in the 50s the Arthur Wontner films were
also available to television, and Wontner's Holmes films were
much faster-paced and intriguing than The Speckled Band,
and so were preferred over the Massey film for broadcasting.

        Two other rare 1931 films are the two Hercule Poirot
mysteries made by Twickenham, the same studio that produced Arthur Wontner's first Holmes picture, The Sleeping
Cardinal.   Starring Austin Trevor as Agatha Christie's brilliant Belgian detective, Alibi, based on the novel The Murder
of Roger Ackroyd, and Black Coffee, based on Christie's
play, were the first two Poirot films of all,[3] and were, in
fact, directed by Leslie Hiscott, who had directed Wontner's
The Sleeping Cardinal, and later two more Wontner-Holmes
films.

        The fourth film version of The Hound of the Basker-
villes was released in 1932.   Produced by Gaumont Pictures

Robert Rendel (center) as Holmes, Sybil Jane as the butler's
wife, and Frederick Lloyd as Watson in the first talking version of The Hound of the Baskervilles (Gaumont 1932).
(Courtesy Ronnie James Collection.)

in England, the feature starred Robert Rendel as Sherlock
Holmes, Frederick Lloyd as Dr. Watson, John Stuart as Sir
Henry Baskerville, Reginald Bach as Stapleton, Wilfred Shine
as Dr. Mortimer, Heather Angel as Beryl Stapleton, Sam
Livesey as Sir Hugo Baskerville, Henry Hallett as Barrymore,
the butler, and Sybil Jane as the butler's wife.   The film
was directed by V. Gareth Gundrey, and written by Gundrey
and Edgar Wallace, one of the most prolific and best-selling
mystery writers of all time.   Still very popular and always
in print, Edgar Wallace's innumerable books and stories have,
in fact, been filmed more times than the works of any other
author of any kind whatsoever; and at least once Wallace even
directed one of his own film versions.   This was British
Lion's 1930 The Squeaker, which starred Gordon Harker,[4]
Anne Gray, and an actor who was just getting started in the
movie business, Nigel Bruce.   Wallace also coauthored the
original King Kong film.

Gaumont's <u>Hound,</u> ineptly directed, was generally panned by audiences and critics alike, and soon disappeared.
The film was also "poorly cast, virtually none of the princi-
pals interpreting the Doyle characters as readers visualize
them," Waly said in <u>Variety</u> (April 19, 1932). At times the
film even seemed a comedy version of the famous story.
Robert Rendel as Sherlock Holmes "was far from the prepos-
sessing figure of fiction," and Frederick Lloyd's Watson was
more or less played for the laughs that seldom came off.

Edgar Wallace's main contribution to the script was
handling the dialogue, and while he did a reasonably good job
of bringing the language up to more modern sounding times,
his work alone did not seem to turn the trick in the picture's
favor.

Gaumont's <u>Hound</u> had little suspense because, according to Waly, "the story hand was tipped so far in advance
that little novelty was left when each situation occurred.
Even when it came to the hound, the audiences had to be tipped that the animal was leashed in the villain's backyard...."

Ironically, the hound was judged the best actor in the
whole film, even though, Waly said, it "bounded over rocks
and walls like a big good natured mongrel rather than a ferocious maneater...."

<h2 style="text-align:center">NOTES</h2>

[1]Warner Oland, the first Fu Manchu of talking pictures, debuted as Sax Rohmer's devil doctor in Paramount's
<u>The Mysterious Dr. Fu Manchu</u> in 1929, encored in
<u>The Return of Fu Manchu</u> in 1930, and closed out his
Fu Manchu years with <u>Daughter of the Dragon</u> in 1931,
costarring Anna May Wong as Fah Lo Suee, the
daughter. Then Oland went to the Fox studios where
that same year he starred in <u>Charlie Chan Carries On,</u>
the first of 16 Chan films that were going to make
him even more famous.

[2]Leigh Lovell was also Watson to a third radio Holmes,
Louis Hector, who took over the part in 1934.

[3]In 1934, Austin Trevor played Hercule Poirot a third time,
in British Real Art's <u>Lord Edgeware Dies</u>, based on
the Agatha Christie novel of the same name.

[4]In 1939 Gordon Harker himself became a screen sleuth. He
     starred as British radio's famous Hornleigh in the
     film Inspector Hornleigh.   Harker then repeated the
     role twice more in films, Inspector Hornleigh on Holi-
     day (1939) and Inspector Hornleigh Goes to It (1941).

Six

ARTHUR WONTNER CARRIES ON

In 1932 Arthur Wontner and Clive Brook both returned to the screen in new Sherlock Holmes adventures. Wontner, in fact, appeared in two different films about London's most famous private inquiry agent.

A British Twickenham film, The Missing Rembrandt was produced by Julius Hagen, directed by Leslie Hiscott, and starred Wontner as Holmes, Ian Fleming as Watson, Philip Hewland as Lestrade, and Minnie Rayner as Mrs. Hudson. Written by Cyril Twyford and H. Fowler Mear, the adventure was partially based on Conan Doyle's "Charles Augustus Milverton" story, and told about a famous Rembrandt painting that had been stolen in Italy and smuggled into England in a chest of tea that also contained other stolen goods. Lestrade and Scotland Yard were quick on the job, though, and raided the Chinese den in Limehouse where the chest was reported located, but by the time they got there the painting was missing. Perplexed about where it might have gone, Lestrade called on his old friend Sherlock Holmes to help look into the matter.

What all this had to do with Conan Doyle's story about the villainous Charles Augustus Milverton, "the worst man in London," was that the painting ended up in the hands of a certain Baron Von Guntermann, an art dealer who was really Milverton--except that the screenwriters had changed his name for the film. But as they say, a rose by any other name ... and so Von Guntermann was as wicked and cunning a scoundrel as the Milverton from the original story. Besides dealing in stolen paintings, he was also blackmailing Lady Violet Lumsden (played by Jane Welsh), an incident taken from the "Milverton" story. Von Guntermann had certain romantic letters of hers that she wished to be kept secret and not become public property that would cause a scandal.

Arthur Wontner as Holmes in The Missing Rembrandt (Twickenham 1932).   (Courtesy George Morgan Collection.)

Von Guntermann was played by Francis L. Sullivan,
who 12 years later was destined to star in another famous
Conan Doyle adventure, playing Professor George Edward
Challenger in a BBC Radio serial version of The Lost World,
written by John Dickson Carr. As Von Guntermann, Sullivan
fared well, although he did have something of a problem in
diction. As Variety noted, "Francis L. Sullivan, an Irish-
man with an English accent trying to do German dialect, is
a bit hard on American ears ..." (Variety, March 29, 1932).

Others in the cast of The Missing Rembrandt included

Miles Mander as Claude Holford, Ben Welden as a detective
working on his own to bring the case to its conclusion, Dino
Galvani as Carlo Ravelli, and Tawase as Chang Wu, a Chinese gangster.   Interestingly enough, when the film opened
in America, it opened at the Strand Theatre in New York
City. (New York's Strand Theatre; Holmes' Strand Magazine.)

     Four months later another Holmes film with Arthur
Wontner was released: The Sign of Four, based on the original novel.   But with the single exception of Wontner himself,
everybody else connected with the film was new to the Wontner-Holmes movie series.

     Produced by British Radio Associated Pictures, The
Sign of Four was directed by Rowland V. Lee and Graham
Cutts, and adapted by W. P. Lipscomb.   Basil Dean was the
producer--the same Basil Dean who had directed the 1929
The Return of Sherlock Holmes with Clive Brook--and his
Sign of Four was a faithful screen version of the book.   The
cast had Ian Hunter as Watson, Gilbert Davis as Athelney
Jones of Scotland Yard, Claire Greet as Mrs. Hudson, Ben
Soutten as Jonathan Small, Isla Bevan as Miss Mary Morstan,
Herbert Lomas as Major Sholto, Miles Malleson as Thaddeus
Sholto, Edgar Norfolk as Captain Morstan, Kynaston Reeves
as Bartholomew Sholto, and Roy Emerton as Bailey.

     The reason Ian Fleming did not again play Watson to
Wontner's Sherlock Holmes in The Sign of Four was the same
as the reason Hubert Willis did not again play Watson to
Eille Norwood's Sherlock Holmes when Stoll Films made the
1923 The Sign of Four: in each case a younger-looking actor
was wanted for the part because it is in this Holmes story
(which they were adapting faithfully) that Watson meets and
marries Miss Mary Morstan, a dainty young woman whom
Watson loved, as he says, "as truly as ever a man loved a
woman. "

     The Sign of Four was another entertaining Holmes ad-
venture, with Wontner shining in the starring role, and it
was followed in theatres by Vitaphone's Sherlock's Home. Directed by Alf Goulding and written by Jack Henley, Sherlock's
Home was a 20-minute short in which the roving documentary
camera toured London--Sherlock's home.   This was followed
less than three weeks later with the release by Fox of an authentic Holmes exploit, Sherlock Holmes.

     DIRECTED BY William K. Howard and written by

Clive Brook as an updated super-scientific Holmes and Miriam Jordan as Alice, his fiancée, in Sherlock Holmes (Fox 1932). (Courtesy Collectors Book Store.)

Bertram Millhauser, who later in the forties would write some really good Holmes films for Basil Rathbone and Nigel Bruce, Fox's Sherlock Holmes was based on William Gillette's play of Holmes, and also the famous Conan Doyle story, "The Red-Headed League." But for the most part it was an original script, and a rather unusual one at that. Featuring Clive Brook as Holmes, Reginald Owen as Watson, Ernest Torrence as Moriarty, Miriam Jordan as Alice Faulkner, Alan Mowbray as Inspector Gore-King of Scotland Yard, and Howard Leeds as Billy the pageboy, Fox's Sherlock Holmes can be seen as an offbeat, not very successful Holmes adventure that contained not only the basic trappings of the Holmesian world but also elements from James Bond, Craig Kennedy, and Nick Carter. Even Dick Tracy.

The film was set in modern times and opened with Holmes about to marry Alice Faulkner, an attractive blonde

whose father owned one of the richest banks in London. Like
America's scientific and Holmesian Craig Kennedy, Clive
Brook's new Holmes was also something of a scientific inventor, as well as detective. One of the Holmesian devices
shown here was a gadget that produced an electric ray that
could stop cars. Before Holmes and his sweetheart Alice
could marry and settle down, however, Moriarty broke out
of prison, and so the game was afoot once again. Leaving
Alice in the lurch (as Dick Tracy did so often to his girlfriend Tess Trueheart when another police case suddenly
came up), Holmes was back in action again at Baker Street.

        Acting not unlike the more recent James Bond neme-
sis, Mr. Auric Goldfinger, Moriarty set up headquarters
again and called a big meeting together of various infamous
criminals and gangsters from all over the world. Soon he
hatched his new plot for murder and robbery. The murder
he was going to have blamed on Sherlock Holmes, and the
robbery he planned was burrowing into the Faulkner bank.
Many of the crooks he imported to London for these chores
were American gangsters, and seeing Holmes matching wits
and bravado in a film with such types reminds one of the
Nick Carter films.

        "Legions of Sherlock Holmes fans may look upon the
picture as sacrilegious despite a fairly good hokumish job
that should please audiences who like blood, thunder and
laughs, in pictures with a sleuth background," Variety said.
"Clive Brook doesn't prove a particularly good Sherlock, and
in scenes where he masquerades as an old woman there's
danger audiences will titter instead of being impressed by
the drama of the thing ..." (October 21, 1932). And because
it seemed as if director Howard had tried his best to kid the
story, the trade magazine even suggested, appropriately
enough, that the studio might do better for themselves by
trying to sell the film as a comedy rather than as a dramatic
Holmes adventure. A later review by Rush in the same paper further pointed out that the picture didn't show Clive
Brook "at his best, particularly in rather sheepish love
scenes ..." (Variety, November 15, 1932).

        Overall, Fox's Sherlock Holmes was an embarassing
exploit featuring Claude King[1] as Sir Albert Hastings, Stanley Fields as Ardetti, an Italian crook; Edward Dillon as Ardetti's henchman; Montagu Shaw as a judge; Roy D'Arcy as
Lopez, a Spanish criminal; and Robert Graves as Gaston
Roux, a French villain.

Besides The Missing Rembrandt, The Sign of Four,
and Sherlock Holmes, there were three other Conan Doyle
films released in 1932: Lelicek in the Service of Sherlock
Holmes, Fires of Fate, and The Lost Special.

Produced by Czechoslovakia's Elekta Films, Lelicek
in the Service of Sherlock Holmes was directed by Karl Lamac, written by Vaclav Wasserman, and starred Martin Fric
as Holmes and Vlasta Burian as secret agent Lelicek, whom
the sleuth from Baker Street sends out to investigate a scandal at the Puerto Rican royal palace.   Wardour's Fires of
Fate, on the other hand, was a British talking picture remake of Gaumont's earlier 1923 silent Fires of Fate, based
on Conan Doyle's novel and play of The Tragedy of the Korosko.   Starring as Colonel Egerton, the man with only one
year to live, in the new adaptation was Lester Matthews,
while included in the cast was Dorothy Bartlam as Kay Byrne,
who was kidnapped in Egypt by Clifford Hearthley playing Abdullah the desert sheik.   The third film, Universal's The
Lost Special, was a 12-chapter serial starring Frank Albertson, Cecilia Parker and Ernie Nevers as three young school
chums out West, investigating a mystery involving an entire
train that seems to have completely vanished off the face of
the earth.   The film (and its original Conan Doyle story) is
interestingly enough not without its Sherlock Holmes connota-
tions.

Directed by Henry MacRae, and written by serial veterans George Plympton, Basil Dickey, Ella O'Neill and
George Morgan, Universal Pictures' The Lost Special was
based on Conan Doyle's story of the same title--a story in
which it is generally acknowledged that it is none other than
Sherlock Holmes himself who is "the amateur reasoner of
some celebrity" who writes a letter to the London Times in
which he attempts "to deal with the matter [of the inexplicably
vanished train] in a critical and semi-scientific manner."
Now whether or not the connection was developed intentionally
on Universal's part when they filmed the story is open to
speculation, but if Holmes can only be vaguely identified in
the original Conan Doyle story, then he can also be vaguely
identified in the Universal film, because playing the part of
Botter Hood, one of the professors at the three students'
school--and the man, in fact, who directs the teenagers to
go out and try their hand at solving the mystery of the vanished train--is none other than Francis Ford, who played
Holmes in the studio's 1914 A Study in Scarlet.

In 1932 Universal also produced <u>The Murders in the
Rue Morgue</u>, the first talking picture version of Poe's famous
story about C. Auguste Dupin, the grandfather of all sleuths.
In this film, however, they changed Dupin's name to Pierre
Dupin, and instead of keeping him a detective or "amateur
reasoner," they made him into a medical student.

Directed by Robert Florey and written by Tom Reed
and Dale Van Avery, with additional dialogue by John Huston,
Universal's <u>The Murders in the Rue Morgue</u> starred Leon
Ames (or Leon Waycoff, as he was billed at the time) as
Dupin, Bela Lugosi as Dr. Mirakle, the owner of a circus
sideshow exhibiting Eric the ape; Sidney Fox as Dupin's lady-
friend, and Arlene Francis as the girl's other friend.   The
story had Dupin tracking down the solution to a number of
murders of young women; women who had originally been kidnapped by Eric the ape, then brought to Dr. Mirakle's weird
underground laboratory, where he used them for strange experiments: injecting each of his helpless female captives
with the blood of gorillas.   But Mirakle's experiments only
kept killing the girls instead.

IN 1933 SOMETHING UNIQUE happened in Holmesian
film worlds: Watson became Sherlock Holmes.   Learning to
become like Holmes, at least to the extent that they tried to
think and reason like Holmes when figuring out a mystery,
was something Watsons often hoped to accomplish in both the
original Conan Doyle stories and in drama of every kind, but
in 1933's <u>A Study in Scarlet</u> film, a Watson actually became
Sherlock Holmes.

Produced by World Wide in Hollywood, <u>A Study in
Scarlet</u> was directed by Edwin L. Marin, written by Robert
Florey, and starred Reginald Owen as Sherlock Holmes.   In
Clive Brook's 1932 <u>Sherlock Holmes</u>, Owen's role of Watson
was in the picture "apparently because this character is as
necessary to Holmes as cabbage to corn beef, [though] sce-
narist gave little for Reginald Owen to do in [the] part"
(<u>Variety</u>, October 21, 1932).   But in <u>A Study in Scarlet</u>,
Reginald Owen was the whole show and he did a fine job of
it too.   In the Clive Brook film, the makeup department had
made him look older by graying his hair and giving him a
moustache, but here as Sherlock Holmes Owen appeared as
his own younger self.   And while he wasn't a terribly energetic Holmes, he nevertheless came off well in the part and
certainly looked like he was enjoying the role.

Reginald Owen, here as Holmes in <u>A Study in Scarlet</u> (World Wide 1933), was the first screen Watson to also play the detective himself.

World Wide's <u>A Study in Scarlet</u> was hardly a screen version of the Conan Doyle novel, however. If anything, it was like something straight out of Edgar Wallace, what with its tale of a secret society whose members were mysteriously meeting death one after the other. The picture (which is also called <u>The Scarlet Ring</u>) featured Alan Mowbray as Lestrade, Temple Piggot as Mrs. Hudson, and Warburton Gamble as Watson. Others were Wyndham Standing as Captain Pyke, Anna May Wong as Mrs. Pyke, Halliwell Hobbs as Malcolm Deering, Billy Bevan as Will Swallow, Tetsu Komai as Ah Yet, Alan Dineheart as Thaddeus Merrydew, and Leila Bennett as Daffy. J. M. Kerrigan was also featured, as Jabez Wilson, the name of a character from Conan Doyle's "The Red-Headed League" adventure. In this film, however, Jabez Wilson didn't come running to Holmes with a mystery to solve; much less did he have a shock of flaming red hair.

In A Study in Scarlet, Jabez was merely one more member
of the Scarlet Ring group, and looking out for his life.

The film was entertaining and easy to take, and as
Char said when reviewing it (Variety, June 6, 1933), "If not
tipped off by the credits trade would think this was an English
made. ... Flavor of England has been particularly well im-
parted via the sets and in the characterizations of the players. ..." Reginald Owen as Holmes was singled out as "fresh
and relieving." Only recently having come to Hollywood from
the legitimate stage, Owen had also worked on the continuity
and dialogue of the film, and he handled the role of Sherlock
Holmes "with a restraint that strengthens" the part.

Warburton Gamble as Watson, Alan Dineheart, Anna
May Wong and the others in the cast were also favorably received. One rather curious thing about World Wide's A
Study in Scarlet, however, was that for some peculiar reason
Sherlock Holmes' address in the film was given as 221A
Baker Street; and while in various publicity photos (including
the one on page 93) Reginald Owen had been seen wearing a
deerstalker, in the film itself he never did. The picture
was set in modern times.

Universal's The Radio Murder Mystery was another
Holmes film released in 1933. Produced by William Rowland
and Monte Brice, and directed by Brice, the picture was
written by H. D. Kusell and starred Richard Gordon as
Holmes, and Leigh Lovell as Watson. The Radio Murder
Mystery was a short, only 18 minutes long, and was unique
in that it was based on NBC's weekly Sherlock Holmes radio
program, a series that also starred Richard Gordon as
Holmes, and Leigh Lovell as Watson. The Radio Murder
Mystery, however, did not actually see Gordon and Lovell
literally playing Holmes and Watson. They were shown
pretty much as themselves, solving a murder mystery taking
place at the same radio studio where they were broadcasting
their Sherlock Holmes radio show.

The year also saw British National Talkies releasing
The Veteran of Waterloo. Based on Conan Doyle's play A
Story of Waterloo, the film version was directed by A. V.
Bramble and starred Jerrold Robertshaw as Colonel Gregory
Brewster, Roger Livesey as Sergeant MacDonald, and Joan
Kemp-Welsh as the colonel's daughter Nora. Also seen in
this tale of Colonel Brewster's adventures at the famous Bat-
tle of Waterloo, was Wontner's Mrs. Hudson, Minnie Rayner,
who had the part of the colonel's next-door neighbor.

Richard Gordon, who played Holmes on NBC Radio, went on
to star in the film, <u>The Radio Murder Mystery</u> (Universal
1933) inspired by the radio show.   (Courtesy Eddie Brandt's
Saturday Matinee.)

There was another offbeat Holmes film released the
following year.   Van Buren Pictures' <u>The Strange Case of</u>
<u>Hennessy</u> in 1934 was directed by Ray McCarey and written
by John Burke and Harold Spina.   The 17-minute musical
short featured a Holmes takeoff character named Silo Dance,
who sang, danced and sleuthed his way through the entire
two-reel comedy.   The film was actually the forerunner of
later Holmesian musical stage adventures like the Sadler's
Wells Ballet Theatre's 1953 <u>The Great Detective,</u> starring
Kenneth Macmillan and Stanley Holden; Alexander H. Cohen's
1964 <u>Baker Street: A Musical Adventure of Sherlock Holmes</u>,
starring Fritz Weaver and Peter Sallis; and Thom Racina's

1971 <u>The Marvelous Misadventure of Sherlock Holmes: A
Musical Mystery for Children</u>, starring Michael Kearns and
Donald Livesay.

     BRITISH REAL ART'S <u>The Triumph of Sherlock Holmes</u>
(in America, called <u>The Valley of Fear</u>) in 1935 returned Arthur Wontner for the fourth time to the role of Holmes.   It
was produced by Julius Hagan, directed by Leslie Hiscott,
and written by Cyril Twyford and H. Fowler Mear--the
same production team that made Wontner's first two
Holmes films.   The new adventure was based on Conan
Doyle's novel <u>The Valley of Fear</u>, and also returned to the
screen Ian Fleming as Dr. Watson, and Minnie Rayner as
Mrs. Hudson.   This time around, however, there was a new
Lestrade: Charles Mortimer.   The film also introduced Lyn
Harding as Professor Moriarty.

     Real Art's film was another good adaptation of a Co-
nan Doyle story; in addition, it elaborated on Moriarty's activities.   (In the book, Moriarty was offstage.)   The film
also introduced the original twist (original, at any rate, to
<u>The Valley of Fear</u> story) of having Holmes in retirement,
but coming out of retirement at the instigation of Lestrade
to look into a crime.   "Professor Moriarty, the arch-crim-
inal and inveterate enemy of Holmes, is the perpetrator of
the crime in this instance, which Holmes deduces from a
code message he receives of the intended murder of John
Douglas, an ex-Pinkerton detective who has wormed his way
into the confidence of a secret society and is hounded for
having brought the criminals to book" (<u>The Triumph of Sherlock Holmes</u>, Ambassador Film Distributors production and
campaign booklet, 1935).   At the climax, Moriarty raced up
to the top of an old tower in an attempt to escape, but Holmes
fired his pistol and brought him tumbling down, down, dead.

     Featured in the cast was Wilfred Caithness as Colonel
Sebastian Moran, Moriarty's ace lieutenant; Leslie Perrins
as John Douglas, Jane Carr as Ettie Douglas, Ernest Lynds
as Jacob Shafter, Michael Shepley as Cecil Barker, Ben Welden as Ted Balding, Roy Emerton as Boss McGinty, Conway
Dixon as Ames, and Edward D'Alby as Captain Marvin.

     The year also saw the release of the first Ellery
Queen mystery film, and two more stirring exploits of Sexton
Blake.

Called the "Logical Successor to Sherlock Holmes" by
mystery writer-critic Anthony Boucher, Ellery Queen was
created by two cousins, Frederic Dannay and Manfred B.
Lee, who wrote all the Queen books and stories under the
name of "Ellery Queen," thereby creating the illusion that
Ellery Queen was a real-life detective who was setting down
on paper his most famous cases.   Many people still think,
in fact, that there really is an Ellery Queen.

A deductive sleuth like Holmes, although more the
college youth than the seasoned professional (particularly in
the early books), Ellery Queen usually comes by his cases
through his constantly harassed father, Inspector Richard
Queen of the New York Police Department, and he first appeared on the crime-sleuthing scene in The Roman Hat Mystery, published in 1929.   His screen debut came six years
later, in Republic's 1935 The Spanish Cape Mystery, which
was based on a Queen novel published earlier that year.   Directed by Lewis D. Collins, The Spanish Cape Mystery starred Donald Cook as Queen, and Berton Churchill as his father,
and saw them investigating the bizarre murder of a man found
dead on a beach.   What made the case bizarre was that the
dead man was wearing a Spanish cape around his shoulders.

The two Sexton Blake films in 1935 were Sexton Blake
and the Bearded Doctor and Sexton Blake and the Mademoiselle, both produced by British Fox and starring George Curzon as Blake, Tony Sympson as Tinker, Blake's young assistant; and Marie Wright as Mrs. Bardell, Blake's Baker Street
landlady.

Directed by George A. Cooper, who had directed three
of the 1928 Blake films, Sexton Blake and the Bearded Doctor
was based on a Blake novel called The Blazing Launch Murder, written by Rex Harding, and costarred John Turnbull as
Inspector Donnell, Henry Oscar as Dr. Gibbs, Lillian Maude
as Janet, and Edward Dignon as Hawkins, a crook.   The
story had Blake up against the villainous Dr. Gibbs, who at
one point murdered a violinist in order to collect on the mu-
sician's insurance policy.   The other film, Sexton Blake and
the Mademoiselle, was directed by Alex Bryce and scripted
by Michael Barringer from another Blake novel, They Shall
Repay, written by G. H. Teed.   It featured Edgar Norfolk as
Inspector Thomas, Vincent Holman as Carruthers, a crooked
financier; Lorraine Grey as Roxanne, and Ian Fleming (of the
Arthur Wontner-Holmes films) as Henry Norman.   The story

saw Blake rescuing Roxanne after she got into considerable
trouble when she decided to go after the crooked Carruthers,
who had earlier ruined her father financially.

      ARTHUR WONTNER'S last film as Sherlock Holmes
was 1936's Silver Blaze, a very interesting and entertaining
adventure.   Although Wontner's Holmes films had in general
been received very well in America, Silver Blaze wasn't released in America until 1941.   And when it did begin its run
in America, it was title-changed to Murder at the Baskervilles to try and cash in on the great popularity and fame of
1939's The Hound of the Baskervilles with Basil Rathbone and
Nigel Bruce.   The title change was not without its legitimate
story values, though, because it was clearly not only an adaptation of Conan Doyle's "Silver Blaze" story, but also a sequel to Doyle's novel about the infamous Baskervilles demon.
Professor Moriarty was also on hand here.

      A Twickenham film, Silver Blaze was produced by
Julius Hagen, directed by Thomas Bentley, and written by
Arthur Macrae and H. Fowler Mear.   Featuring the familiar
Baker Street team of Wontner as Holmes, Ian Fleming as
Watson,. and Minnie Rayner as Mrs. Hudson, the film intro-
duced John Turnbull as Lestrade.   Turnbull had some exper-
ience for the part, though, because the year before he'd star-
red as Inspector Donnell in Sexton Blake and the Bearded
Doctor.

      With Lyn Harding once again playing Moriarty, and
Arthur Goulet now playing Colonel Sebastian Moran, Silver
Blaze opened with Holmes receiving a letter from Sir Henry
Baskerville (Lawrence Grossmith).   It was now ten years
after Holmes and Watson had first gone to Devonshire to
track down and destroy the Hound, and to celebrate the tenth
anniversary of that most famous adventure, Sir Henry and
his wife Lady Diana (Judy Gunn) were now inviting Holmes
and Watson to return to Baskerville Hall for a festive reunion.
But when they arrived at Baskerville Hall, Holmes and Watson found there was once again trouble afoot.   Besides its
being the tenth anniversary of the destruction of the Hound,
it was also the time of the annual running of the big Devonshire horse race, and someone had now stolen the neighboring Colonel Ross' (Robert Horton's) prize race horse, Silver
Blaze.   Investigating the business, though, Holmes learned it
was none other than his arch enemy Moriarty who was behind
the theft; and before it was all over he wrote finis to the

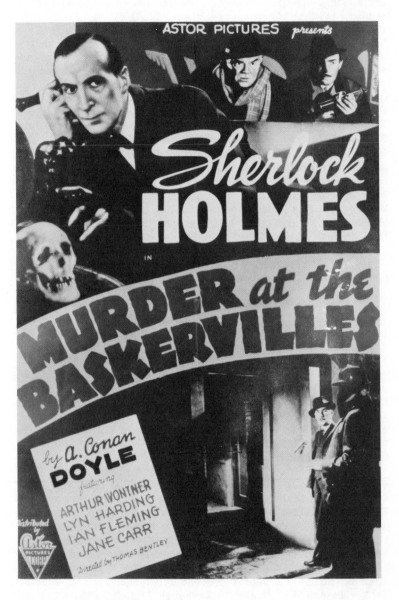

Advertisement for Wontner's last Holmes film, <u>Silver Blaze</u> (Twickenham 1936), retitled <u>Murder at the Baskervilles</u> for its U.S. release (Astor 1941).

professor's schemes and restored the horse to its rightful
owner.

Silver Blaze was a very clever working of Conan Doyle
stories, with new elements and situations written in just as
cleverly. Martin Walker was seen as Straker, Eve Gray
played his wife, and Arthur Macrae, the co-writer of the picture, played the part of Jack Trevor. But even though it
marked Arthur Wontner's last film appearance as Sherlock
Holmes, Wontner did play Holmes one more time. On July
3, 1943, Wontner starred as Holmes on BBC Radio, in a 50-
minute version of "The Boscombe Valley Mystery." His Watson on this occasion was Carleton Hobbs, who later went on
to become the Sherlock Holmes of British radio, playing the
part in more than 75 adventures, with Norman Shelley as
Watson. Hobbs' radio shows, first broadcast from 1952
through 1969, are still playing on the air in various cities
in America.

The first Nero Wolfe film, and another exploit of
Craig Kennedy were also released in 1936.

Directed by Herbert Biberman, Columbia's Meet Nero
Wolfe was based on Rex Stout's first Wolfe novel, Fer-de-
Lance, published two years earlier, and starred Edward Arnold as Nero Wolfe,[2] that orchid-loving, work-hating, New
York City detective whom some believe is actually the son
of Sherlock Holmes and Miss Irene Adler. Meet Nero Wolfe
costarred Lionel Stander as Archie Goodwin, Wolfe's everlastingly energetic legman, and featured Victor Jory and Joan
Perry in a story that saw Nero Wolfe solving the mystery of
a college president who was murdered on a golf course. But
today the film is as obscure as many of the early Holmes
films themselves.

The Craig Kennedy adventure was The Clutching Hand,
a 15-chapter serial produced by Stage & Screen Pictures.
Directed by Albert Herman, and written by Leon D'Usseau
and Dallas Fitzgerald, The Clutching Hand starred Jack Mulhall as Kennedy, Rex Lease as reporter Walter Jameson,
and saw America's scientific Sherlock Holmes and his associate battling their old enemy the Clutching Hand, who was
after an inventor's secret process for manufacturing synthetic
gold. Joseph W. Girard, Mae Busch, Robert Frazer, William Farnum, Richard Alexander and Ruth Mix, the daughter
of cowboy star Tom Mix, were also featured in this sometimes exciting cliffhanger.

Three new Holmes films were released in 1937, and they were all made in Germany. Bayerische's The Hound of the Baskervilles, starring Bruno Guttner as Holmes and Fritz Odemar as Watson, was the first of the trio.

Today still another lost, even though comparatively recent, movie, Bayerische's 1937 Hound, was produced and directed by Karl Lamac, who had directed the 1932 Lelicek in the Service of Sherlock Holmes. It featured Peter Voss as Sir Henry Baskerville, Ernest Rotmund as Dr. Mortimer, Erich Ponto as Stapleton, Arthur Malkowski as Sir Hugo Baskerville, and Lilly Schonberg as Mrs. Barrymore. The picture was written by Carla Von Stackelberg, and also featured Fritz Rasp as Barrymore, the butler. In 1929 Rasp had played Stapleton in the third screen version of the Hound novel.

The second German Sherlock Holmes film released in 1937 is also a vanished film today: Terra-Filmkunst's Sherlock Holmes and the Grey Lady. Produced and directed by Erich Engels, and written by Engels and Hans Heuer, the picture starred Hermann Speelmans as Holmes, Trude Marlen as Maria Iretzkaja, the lady of the title; Ernst Krakow as Inspector Brown, Edwin Jurgensen as Baronoff, and Henry Lorenzen as Peppercorn. Germany's third Sherlock Holmes film that year is, however, still around.

Produced by UFA Pictures, The Man Who Was Sherlock Holmes was directed by Karl Hartl, written by Hartl and Robert Stemmle, and starred Hans Albers and Heinz Ruhmann. According to Hollywood film producer Alex Gordon, however, "Hans Albers and Heinz Ruhmann did not actually play Holmes and Watson.... They dressed and were mistaken--like and for--the two and never denied it, but were not actually those two characters" ("Letters," E-Go Collectors Series 4, September, 1976).

The reason Albers and Ruhmann were masquerading as Holmes and Watson (at one point, tracking down a stolen stamp) was simple enough: as detectives they weren't getting very many clients, so they decided that if people thought they were Sherlock Holmes and Dr. Watson, the famous sleuths, they'd get more. They fooled many people this way, but at various points in the story they kept running into one particular individual who knew they were imposters; and at the end of the film this man (played by Paul Bildt) revealed himself to be none other than Sir Arthur Conan Doyle himself.

The year 1937 also marked another first for Sherlock
Holmes: on November 27, 1937, the detective made his debut as a television star. The first words he ever spoke in
front of a television camera were, "Friend Watson. Have
you ever heard of a Garrideb?"

TAKEN FROM THE STORY by Doyle, NBC-TV's The
Three Garridebs was a 30-minute program broadcast from
Radio City, and was, as The New York Times put it, "the
most ambitious experiment in tele-showmanship so far attempted over New York. The shadow reincarnation of Conan
Doyle's master detective ... served to introduce the first
full-length dramatic presentation of the Radio City showmen
...." A broadcast that used film clips of exterior scenes to
bridge the "Live" sequences coming from the television studio
itself, the Sherlock Holmes program "offered an interesting
glimpse into the future of a new form of dramatic art ..."
("Shadowing a Sleuth; Holmes Stalks the City by Television--
Football Pictures Are Clear," November 28, 1937).

A truly historically important television program that
is nearly always completely overlooked in histories of television, NBC's The Three Garridebs had been authorized by
the Conan Doyle Estate, through Lady Jean Conan Doyle, and
adapted by Thomas H. Hutchinson. It was a very faithful
version of the adventure of Mr. John Garrideb, Counsellor-
at-Law, who requested that Sherlock Holmes help him locate
two other men named Garrideb, so all three of them could
split up a fortune left in the rather unique will of a wealthy
man who was also named Garrideb.

The program starred Louis Hector as Holmes, complete with cape and deerstalker, and featured William Podmore as Watson. Louis Hector gave a very convincing,
forceful performance as Holmes, while Podmore's Watson
was by contrast rather mild-mannered. They both came off
well, however. Louis Hector was anything but a stranger to
Holmes: he had originally played the role on NBC Radio in
29 Holmes adventures during the 1934-1935 season.

The Three Garridebs costarred Arthur Maitland as
John Garrideb, Eustace Wyatt as Inspector Lestrade, Violet
Besson as Mrs. Hudson, James Spottswood as Nathan Garrideb, and Selma Hall as Mrs. Saunders, and opened with a
shot of the London skyline, after which it shifted "to the 'live'
studio where ... Sherlock Holmes was seen looking out of his

Louis Hector (left) as television's first Sherlock Holmes, seen
here with Arthur Maitland as John Garrideb in The Three
Garridebs (NBC 1937). (Courtesy Eddie Brandt's Saturday
Matinee.)

Baker Street window...." The story locations were mainly
confined to "two studio sets, one representing the detective's
apartment and the second the home of John Garrideb...."
Other film clips showed "Holmes and Watson riding in a hansom cab through the streets of London to the home of Garrideb in search of a new clue ..." (New York Times, November 28, 1937).

        NBC's big night of experimental television[3] in 1937
also included the song and dance team of Lucille and Lanny,
singer Sylvia Bruce, and then newsreels featuring in one segment football highlights of a game between Yale and Harvard.
The year also saw the first films of detectives Dick Tracy
and Mr. Moto playing in theatres.

Chester Gould's indomitable, square-jawed police
sleuth arrived on screen in Dick Tracy, a Republic serial
directed by Ray Taylor and Alan James, and written by Barry
Shipman, Winston Miller, George Morgan, and Morgan Cox.
The 15 chapters starred Ralph Byrd as Tracy[4] and Lee Van
Atta as Junior, and had Tracy battling a fiendish master criminal named the Lame One, who terrorized the nation with such
devices as a gadget that zapped out destructive sound waves.
The Lame One also had a handy gadget that could turn men
into zombies.

Fox's Think Fast, Mr. Moto was directed by Norman
Foster, and was based on John P. Marquand's novel that saw
Moto, the polite and deductive Japanese secret agent, trying
to discover the identity of international smugglers who were
smuggling great sums of American money into Manchuria.
The Fox movie had Moto, played by Peter Lorre,[5] going to
Shanghai from San Francisco to round up men who were smuggling diamonds; and from that point on the film version took
more original story turns.

There weren't any new Sherlock Holmes films made
in 1938, but on April 28th of that year Britain did broadcast
its very first Sherlock Holmes radio program. Heard over
the Detectives in Fiction series, Silver Blaze was a half-
hour version of the Conan Doyle story, starring F. Wyndham
Goodie as Holmes, and Hugh Harben as Watson. Eastman
Kodak in America also released A Lost World in 1938. Produced and directed by Kenneth R. Edwards, this was a ten-
minute documentary teaching film that used excerpts from
First National's 1925 The Lost World feature release. The
year also saw a new Sexton Blake adventure, and the first
Saint and Mr. Wong films.

Released by King Pictures, the British Sexton Blake
and the Hooded Terror was produced and directed by George
King, and starred George Curzon as Blake for the third time.
The picture was written by A. R. Rawlinson from the novel
The Hooded Terror by Pierre Quiroule, and featured Tony
Sympson as Tinker, and Marie Wright as Mrs. Bardell. The
story had Blake up against the machinations of one Charles
Oliver, a master criminal heading a secret, masked terror
society.

Besides its being a decent thriller, perhaps the most
interesting thing about the film--at least insofar as matters
Holmesian are concerned--was that the villainous hooded

terror was played by Tod Slaughter, who himself had once played Sherlock Holmes. That had been ten years earlier, on stage in 1923 in <u>The Return of Sherlock Holmes</u>, the very same play in which Eille Norwood had made his final bow as Holmes. Slaughter had toured England with this play in 1928. His everlasting fame lies with his many excellently melodramatic roles of villainy on both stage and screen, however.

Leslie Charteris' debonair Simon Templar came to life on screen in RKO's <u>The Saint in New York.</u> Based on Charteris' novel about the Saint battling and outwitting American gangsters in Manhattan, the 1938 film was directed by Ben Holmes and starred Louis Hayward as the Robin Hood of Modern Crime. It was an engaging debut for Templar, the crime adventurer and sometime out-and-out sleuth, and though Louis Hayward left the part after this one film, he returned to it years later in another RKO film, <u>The Saint's Girl Friday</u>, released in 1954. By that time, however, there had been many more Saint films made, starring the likes of George Sanders and Hugh Sinclair.

Mr. Wong, Hugh Wiley's Oriental sleuth, debuted at the movies in <u>Mr. Wong, Detective.</u> Wiley had originally created Mr. Wong in <u>Collier's Magazine</u> stories, and the character of Wong was in the tradition of Charlie Chan and Mr. Moto. The film version from Monogram starred Boris Karloff[6] and was directed by William Nigh. It featured Grant Withers as Wong's policeman friend, Captain Street of the Homicide Division, and had the softly spoken, kindly and gracious Wong methodically tracking down the murderous mastermind behind the triple slaying of three wealthy, and very powerful industrialists.

NOTES

[1] In 1910 Claude King had played Watson to H. A. Saintsbury's Holmes on stage in Conan Doyle's <u>The Speckled Band: An Adventure of Sherlock Holmes</u>, at the Adelphi Theatre in London.

[2] Besides Nero Wolfe, Edward Arnold also played Captain Duncan MacLain, the blind detective, in films. Arnold's two outings as Bayard H. Kendrick's New York City sleuth were MGM's <u>Eyes in the Night</u> in 1942, and then <u>The Hidden Eye</u> in 1945.

[3]Interestingly enough, it was none other than Maurice LeBlanc, the creator of Arsene Lupin, France's national thief, who was one of television's founding fathers. As far back as 1880, LeBlanc had been developing a theory about transmitting pictures through the air; a theory which in fact became one of the fundamentals of telecasting.

[4]Ralph Byrd practically made a career out of playing Dick Tracy. In 1938 he encored in Dick Tracy Returns, then played the role in two more Republic serials, Dick Tracy's G-Men (1939) and Dick Tracy vs Crime Inc. (1941). Then Byrd starred in two feature films made by RKO Radio Pictures, Dick Tracy Meets Gruesome and Dick Tracy's Dilemma, both released in 1947. Finally, on television in 1951 he starred in 26 half-hour episodes of The Adventures of Dick Tracy.

[5]Like Ralph Byrd with Dick Tracy, Peter Lorre also made something of a career out of playing Mr. Moto in the movies. Lorre, however, made all his Moto films within two years' time. All Fox productions, and well produced, these pictures were Thank You, Mr. Moto, Mysterious Mr. Moto, Mr. Moto Takes a Chance, and Mr. Moto's Gamble, all made in 1938; and Mr. Moto in Danger Island, Mr. Moto's Last Warning, and Mr. Moto Takes a Vacation, all made in 1939.

[6]Boris Karloff went on to make four other Monogram-Wong films: The Mystery of Mr. Wong, Mr. Wong in China-town, and The Fatal Hour (all released in 1939); and then Doomed to Die (in 1940).

Seven

RATHBONE AND BRUCE
ARRIVE ON THE SCENE

With the release of 20th Century-Fox's The Hound of
the Baskervilles in 1939, Basil Rathbone and Nigel Bruce began making a series of 14 Sherlock Holmes films that without
question are the most famous, and most popular Holmes films
ever made.

Mysterious, challenging, usually bizarre but always
entertaining, these adventures from 1939 through 1946 had
Rathbone and Bruce coming up against not only favorite, time-
honored villains like Moriarty and Colonel Sebastian Moran,
even the notorious Hound of the Baskervilles itself, but also
many original and colorful new purveyors of heinousness like
the Spider Woman, the Scarlet Claw, the Voice of Terror,
the Creeper; Lydia Marlowe, the hypnotizing murderess;
Giles Conover and Naomi Drake, the jewel thieves; and among
others, Miss Hilda Courtney and her murder gang.   These
films have really become so famous, in fact, that simply
mention the names of Sherlock Holmes and Dr. Watson to
just about anybody anywhere in the world, and you're more
likely to get as a response "Oh yes, Basil Rathbone and
Nigel Bruce" than "Sir Arthur Conan Doyle."

Over the years Rathbone and Bruce have become as
identified with the Great Detective and the Good Doctor as
Hershey is with chocolate bars, Ford with cars, or Howard
Hughes with money.   On a 1975 Los Angeles KNBC-TV news
program, in fact, even newscaster Paul Moyer found himself
interchanging the names of Sherlock Holmes, Basil Rathbone,
Dr. Watson, and Nigel Bruce without so much as blinking an
eye; without a single bit of self-consciousness, and in all perfect honesty.

What happened was that for this particular evening's

new's show, KNBC had sent a cameraman to Century City
Plaza in Beverly Hills to cover an exhibition of world famous
rooms, which included a fine recreation of the famous digs
at Baker Street. For this special television coverage the
station had asked Luther Norris and Captain Cecil A. Ryder,
two well known Sherlockians, to portray Holmes and Watson
in person in the Baker Street sitting room. Complete with
deerstalker, Inverness and magnifying glass, and with top hat
and black medical bag, Norris and Ryder had often played
Holmes and Watson at special doings, and now as the TV
camera slowly panned Century City's Baker Street room,
newsman Moyer told viewers that here we are now at the famous rooms occupied in London by Sherlock Holmes and Dr.
Watson.   Then as the TV camera panned over to where Luther Norris and Cecil Ryder were standing in the room and
looking back at the viewers, Moyer said that, and surprise
of surprises, here they were now, in person, the famous occupants themselves: Sherlock Holmes and Dr. Watson--with
Luther Norris playing Basil Rathbone, and Cecil Ryder taking
the part of Nigel Bruce.

Quote unquote.

During a 1962 press interview, Basil Rathbone had
said, "I liked Holmes. Well ... I was Holmes. All the
same, he did have some bad habits, you know, and he was
awfully pompous. I don't know how Watson put up with him
all those years. I don't know how I did. The only mystery
I couldn't solve was the same one Conan Doyle had: how to
get rid of the man!" (The Magic Sword, a Bert I. Gordon
Production; United Artists Press Interview, 1962).

Which was true enough. Because for all the worldwide acclaim and income it brought him over the years, Rathbone did after awhile become very upset about Holmes. Besides playing him in 14 movies and one guest appearance in
a film, Rathbone also was Sherlock Holmes in 219 radio programs, two television shows, once on the stage, and in various recordings. Having become identified with the character,
he found it difficult to escape the inevitable typecasting. Producers and audiences, especially in the late 1940s, had come
to think of him as Holmes and not Rathbone. It was virtually

Opposite: Basil Rathbone and Nigel Bruce, the most famous
Holmes and Watson of all, in 1939. (Courtesy George Morgan Collection.)

the same complaint, as Rathbone has pointed out, that piqued
Conan Doyle after a while: the world was thinking of Doyle
as simply the creator of Sherlock Holmes, and not as a serious author who also wrote Holmes stories.

Rathbone's irritation with Holmes was never a lasting
thing, however. In later years he was again speaking kindly
and warmly about the detective--just as he'd been talking
about him while making his first Holmes film in 1939.

"I THINK THAT HOLMES is one of the greatest characters in fiction," Basil Rathbone said while making The
Hound of the Baskervilles for Fox. "With all the thousands
of detective and mystery stories that have been written since,
the name of Sherlock Holmes still stands at the head of the
roster of famous sleuths. It is synonymous with the very
word 'detective.' To play such a character means as much
to me as ten Hamlets!

"Ever since I was a boy and first got acquainted with
the great detective," Rathbone went on, "I wanted to be like
him. My desire to be an actor also began when I was a
youngster, so it was only natural to combine the two--and
here I am!" (20th Century-Fox Press Interview, 1939).

And there he was, playing Sherlock Holmes with Nigel
Bruce as Watson, Richard Greene as Sir Henry Baskerville,
and Wendy Barrie as Beryl Stapleton in Fox's well-produced,
large-scale film about the giant unearthly monster Hound that
roamed the fog-shrouded countryside of Dartmoor with eyes
blazing and fangs bared. The studio's publicity at the time
described the "tall, spare, hawklike Basil Rathbone" as having "the perfect-fitting role," and garbed in deerstalker cap
and Inverness, with pipe and magnifying glass in hand, and
Watson at his side, Rathbone certainly did present a picture
every bit of Holmes. He showed a sharp, enthusiastic sleuth,
and in effect it looked like Holmes himself had stepped out
from the pages of the Conan Doyle stories to recreate his
many adventures for the movie camera now. Nigel Bruce's
Watson was also a classic portrayal. What Bruce did for
the Holmes films here was not only to show a Watson one
liked immediately as simply a person, a Watson one felt instantly comfortable with and even sympathetic towards, but
also a Watson (unlike previous incarnations on screen) who
conveyed all the warmth, charm and flavor that are the Doyle
stories. His Watson was very much his own man.

Newspaper advertisement for Rathbone's and Bruce's first (1939).

"There is no question in my mind that Nigel Bruce was the ideal Watson," Rathbone said (in his In and Out of Character, Doubleday, 1962), "not only of his time but possibly of and for all time. There was an endearing quality to his performance that to a very large extent ... humanized the relationship between Dr. Watson and Mr. Holmes." Rathbone always believed it was "more than possible that our 'adventures' might have met with a less kindly public acceptance had they been recorded by a less lovable companion to Holmes than was Nigel's Dr. Watson...."

They had been friends for years before the Holmes films brought them together professionally, and when "Willy" Bruce died suddenly in 1953 Rathbone recalled that it had been "a painful shock to all of us who had experienced with him his great joy in Elizabethan humor...."

Rathbone's own greatest fame will always be Sherlock Holmes, and ironically his very first films--Innocent and The Fruitful Vine--were made for the Stoll company in England the very year (1921) they embraked on their first series of Sherlock Holmes two-reelers. What's more, Rathbone's original films were even directed and written by Maurice Elvey and William J. Elliott, the creators of the Eille Norwood and Hubert Willis series, and featured in their respective casts many of the Stoll-Sherlock Holmes players.

Innocent, Rathbone's first film, costarred Madge Stuart and had Rathbone playing the part of a selfish painter whom she loved. Filmed two months before Elvey and Elliott made their first Holmes film, Innocent featured Mme. d'Esterre, who was shortly going to become Mrs. Hudson in the Holmes series. Rathbone's second picture, The Fruitful Vine, was released after Stoll made their Hound of the Baskervilles, and costarred Miss Valya as Rathbone's married lover. Robert English and Fred Raynham (Dr. Mortimer and butler Barrymore in The Hound) were both in The Fruitful Vine, as well as other Stoll-Holmes players like Teddy Arundell (Inspector Hopkins of Scotland Yard), Irene Rooke, and Paulette del Baye; and all in all, for Rathbone it was quite a double debut in movies.

Fox's The Hound of the Baskervilles was released in March 1939. A gripping mystery film that many consider the best Holmes ever made, it had plenty of general entertainment value and was an immediate, even overwhelming success that gained for itself a very large, worldwide main-

stream audience. Variety had reviewed it as "a strong programmer that will find many bookings on top spots of key
dualers that attract thriller-mystery patronage ..." (March
23, 1939) but its success went far beyond its appeal to only
those who liked mystery and detective films.

Produced by Darryl F. Zanuck, directed by Sidney
Lanfield and written by Ernest Pascal, Fox's The Hound of
the Baskervilles featured Mary Gordon as Mrs. Hudson, Lionel Atwill as Dr. Mortimer, Morton Lowry as Stapleton,
John Carradine as Barrymore the butler, and Elly Malyon as
his wife. Others in the cast were Ralph Forbes as Sir Hugo
Baskerville, Nigel de Brulier as Selden, the escaped convict;
Beryl Mercer as Dr. Mortimer's wife, Jennifer, Barlowe
Borland as Frankland, Ian MacLaren as Sir Charles Baskerville, and E. E. Clive as a London cabby. The film remains
a very impressive one that seems to get even better as the
years go by.

Set completely in period, the picture was diabolically
menacing, more so than any other Holmes film, past or present. It was powerfully cloaked with a consistently oppres-
sive atmosphere of deep brooding and Gothic foreboding all the
way from Baker Street in the opening reels to Dartmoor and
Baskerville Hall later on, then finally to the classic finale
that saw Holmes and Watson out on the fog-shrouded moors
of Grimpen Mire stalking the legendary Hound with pistol,
lantern and stealth. The Hound itself was played down somewhat, and wasn't quite the equal of the terrifying beast as
described by Conan Doyle in the original novel, but it nevertheless came off well. What so very nearly stole the whole
show, however, was not one of the actors or even the Hound,
but Fox's mammoth reproduction of the great barren moor
country. The set was sprawled over an entire soundstage
and artfully and atmospherically depicted an acre of extremely
depressing-looking landscape of scrubby, leafless trees, rolling gray plains, and even a backdrop of heavily overcast sky.
Fog machines provided the rolling layers of fog that constantly
swept the moor, and when he was interviewed at the time
Richard Greene (Sir Henry Baskerville) said, in fact, that the
set felt very authentic to him because while he was still living in England he would often take a trip to the country of
Dartmoor, where he would spend the day walking through the
great desolate countryside.

"One of my greatest pleasures," Greene recalled (The
Hound of the Baskervilles; 20th Century-Fox Press Interview,

1939), "was to duck out for a day in the country. I'd usually
go to Dartmoor, which is the scene of the action in this film,
and stride across the barren ground with my thoughts running
wild over the idea of the many ancients who lived there thousands of years ago. The forbidding aspect of the area always
took on an additional note of grim mystery from the strange
stone structures erected by the Druids in prehistoric times.

"I can see how such a legend as the Hound of the Baskervilles could have grown in the neighborhood. But I loved
it anyway...."

The film was not without some controversy, though.
"As a concession to the censors the astute British detective
is here seen without his narcotic needle," Hollywood columnist Dorothy Manners wrote, "but excepting this bare detail
Basil Rathbone does a swell job of creating Sherlock right
down to the teeth ..." (Los Angeles Examiner, May 4, 1939).

What happened was that the Hays Office, Hollywood's
film censorship board of the time, objected to the last line
of the film where after having successfully wrapped up the
adventure of the devil hound, Holmes left the room in Baskerville Hall and then returned for a fast moment to say,
"The needle, Watson!" Then he left the scene again, and
presumably Watson was going to follow after him with the
hypodermic. But when the picture went into the release,
Holmes' line was blipped from the soundtrack. When Specialty Films Inc. reissued The Hound of the Baskervilles to
theatres in 1975, however, they presented "the uncensored
original version...."

Talking about the stars of the film in her review,
Miss Manners went on to say that "Rathbone, an acting
smoothie if there ever was one, is a delight as the pipe-
smoking Sherlock--but if it were possible for anyone to steal
scenes from him it would be Nigel Bruce, who is perfection
itself as Dr. Watson...." Six months after The Hound of
the Baskervilles was released, Nigel Bruce again had the
chance to "steal scenes" when he and Rathbone were back on

Opposite: Holmes (Rathbone, second from left) leaves young
Sir Henry (Richard Greene, left) in the care of Watson
(Bruce, right) as Dr. Mortimer (Lionel Atwill) looks on.
The Hound of the Baskervilles (20th Century-Fox 1939).
(Courtesy George Morgan Collection.)

screen again in their second Holmes exploit, which certainly rivals The Hound for the best Holmes picture ever.

PRODUCED BY DARRYL F. ZANUCK, and directed by Alfred Werker,[1] The Adventures of Sherlock Holmes was another big Fox film. Scripted by Edwin Blum and William Drake from William Gillette's stageplay, the picture was in many ways really better than Rathbone's Hound film. For one thing, all the action this time was centered around London and the Baker Street digs, and the story was complete with many amazing Holmes deductions and complex, intriguing problems for him to solve. Besides in general capturing well the spirit of the sleuth, and also the hustle and bustle of Holmes' London at the turn of the century, the film also presented the masterful villainy of the arch fiend Moriarty, who was extremely well played by George Zucco: appropriately menacing and diabolically insidious; the very epitome of subtle, chortling, plotting evil.

"Latest screen treatment of Sir Arthur Conan Doyle's super-sleuth is about the neatest package in several attempts to make Sherlock Holmes exciting on the screen," Wear said. "It is considerably better than the last in this group and should prove a healthy buildup for others in this line of detective yarns.... Well conceived and grippingly presented. Plenty of ingenuity is concentrated into two concurrent mysteries with the impossible clues not made too absurd or too obvious for mystery devotees....

"Realistic production.... Aldred Werker's direction is nicely paced and clear-cut. He never allows the action to drag even in the subdued episodes..." (Variety, September 6, 1939).

The Adventures of Sherlock Holmes costarred Ida Lupino as Ann Brandon, the much put-upon heroine; Henry Stephenson as Sir Ronald Ramsgate of the Tower of London; Alan Marshall as Jerrold Hunter, the Brandon family's attorney; E. E. Clive as Inspector Bristol of Scotland Yard; Mary Gordon as Mrs. Hudson; Terry Kilburn as Billy, the Baker Street pageboy; Peter Willes as Lloyd Brandon, Ann's doomed brother; Arthur Hohl as Moriarty's chief lieutenant, Bassick; Mary Forbes as Lady Conyngham; and George Regas as Mateo, a menacing clubfoot South American gaucho who murdered people with swiftly hurtling bolos.

Rathbone, Ida Lupino (as Ann Brandon), and Bruce in a publicity still from The Adventures of Sherlock Holmes (20th
Century-Fox 1939).   (Courtesy Eddie Brandt's Saturday Matinee.)

Although it was based on the Gillette play, there was
much new in the story, which had Moriarty promising Sherlock Holmes that he was going to break him.   "I'm going to
bring off," the professor vowed, "right under your nose, the
most incredible crime of the century!   And you'll never suspect it, until it is too late!   That will be the end of you,
Mr. Sherlock Holmes!"

Moriarty planned to accomplish Holmes' downfall by
first secretly presenting Holmes with such an intriguing problem to bother himself with that he would completely disregard
a lesser mystery; one that was going eventually to show itself
as that "incredible crime" of which the professor had spoken:
the theft of the Crown Jewels of England from the Tower of
London.

The red herring mystery that Moriarty thought up to throw Holmes off the track was unknowingly handed to Holmes by Miss Ann Brandon, who was fearing then not only for her own life, but her brother's as well. The problem was a dilly that involved an ancient Inca funeral dirge, murders by a strange and baffling killer who used an equally mysterious murder weapon, and also death threat messages that contained drawings of a man with a dead albatross hanging around his neck. But needless to say, before it was all over Sherlock Holmes had not only solved the red herring mystery but also realized the clever game Moriarty had been playing with him; and dashing off with Watson to the Tower of London, Holmes caught the wily professor in the very act of commiting his perfect crime.

In a sequence highly reminiscent of the great Holmes-Moriarty confrontation at the Reichenbach Falls in Switzerland, in the story "The Final Problem," the climax of The Adventures of Sherlock Holmes saw Holmes and Moriarty struggling wildly with one another high atop the Tower of London. Then suddenly Holmes managed to thrust the grappling Napoleon of Crime off the Tower, and Moriarty went plunging into the abysmal black of the Thames so far below.

The film opened with Moriarty standing trial at Old Bailey Court for the murder of a man named Lariat. Because he had an alibi for the time of the murder, however, the professor was declared innocent of the charge. Then there was a commotion at the back of the courtroom and in burst Sherlock Holmes, crying out that he could destroy Moriarty's unshakable alibi and prove him guilty of murdering Lariat. But because Moriarty had already been acquitted, he could not be tried again on the same charge, and so he was a free man; and at this point in the story, the film dissolved to a scene showing Holmes and Moriarty standing together outside the Criminal Courts Building, waiting for hansom cabs to take them their separate ways; and the film as released never did explain exactly what was Moriarty's foolproof alibi, nor how Sherlock Holmes had managed to smash it. These explanatory scenes had been filmed, however, and it is unfortunate they ended up on the cutting room floor because Moriarty's cunning alibi, and Holmes' deduction of the truth, were both extraordinary, and worthy of each of them.

According to the scenes that never reached the theatre screen, Moriarty's alibi for the time of the murder of Lariat was that he was at that time lecturing at the Royal

At the British Museum, the Baker Street sleuth (Rathbone)
and Miss Brandon (Ida Lupino) come across a vital clue in
the form of a stuffed albatross. The Adventures of Sherlock
Holmes (20th Century-Fox 1939). (Courtesy Collectors Book
Store.)

Society to an audience of more than 300 members.   Not only
that. but there was even an official clock in view at all times.
Nevertheless, Holmes' brilliant explanation completely shat-
tered Moriarty's alibi and would have sent the man to the
gallows had Holmes arrived in court only moments sooner.

Speaking out in court (even though the explanation
could do Justice no good because Moriarty had already been
judged innocent) Holmes announced that between the hours of
seven and eleven-thirty of the night Moriarty had lectured at
the Royal Society and Larait was murdered, the master clock
motor at the Greenwich Observatory--the clock that controlled
the standard chronometers in every part of the United King-
dom (including the official clock at the Royal Society)--this
clock had gone mad.

Since Moriarty's alibi was based on the fact that he
was lecturing at the Royal Society at the very time the crime
was committed, and the fact that the clock behind Moriarty
on the stage was operating on directly-wired Greenwich time,
Holmes had gone to the Observatory where he learned that
Dr. Gates, the chief astronomer, was already very much
puzzled by certain discrepancies in celestial observations
made during the night of Moriarty's lecture and Larait's murder.   Working together then, Holmes and Dr. Gates figured
out mathematically that Professor Moriarty had that night of
the lecture and murder tampered with the Greenwich control
clock; that Moriarty had succeeded in accomplishing a time
fluctuation by concentrating a counter-magnetic field to sufficient intensity to affect the Observatory clock motor.   This
caused a deviation in clock-time, and thus established his
alibi of Time.

One other particularly startling (and entertaining) sequence did, however, appear in the final release print.   This
was at a garden party at Lady Conyngham's home, where a
song-and-dance man was entertaining the guests.   With the
camera full on him, the song-and-dance man strutted about
doing his number, and afterwards this happy-go-lucky chap
revealed himself to be none other than Sherlock Holmes in
disguise.   What is certainly unique about this scene is that
Basil Rathbone carried off the song and dance act so brilliantly that even after seeing the film a number of times,
many in the movie audience will still absolutely forget that
it is Rathbone up there singing and dancing away.   Always
it seems a surprise when the entertainer later whips off his
false nose and whiskers to reveal his true identity.   On the

printed page, of course, disguises are easy to pull off and
fool somebody with, but the movie camera has an all-seeing
eye and it's to Rathbone's everlasting credit as an actor and
showman how well he managed the feat.   Holmes' penchant
for disguises had first surfaced in The Hound of the Baskervilles, where he fooled Watson on the moor with the disguise
of a rather aggressive ragman, and later Holmes films were
generally always highlighted by other fine Rathbone disguises
--everything from a hardboiled seaman to a distinguished
East Indian army officer, an obnoxious antique collector, an
impatient rare book dealer, and more--but Rathbone's disguise as the song-and-dance man must surely stand out as
his ultimate stint.

        Fox's The Adventures of Sherlock Holmes was every
bit as successful as the studio's The Hound of the Baskervilles, but they didn't follow it up with a third film, which,
considering the success of their Holmes films, was odd for
a studio that had been doing rather well producing mystery
series films in addition to their regular features.   Already
Fox was releasing a long string of Charlie Chan films first
with Warner Oland and then Sidney Toler,[2] and they would
have produced even more Mr. Moto films with Peter Lorre
had it not been deemed advisable and patriotic at that point
in world history to stop production on films that starred a
Japanese Hero.   Fox had also produced a series of Nancy
Drew mysteries in 1938-39,[3] and the year after The Hound
of the Baskervilles and The Adventures of Sherlock Holmes
they started, in fact, a brand new mystery film series based
on the exploits of Brett Halliday's private detective Michael
Shayne, played by Lloyd Nolan.[4]   But for some reason Fox
never did make any more Sherlock Holmes films with Rathbone and Bruce, and the next time Rathbone and Bruce
sleuthed as Holmes and Watson on screen was three years
later, in 1942 when they began a series of 12 very popular
and very entertaining Holmes films for Universal Pictures.
These new films, however, were all set in modern times
and not in period like the two Fox films, and so were hardly
a direct continuation of the Fox-Holmes pictures.

        The years in-between were not without the Holmes
and Watson of Basil Rathbone and Nigel Bruce, though, because one month after Fox released The Adventures of Sherlock Holmes film, Rathbone and Bruce started appearing on
a weekly Sherlock Holmes radio series that was eventually
broadcast through 1946, when Rathbone finally decided to quit
playing Sherlock Holmes in both films and on radio, and try
breaking the type-casting mold the sleuth had put him in.

Nigel Bruce as Watson in 1940 NBC's Sherlock Holmes radio series.   (Courtesy Eddie Brandt's Saturday Matinee.)

THE RADIO PROGRAM, The Adventures of Sherlock Holmes, with Basil Rathbone and Nigel Bruce, and Mary Gordon as Mrs. Hudson, was first broadcast over NBC on October 2, 1939, and in the opening weeks the show presented the adventures of the Sussex Vampire, Silver Blaze, the Speckled Band, the Man with the Twisted Lip, the Devil's Foot, the Bruce-Partington Plans, the Lion's Mane, the Dying Detective, the Creeping Man, Charles Augustus Milverton, the Musgrave Ritual, and Wisteria Lodge.   The Conan Doyle story adaptations by Edith Meiser continued through

the years with the Adventure of the Empty House, the Red-
Headed League, the Boscombe Valley Mystery, the Reigates
Squires and more, and in 1942 Rathbone and Bruce even starred in a special six-part radio-serial version of The Hound
of the Baskervilles.

The first installment was broadcast on January 12th of
that year, and recalling those programs, writer-radio historian Jim Harmon said: "I will never forget those evenings,
listening to the episodes about the cursed Baskerville family
and their private demon.... On radio, [the Hound] was real
--more real than the movies were ever able to make him,
for who could match the befanged ghastlies blooming in the
imagination of a six-year-old boy and nourished by the genius
of some of the greatest of all mystery writers, the stylish
melodramatics of a Basil Rathbone, and the matchless skill
of an anonymous sound effects man in a cramped radio studio."[5]

There were other Rathbone-Bruce radio adaptations of
Conan Doyle's original Holmes stories, but by the time they
completed their 219th and final radio adventure on May 27,
1946, many new exploits had been written for them and dra-
matized over the air, including the Giant Rat of Sumatra, the
Murder in the Wax Works, the Vampire of Cadiz, Murder
Under the Big Top, the Case of the Red Leeches, the Notor-
ious Canary Trainer; Sweeney Todd, the Demon Barber of
Fleet Street; the Walking Corpse, the Phantom Iceberg, the
Fingerprints that Couldn't Lie, the Case of Mrs. Farintosh's
Opal Tiara, the Hampton Heath Killer, the Telltale Pigeon
Feathers, the Amateur Mendicant Society, the Monster of
Gyre; the Case of the Aluminum Crutch, the Frightened Poli-
tician, and the Trained Cormorant (all one title); Murder in
the Himalayas, the Vanishing Elephant, the Paradol Chamber,
the Werewolf of Vair, the Secret of Stonehenge, the Peculiar
Persecution of John Vincent Harding, the Voodoo Mystery,
the Case of the Dying Rosebush, the Third Hunchback, Mur-
der by Remote Control, The Island of Uffa, the Haunting of
Sherlock Holmes, the Invisible Necklace, Murder at the
Opera, Death on the Scottish Express, the African Leopard
Men, the Limping Ghost, the Syrian Mummy, the Camberwell
Poisoning Case, the Viennese Strangler, the Dentist Who Used
Wolfbane, and Murder in the Casbah among so many others.

These original Holmes radio stories--some were
(vaguely) inspired by the original Conan Doyle stories--were
variously written by Bruce Taylor, Anthony Boucher, Denis
Green, and Edith Mesier, the last of whom has the distinction

of having written the first of all Holmes radio shows, NBC's
The Adventure of the Speckled Band on October 20, 1930,
starring William Gillette and Leigh Lovell.   Of special note,
though, is the Rathbone-Bruce radio series scripter Bruce
Taylor--who was in reality Leslie Charteris, the creator of
the Saint.

   The Sherlock Holmes films Basil Rathbone and Nigel
Bruce started appearing in for Universal Pictures in 1942
were all set in the modern 1940s, but their radio adventures,
like their two Fox films, were period exploits.   Rathbone and
Bruce even appeared in deerstalker and top hat in various
radio publicity photos of the time, and during the forties what
all this amounted to was that you could actually get two Sherlock Holmeses and two Dr. Watsons for the price of one:
Rathbone and Bruce in modern times in the films, and simultaneously Rathbone and Bruce in the gaslight era on radio.

NOTES

[1] Alfred Werker previously directed a Sherlock Holmes player
   when in 1936 he directed Clive Brook in British Capitol's Love in Exile, a romantic comedy in which Brook
   had the role of King Regis VI.

[2] After completing Charlie Chan at Monte Carlo in 1938, his
   16th Chan film, Warner Oland died, and Fox continued
   the series with Charlie Chan in Honolulu, starring Sidney Toler, who went on to make 11 more Chan films
   for them.   Fox dropped the series in 1942, but Monogram Pictures picked it up then for yet 11 more Chan
   films with Toler.

[3] Based on the novels by Carolyn Keene, which are still published and widely read today, Fox's Nancy Drew films
   starred Bonita Granville as the intrepid teenage sleuth,
   John Litel as her attorney father Carson Drew, and
   Frankie Thomas as her boyfriend Ned.   The Fox films
   were Nancy Drew, Detective (1938); and Nancy Drew,
   Reporter; Nancy Drew, Troubleshooter; and Nancy
   Drew and the Hidden Staircase (all 1939).   The last
   title was based on one of Keene's most famous published stories.

[4] Fox produced seven Michael Shayne films with Lloyd Nolan:
   Michael Shayne, Private Detective (1940); Sleepers

West, Dressed to Kill, and Blue, White and Perfect
(all 1941); and The Man Who Wouldn't Die, Just Off
Broadway, and Time to Kill (all 1942).

[5]"For Armchair Detectives Only," The Great Radio Heroes
by Jim Harmon; Doubleday, 1967. In 1975 Harmon
produced his own Holmes radio story as an episode of
Trail of Mystery, starring Curley Bradley, the "Tom
Mix of Radio," Harmon himself as Deputy Dallas Jud-
son, and George De Normand as their adventurer pal,
Ringo. In the story, "The Man Who Was Not Sherlock
Holmes," Kirk Alyn played "Sherlock Holmes." For-
merly Alyn had played Superman and Blackhawk in
film serials. Richard Gulla was cofeatured as "Dr.
Watson" and Patrick Culliton played "Moriarty."

Eight

THE MYSTERY MASTERS
AT UNIVERSAL PICTURES

"Temptress of Pleasure, or Mistress of Murder?"

That was one of the more provocative advertising
catchlines used by Universal Pictures to announce their 1942
release of <u>Sherlock Holmes and the Voice of Terror</u>, the
first of their 12 new Holmes thrillers starring Basil Rathbone
and Nigel Bruce, with Mary Gordon continuing as Mrs. Hudson. The adline was a bit misleading, though, because the
film was actually about Holmes and Watson battling Nazi spies,
and it really didn't offer any female character who could
properly be described by anyone other than a studio publicist
as either a "temptress of pleasure" or "mistress of murder."

Directed by John Rawlins, and written by Lynn Riggs
and John Bright, <u>Sherlock Holmes and the Voice of Terror</u>
set Holmes and Watson squarely in modern 1940s wartime
and saw them foiling the mysterious "Voice," whose frightening radio broadcasts always accurately foretold Nazi sabotage
attacks in England. In reality, the Voice was a top Nazi spy
named Von Bork who was secretly posing as a member of
Britain's top security council--the same group of men who
called Holmes in to capture the unknown agent. The Voice's
jeering broadcasts (which Holmes later deduced were not actually "live" performances on the air, but pre-recorded messages that were then broadcast at the proper time) dared all
England to try and stop the Nazi sabotaging of railroads and
munitions factories, for example. But because of the success of these many Nazi raids on the homefront--and also because of the mocking Voice's gleeful warnings that soon the
whole country itself was going to fall to the Master Race--
the British people were feeling greatly demoralized and on
the brink of even greater despair. So it was up to Sherlock
Holmes to stop the Voice, bring him to justice, and thus re-
store British morale.

126

	The cast featured Reginald Denny as Sir Evan Braham,
Henry Daniell as Anthony Lloyd, Montagu Love as General
Lawford, and Leyland Hodgson as Captain Shore; all members
of Britain's Intelligence Inner Council, one of whom was
really the Voice of Terror. The picture also cast veteran
character actor Thomas Gomez as Meade, one of the saboteurs, and Evelyn Ankers as Kitty, the only girl in the film
who could conceivably be likened to a "temptress of pleasure,"
though even at that, hardly a "mistress of murder." Kitty
was a dancehall girl, working out of the dismal and rough
Thomas River waterfront territory, and in a number of in-
stances in the story she proved invaluable to Holmes by se-
curing information he could use in his war on the nefarious
Voice.

	Universal's Sherlock Holmes and the Voice of Terror
was a fast-paced, enjoyable thriller that set the tone and style
for the 11 other Rathbone-Bruce films that were going
to follow from Universal during the next four years; and like
nearly all these other films in this memorable and classic
series, Sherlock Holmes and the Voice of Terror was also
based to some extent on one of the original Conan Doyle
stories. In this case, the Riggs-Bright script came from
Robert D. Andrews' adaptation of "His Last Bow," the epi-
logue of Sherlock Holmes that featured Holmes against a German enemy spy named Von Bork. The film version ended
with the famous closing lines from the original story as
Holmes and Watson looked out over the North Sea from the
ruins of a bombed-out church, after Holmes had ended the
manace of the voice.

	"Good old Watson! You are the one fixed point in a
changing age. There's an east wind coming all the same,
such a wind as never blew on England yet. It will be cold
and bitter, Watson, and a good many of us may wither before its blast. But it's God's own wind none the less, and
a cleaner, better, stronger land will lie in the sunshine when
the storm has cleared...."

	Actually none of the Universal-Holmes films (Howard
Benedict was the Executive Producer of the entire series)
were wholly based on any of the Conan Doyle stories. Mostly
the generally well-written, and thoughtfully conceived mystery
screenplays only borrowed certain incidents or characters
from any of the 60 Conan Doyle adventures, and then used
them as foundations or pivotal plot elements for what amounted
to new and original screen stories. Regardless, the scripts

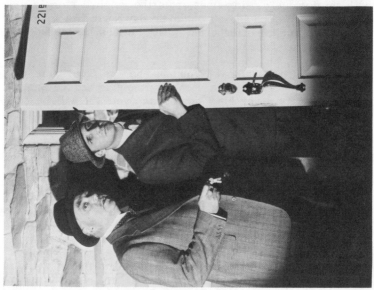

were remarkably Doylesque in concept, loaded with Baker
Street flavor and excitement, and they very faithfully captured
and conveyed the essence and spirit of Conan Doyle. Faithfully updating Holmes had been the studio's intention right
from the start, however, as witness the special prologue that
appeared on screen at the opening of Sherlock Holmes and
the Voice of Terror, and then was repeated in the next two
films:

> "Sherlock Holmes, the immortal character of fiction
> created by Sir Arthur Conan Doyle, is ageless, invincible
> and unchanging. In solving the significant problems of the
> present day he remains--as ever--the supreme master of de-
> ductive reasoning...."[1]

Except to purists, Universal's change of era for Sherlock Holmes and Dr. Watson never really mattered one iota.
As far as the general film audiences were concerned, Universal was making very entertaining mystery films that very
successfully managed to transport Holmes and Watson into
the modern era, and if high-speed taxis replaced hansom
cabs, or telephones took the place of messengers, it was
nevertheless the same familiar figure of Conan Doyle's Sherlock Holmes who could be seen working out problems at
Baker Street. Too, the Universal films were all creatively
mounted to at least express the basic flavor of those bygone
days, and so they were for the most part all wonderfully atmospheric with menacing fog and shadow, gaslight-type mystery. Some of the films even nicely acknowledged the past
era by showing Holmes' famous deerstalker hanging from a
peg of the hat tree at Baker Street. In Sherlock Holmes and
the Voice of Terror, in fact, on his way out the door with
Watson for an important meeting of the Intelligence Inner
Council, Holmes even reached to that hat tree to pluck up
the deerstalker and put it on. But Watson quickly intervened,
"Now, Holmes, you promised...." Whereupon Holmes nod-
ded, glanced fondly at the deerstalker for a moment, then
grabbed up a more modern styled hat to wear into the new
world.

Opposite, left: Rathbone and Bruce sleuthing in the contem-
porary 1940s for Universal. (Photo from 1944). Right:
The two show Holmes' new walking stick to Evelyn Ankers,
(Kitty, the dancehall girl) on a break from filming Sherlock
Holmes and the Voice of Terror (Universal 1942).

At the very outset of the series, though, there was
concern about what Universal might be doing to Holmes by
updating him.

"Here's Sherlock Holmes today fighting the Nazis,"
Frederick C. Othman said, while Sherlock Holmes and the
Voice of Terror was still in production. "Without his two-
way cap, or his calabash pipe, or his magnifying glass.
Tch-tch-tch, or what is this world coming to? This new
Sherlock Holmes even has a telephone in his diggings at 221B
Baker St. He wears a fedora hat, with the brim turned down
front and back. He has a pipe, but it is a briar and in place
of his magnifying glass he's got a microscope....   Shades of
A. Conan Doyle! These movie makers just seem to be going
out of their way for trouble. In the United States alone, according to Rathbone, there are more than 1,000,000 members
of the Sherlock Holmes Club, known as the Baker Street Irregulars ..." and because there were countless millions of
other Irregulars all around the world, Othman warned that if
there was anything wrong with this new, modernized version
of Sherlock Holmes, "Universal will be in a bad way.   Producer Howard Benedict will be looking for a new job.   Director John Rawlins will go back to directing the pretty-pretties,
while good old Sherlock and Dr. Watson probably will have
to go into hiding ..." ("Sherlock Modernized for Films,"
Hollywood Citizen News, May 20, 1942).

At the time of the column, the film was shooting under the title Sherlock Holmes Saves London and to be fair
about it, Othman was quick to point out that Universal did
seem to care about doing a good job with their new version
of Holmes because they'd hired "Thomas McKnight, one of
the world's leading authorities on Holmes, as technical director, and they only hope the Baker St. Irregulars look
upon their undertaking sympathetically...." So Othman suggested, everyone give Universal a chance to see what they
can do, "maybe this picture'll be a masterpiece...."

When the film was completed and released, however,
the reviews were extremely favorable. The Hollywood Reporter even said (September 4, 1942), "The Baker Street Irregulars should admit to membership Lynn Riggs and Robert
D. Andrews [the writers] for the care with which Holmes is
brought up to date without sacrifice for his methods of deductions that capture the imagination...." Variety said that the
direction "by John Rawlins is high grade.... Woody Bredell's
photography is on the low key side, and hits good quality

throughout.... Rathbone carries the Sherlock Holmes role
in great style, getting able assistance from the flustery Bruce
as Dr. Watson. Evelyn Ankers does a fine job characterizing
a Limehouse girl ... while good support is provided by Reginald Denny, Thomas Gomez, Montagu Love, Henry Daniell,
Olaf Hytten and Leyland Hodgson ..." (September 4, 1942).

The picture was a hit.

ALL THE UNIVERSAL films about Sherlock Holmes
were both popular and financially profitable, and the success
story continues healthily through today. For in spite of a
change of era, it is still these Universal films that stand out
as the definitive Sherlock Holmes movies. Every Sherlock
Holmes adventure to come along since (and even the earlier
Holmes films when seen again today) are inevitably compared
to the Universal stories. Even the two Rathbone films made
at Fox in 1939 are compared to the Universal product. The
votes of the general public have always put the Universal-
Holmes films on top.

Universal Pictures, in fact, always had good fortune
updating famous fictional characters. Besides Sherlock
Holmes, their Frankenstein, Dracula, Invisible Man, Mummy,
and Wolf Man films (all set in contemporary times) have also
gone on to become classics of the screen, continuing to gather
new fans and viewers decade after decade. An idea of what
the Universal Holmes films might have looked like had they
been set in the 1890s can, however, be obtained from viewing their film, The Mystery of Marie Roget.

Released the same year as Sherlock Holmes and the
Voice of Terror, The Mystery of Marie Roget was a period
mystery film based on Edgar Allan Poe's story of the same
title. Directed by Phil Rosen, and written by Michael Jacoby, it starred Patric Knowles as Dupin, Poe's investigator,
and Maria Montez as the vanishing Marie Roget. Although it
wasn't a terribly exciting film, The Mystery of Marie Roget
was still a very playable programmer budgeted at about the
same figure as any of the studio's Holmes films, or other
program features. The period art direction and costuming
were fine (though of course half a century before Holmes
heyday), and there can be little doubt that had Universal
wanted, they could easily have set Holmes, Watson and Mrs.
Hudson in their original period.

Top: Professor Moriarty (Lionel Atwill) gets the drop on Rathbone and Bruce. (Courtesy Eddie Brandt's Saturday Matinee.) Bottom: Rathbone (center, in disguise as a rare book dealer, tries to interest Moriarty's agents. <u>Sherlock Holmes and the Secret Weapon</u> (Universal 1943). (Courtesy Larry Edmunds Cinema Shop.)

The second film was <u>Sherlock Holmes and the Secret
Weapon</u>. With Roy William Neill directing, the 1943 adventure was written by Edward T. Lowe, W. Scott Darling and
Edmund L. Hartmann from an adaptation by Darling and Lowe
of the story "The Adventure of the Dancing Men." The film
introduced Inspector Lestrade into the series, and also rein-
troduced Professor Moriarty. Although Rathbone's Holmes
had first met and triumphed over Moriarty back in the late
Victorian era of <u>The Adventures of Sherlock Holmes</u> at 20th
Century-Fox in 1939, there was yet a fine gesture at continuity here in the new film when references were made to
Moriarty's present known whereabouts: the bottom of the
Thames River (where he had plunged after battling Holmes
atop the Tower of London in the Fox film). Now, though,
it was shown that he had escaped death in the Thames, and
was once again on the loose.

The cast featured Mary Gordon as Mrs. Hudson, Dennis Hoey as Inspector Lestrade, and Lionel Atwill as Moriarty. Others included Paul Fix as Mueller, Holmes Herbert
as Sir Reginald, Phillip Van Zandt as Kurt, Harold De Becker
as Pegleg, and Harry Cording as Brady. The story had
Moriarty and his henchmen trying to get their treacherous
hands on "the secret weapon," a new and vitally important
airplane bombsight invented by Dr. Franz Tobel (William
Post, Jr.). Moriarty wanted to sell the bombsight to the
Nazis, but after using various disguises and much deduction
--including the deciphering of a complicated code message
made up of "dancing" stick figures--a code presented to
Holmes by Charlotte Eberli (Kaaren Verne), the missing inventor's girlfriend--Sherlock Holmes finally tracked Moriarty's
agents to their headquarters, where Holmes was duly captured
and then met Moriarty face-to-face again. In a last-ditch effort to try and talk the professor out of selling out their native England to the Nazis, Holmes tried appealing to Moriarty's patriotism, but the man would have none of it. He was
going to sell the precious bombsight to Germany, make a lot
of money out of the deal, and England could therefore go blow
in the wind for all <u>he</u> cared. Before he made the sale,
though, Moriarty decided to eliminate the bothersome Sherlock
Holmes once and for all.

Moriarty's fiendish scheme in <u>Sherlock Holmes and
the Secret Weapon</u> was to strap Holmes to an operating table
in his laboratory and drain the sleuth of every last drop of
his blood, while standing by and gloating over Holmes' ago-
nizing death throes. Holmes, however, escaped this terrible

death, thanks to the timely intervention of Watson and Lestrade,
and during the ensuing melee Moriarty lost his own life (apparently) when he plunged through a trapdoor death device
he'd previously set up for his enemies.

Sherlock Holmes and the Secret Weapon was every bit
as entertaining (if not more so) as The Voice of Terror, and
director Roy William Neill stayed on eventually to direct all
the remaining Rathbone titles. Neill had a fine master's
touch with the series and even though his Sherlock Holmes
pictures really were basically produced as B-mystery program features, Neill and his crew of writers and technicians
seemed to wrest as much well-constructed story and production values from their Holmes stories as could be seen in
much bigger budgeted films. Neill's Holmes adventures usually all had plenty of moody, suspenseful Gothic overtones
and the series' lighting alone was as fine as you could get
anywhere, and better than that seen in even most of today's
million dollar epics.

Neill had been directing films for some years before
he took on the Baker Street exploits. One of his most remembered hits was the 1935 The Black Room for Columbia--
a Boris Karloff thriller, one of his very best. It was set
completely in period and told the Gothic tale of a legend that
said when twins were born to the De Berghmann family, the
family line would cease to exist with the murder by the
younger twin of the older in the castle's infamous Black
Room. Karloff played both twins, and it was a very eerie
film. Then later Neill went to England where most of his
films were light-hearted comedy exploits with Reginald Purdell and Claude Hulbert. In 1938, Quiet Please with Purdell,
Lesley Brooks and Ian Fleming (Arthur Wontner's Watson)
was a comedy about a gem theft. Simply Terrific had Purdell and Claude Hulbert involved with a cure for hangovers.
The Viper saw Purdell and Hulbert as detectives, using disguises to capture an escaped convict who'd stolen the heroine's
valuable diamond. Double or Quits (also 1938) was a straight
mystery caper, though, with Frank Fox, Patricia Medina and
Ian Fleming in a story about a thief who absconds with a rare
stamp while aboard a transatlantic ocean liner. (Later the
film would be recalled somewhat with the making of Neill's
Pursuit to Algiers with Rathbone and Bruce.) Then Neill
made yet another comedy with Purdell and Hulbert, Many
Tanks, Mr. Atkins (1938), which had them saving a newly
invented tank superweapon from spies.

Besides Neill's directing, Dennis Hoey's Lestrade was also a formidable and welcome addition to the series, and after debuting in <u>The Secret Weapon</u> Hoey reappeared as the popular Lestrade in many of the later films.   While he wasn't quite a faithful recreation of the Lestrade from the original Conan Doyle stories, Hoey's blustery and brazen inspector nevertheless entertainingly completed the basic Baker Street unit of four (with Holmes, Watson and Mrs. Hudson) and he provided a fine foil for both the sleuth and the doctor.   Lestrade was, in fact, portrayed as being even less bright than Nigel Bruce's Watson, and so Watson's little moments of deductive triumph over the ever-dumb, but lovable Lestrade in various of the adventures were memorable moments.

Courtesy of Roy William Neill, Dennis Hoey's "Lestrade" was featured in another Universal film that year.   With Neill directing, <u>Frankenstein Meets the Wolf Man</u> starred Lon Chaney as the lycanthropic Lawrence Talbot and Bela Lugosi as the Monster, and the picture saw Hoey in the opening reels interrogating a hospitalized Talbot about his startling claim of identity (Talbot was claiming he was Lawrence Talbot, but Lawrence Talbot was supposed to have been dead and buried for three years then).   Hoey's police inspector was named Owen, but for all practical purposes it was Lestrade himself, complete with familiar bowler, raincoat and brazen personality.

One can only wonder why "Lestrade" here chose not to reveal his true identity to either Talbot or the staff at the hospital; but he must have had his good reasons.

Universal made two other Sherlock Holmes films in 1943: <u>Sherlock Holmes in Washington</u> and <u>Sherlock Holmes Faces Death</u>.   The Washington adventure was written by Bertram Millhauser and Lynn Riggs, and turned out to be the last time Holmes took on enemy agents at Universal.   Its story had Holmes and Watson traveling to Washington, D. C. , to solve the disappearance of an important document that had been brought to America by Alfred Pettibone (Gerald Hamer), a British secret service agent mysteriously abducted from a train bound for the nation's capitol.   Holmes figured out the secret document had been put on microfilm while Pettibone was still in London, and then deduced the clever agent had concealed the microfilm between the covers of a matchbook; arriving in Washington, the sleuth from Baker Street investigated the train from which Pettibone had been kidnapped, and

after talking with the porter in charge of the club car, deduced further that Pettibone had given the matchbook to society's own Nancy Partridge (Marjorie Lord), who didn't know
the matchbook was anything more than a matchbook.

Tracing the Partridge girl and the elusive little matchbook that kept traveling from one unknowing person to another,
Holmes' search eventually led him to the antique shop of William Stanley (George Zucco), an enemy agent who saw through
Holmes' disguise of a persnickety antique collector, and captured him.   Stanley had previously kidnapped Nancy Partridge
as well, and she had the matchbook back in her purse again,
but though Stanley absently fooled with the matchbook he never
guessed that it contained what he was after.   At the climax,
it was Holmes himself who showed Stanley how stupid he'd
been.

The others in the cast included Henry Daniell as William Easter, one of Stanley's henchmen; John Archer as Lieutenant Peter Merriam, Nancy's boyfriend; Edmund MacDonald as
Detective-Lieutenant Grogan of the Washington police; Thurston Hall as Senator Babcock; and Don Terry as Howe, another
of Stanley's thugs.

The next film, Sherlock Holmes Faces Death, returned
Holmes and Watson to the kind of bizarre mystery exploits
for which they'd always been famous.   Based on "The Musgrave Ritual," Sherlock Holmes Faces Death was written by
Bertram Millhauser and was a very effective, atmospheric
"old dark house"-type thriller about ancient Musgrave Manor,
which was being used now as a home for shell-shocked British officers returning from the war that was still very much
raging across real-life Europe.   Watson himself was in
charge of the treatment of these mentally-disturbed, or
nerve-wracked, men but when the head of the house, old
Geoffrey Musgrave (Frederick Worlock), was found murdered
under very strange circumstances, Holmes himself stepped
into the scene.   Close on his heels came Lestrade (Dennis
Hoey).

The story that followed was certainly a clever one,
about a very old, cryptic, spoken family ritual that Holmes
believed held the key to a long buried family secret of great
value, and thus the reason for murder.   Finally deducing
that the ritual was a code to be played out by human chess
pieces on a giant chessboard that was actually the floor of
Musgrave Manor, Holmes' investigations led him to the dis-

covery of a subterranean crypt where later he set a trap for
the murderer; a trap that shortly seemed to backfire when
the fiend swiped Holmes' gun away from him, and turned on
the sleuth himself--thus facing Sherlock Holmes with death.

Besides Rathbone, Bruce and Hoey, the cast included
Gavin Muir as Phillip Musgrave, Milburn Stone as Captain
Vickery, Hillary Brooke as Sally Musgrave, Arthur Marget-
son as Dr. Sexton, Halliwell Hobbs as Brunton the butler,
Minna Phillips as Brunton's wife; and Gerald Hamer as Major
Langford, Vernon Downing as Lieutenant Clavering, and Olay
Hytten as Captain Mackintosh--war veterans all.

As Holmes and Watson, Rathbone and Bruce also made
guest appearances in a non-Holmes Universal film that year:
Crazy House, a madcap Olsen and Johnson comedy that saw
the two comedians coming to Hollywood to make a movie.
This was big news, their coming, and the word spread rapidly everywhere. When Watson heard about it, he naturally
rushed back to Holmes to tell him, but Holmes interrupted
the good doctor to say he already knew that Olsen and Johnson were coming to town. How did he know? Why, he was
Sherlock Holmes and he knew everything! Other guest stars
like Edgar Kennedy, Billy Gilbert, Andy Devine and Count
Basie & His Orchestra also had cameos in Crazy House.

During the Christmas season that year Rathbone and
Bruce made another appearance as Holmes and Watson. This
was in Hollywood's annual Santa Claus Lane parade. Complete with deerstalker, Inverness, and high top hat, Rathbone
and Bruce rode along in a horse-drawn carriage waving to
the crowds along Hollywood Boulevard.

The year 1943 also saw the first Crime Doctor film.
Created on radio by Max Marcin, the Crime Doctor was Robert Ordway, a psychiatric sleuth. Played in films by Warner
Baxter, the character debuted in Columbia's The Crime Doctor, costarring John Litel, Ray Collins and Margaret Lindsay
(Nikki Porter in Columbia's 1940s Ellery Queen films). The
Crime Doctor was directed by Michael Gordon and told Ordway's origin: that he was a criminal leader who had suffered
amnesia, and who then went on to become a force working
against the underworld. 2

"A FEMALE MORIARTY ...": that was how Sherlock
Holmes characterized Miss Adrea Spedding to Watson in
1944's The Spider Woman.

Well played by Gale Sondergaard, whose fame in the
Spider Woman role has been long lasting and has become, in
fact, even more classically established as the years go by.
Miss Spedding was a sinister, aristocratic woman who was
using large, vicious, hairy-legged spiders to perpetrate the
fiendish "Pajama Suicides," which had all London aghast.
The spidery horrors were of the <u>Lycosa carnivore</u> variety,
and the deaths Adrea caused for insurance policy purposes
had been so-named because all of her wealthy victims, when
bitten by her visiting spiders in the dead of night, instantly
suffered such monstrous pain they were helplessly driven to
self-destruction--usually by leaping right straight out their
bedroom windows while still in their pajamas.

Written by Bertram Millhauser, <u>The Spider Woman</u>
presented Holmes with one of the most memorable evildoers
he had ever faced, whether in books, films, television, radio
or anywhere. [3]   As Holmes himself told Watson, Adrea was
a female Moriarty; one of the most dangerous criminal brains
alive in Europe; a lady who was as "audacious and deadly as
any of her spiders"; and he got on her trail in the film after
faking his own death while with Watson on a fishing vacation
in Switzerland.   The scene was inspired by Holmes' "plunge"
into the Reichenbach Falls in "The Final Problem" story.
But now that Miss Spedding, and all the rest of the world
too thought him dead, Holmes was at last free to return to
London to lay a trap for her, and when he arrived back at
Baker Street (to shock both Watson and Lestrade) it was in
the disguise of a wizened, nosy mailman.   Then later he disguised himself as Ram Singh, a wealthy officer in His Ma-
jesty's Indian Army, and really got down to the business of
catching the Spider Woman and bringing her to justice.

The film was one of the best in the series.   "It comes
complete with a sterling set of characters," the <u>Hollywood
Reporter</u> said, "and thrills guaranteed to satisfy the most de-
manding of the Baker Street regulars, and enough excitement
to keep the ordinary movie-goer glued to his seat until the
villain is snared and Holmes fades into a crowd, spilling
philosophy, in search of a new adventure.... More to the
point, this is one of the better films based on the tales of
Sir Arthur Conan Doyle.   Credit can be equally divided between Roy William Neill, who produced and directed, and
whoever was responsible for the special effects, which do
much to lift the picture above the standard level and give it
the stamp of thoughtful production ..." (January 6, 1944--
the 90th anniversary of Sherlock Holmes' birthday).

Inspector Lestrade (left, Dennis Hoey) and Holmes (Rathbone)
collar the villainous Adrea Spedding (Gale Sondergaard) in
The Spider Woman (Universal 1944). (Courtesy The Sherlock
Company.)

Variety also praised the adventure, saying that while
it carried the imprint of past successes, it has "chiller action all its own, to elevate this meller as topper of series
thus far. Basil Rathbone and Nigel Bruce ... score in action which is both unique and typical of Sir Arthur Conan
Doyle style.... Series is becoming more and more Doyle-ish
with each successive edition. Current production is an exciting and well worked-out adventure in the career of Sherlock Holmes which brings him as near death as sleuth ever
faced.... Story as worked out by Bertram Millhauser is engaging piece of writing and serves as excellent setting for
realistic action on part of entire cast. Miss Sondergaard
acquits herself with menacing charm, and Dennis Hoey again
portrays series character of Scotland Yard Inspector Lestrade
with his usual aplomb.... Roy William Neill ... must be

singled out for outstandingly good piece of endeavor. Neill
builds up to strong climax, never allowing action or interest
to falter, with result picture marks signal triumph for him
..." (January 6, 1944).

Arthur Hohl played Adam Gilflower, a noted entomolo-
gist, and Alec Craig played Radik, one of Miss Spedding's
infamous gang. Another member of the Spider Woman's insidious retinue was an ugly pygmy played by Angelo Rossitto;
a character doubtlessly inspired by Tonga, the pygmy in the
novel The Sign of the Four. But although Sherlock Holmes
did finally best the Spider Woman at the clever climax, she
returned to the screen two years later to plot anew. In Universal's The Spider Woman Strikes Back Gale Sondergaard
took on the role again, though now her name wasn't Adrea
Spedding but Zenobia Dallard, who was living in an isolated
mansion on the outskirts of a small southwestern England
city. In this non-Holmes horror film, busy draining off the
blood from her various victims, the Spider Woman was using
her ill-gotten blood to feed a large carnivorous plant from
which she was distilling a poison. In turn, she used this
poisonous extract to kill off her neighbors' cattle in an effort
to force the nearby ranchers into ruination, so she could then
claim their lands for her own.

The Spider Woman Strikes Back wasn't anywhere near
as effective as the Sherlock Holmes outing, but it did return
Gale Sondergaard, always a fine performer, to movies once
more as the infamous Spider Woman. The film also sported
an interesting cast of other players, with hero Kirby Grant
(later to become television's Sky King), heroine Brenda Joyce
(then also playing Jane in Johnny Weissmuller's Tarzan films),
and Rondo Hatton as Miss Sondergaard's hulking henchman.

After The Spider Woman exploit, Holmes and Watson
took on other horrific doings. In The Scarlet Claw (1944)
they journeyed to the fog draped marshes of La Morte Rouge,
a small village near Quebec, Canada, where the Scarlet Claw
(a legendary 100-year-old, glowing monster of the marshes)
was once again on the prowl, slashing open the throats of
men, women, and farm animals. Typically though, Holmes
wouldn't accept the local theory that psychic phenomena were
responsible for the gruesome deaths in the area, and later
he ventured out onto the foggy marshes himself to try and
capture the elusive horror that glowed in the night and committed brutal murder.

Directed very atmospherically by Neill, The Scarlet Claw was written by Edmund L. Hartmann from an original story by Paul Gangelin and Brenda Weisberg, and was styled after The Hound of the Baskervilles. There were many well-lit, well-photographed scenes on the foggy marshes, while the monster itself (like the Baskervilles' hound) was eventually revealed by Holmes to be a real-enough, flesh-and-blood murderer who'd been dressing up in phosphorescent clothing and using a sharply-honed gardener's hand rake to slash up his victims. The cast included Paul Cavanagh as Lord Penrose, Gertrude Astor as Lady Penrose (one of the Scarlet Claw's victims), Miles Mander as Judge Brisson, Gerald Hamer as Potts the mailman, David Clyde as Sergeant Thompson, Arthur Hohl as barkeeper Journet, and Kay Harding as his daughter Kay (who became another victim). Neither Lestrade nor Mrs. Hudson appeared in this film, which remains one of the best in the series.

In The Pearl of Death (also released in 1944) Holmes and Watson again encountered one of their more memorable villains: the Creeper, a hulking brute played by Rondo Hatton. Based on "The Adventure of the Six Napoleons," the screenplay for The Pearl of Death was written by Bertram Millhauser and saw Holmes and Watson at first matching wits with Giles Conover (Miles Mander) and Naomi Drake (Evelyn Ankers), two notorious jewel thieves who were after the infamous Pearl of Death, a valuable gem that had been causing murder and misfortune ever since the days of the Borgias.

Actually, Conover was successful in stealing the pearl from the London museum where it was on display, but when he was pursued by police he was forced to dash into a statue-making establishment where he quickly hid the Pearl in one of six plaster busts of Napoleon. Later his pretty but dangerous accomplice Naomi started seeking out the various people who had meanwhile bought the six busts, and then Conover sent the Creeper after them. A gargantuan imbecile who loved Naomi (who was understandably in terror of him), the Creeper not only broke the Napoleon busts to find the Pearl that was hidden in one of them, but he also broke the backs of the innocent people who were by now the owners of the statues. In the finale, it was Holmes himself who had possession of the last statue (which contained the Pearl), and it was all the sleuth could do to stop the Creeper from snapping his spine too.

With The Pearl of Death, Dennis Hoey as Lestrade

With The Pearl of Death (1944), Universal began advertising
their Holmes films not so much as new adventures of the detective and Dr. Watson, but new exploits of Rathbone and
Bruce. (Courtesy Eddie Brandt's Saturday Matinee.)

---

and Mary Gordon as Mrs. Hudson both returned to the series;
others in the cast were Holmes Herbert, Ian Wolfe, Richard
Nugent and Charles Francis. Besides being a good thriller,
however, The Pearl of Death is noteworthy because it was at
this point in the series that Universal practically eliminated
the names of Holmes and Watson from their advertising.
From here on out the Sherlock Holmes films Universal made
weren't advertised with typical blurbs like "Basil Rathbone
as Sherlock Holmes" and "Nigel Bruce as Dr. Watson," but
with "Basil Rathbone and Nigel Bruce Crack the Mystery of
--The Pearl of Death!" Generally the name of Conan Doyle
was retained somewhere in the respective ads, but for all
practical purposes the advertising for The Pearl of Death and
the five other films to come only heralded the release of a
new Rathbone-Bruce film, not a new Holmes-Watson exploit.

The names and identities of the actors had become so synonymous with those of the characters that so far as Universal
was concerned (and the public too), using one name was as
good as another.

The climax of The Pearl of Death saw the Creeper
shot down; however, like the Spider Woman before him, popularity brought him back to life again. In 1946 Rondo Hatton
encored as the Creeper in Universal's The House of Horrors.
Costarring Robert Lowery (who was shortly to play Batman
in movie seriels) and Virginia Grey, The House of Horrors
was about a mad sculptor, played by Martin Kosleck, who
was using the Creeper to avenge himself on art critics who
didn't like his work. And perhaps there would have been
even more Creeper films had not Rondo Hatton died shortly
after finishing the picture. The Creeper was and still is a
favorite character.

After The Pearl of Death, Rathbone and Bruce went
to Paramount Pictures to make Frenchman's Creek. Based
on the Daphne du Maurier novel, Frenchman's Creek was a
period costume adventure film starring Joan Fontaine and
Arturo de Cordova. Rathbone had the part of Lord Rocking-
ham, an aristocratic scoundrel who was lusting after Miss
Fontaine, while Nigel Bruce played Lord Goldolphin, a country squire, a good fellow. Rathbone and Bruce were in at
least one scene together, but in it they hardly even acknowledged each other.

A new Sexton Blake film was also released in 1944.
Produced by Louis H. Jackson, and written and directed by
John Harlow, British National-Strand's Meet Sexton Blake
starred David Farrar as Blake, John Varley as Tinker, and
Kathleen Harrison as Mrs. Bardell. Farrar had debuted in
Sexton Blake films with a small part in the 1938 Sexton Blake
and the Hooded Terror, but now he was the sleuth himself,
battling enemy agents who were after a formula for a new
airplane alloy that was vital to the war effort. The cast
featured Dennis Arundell as Johann Sudd, the alloy inventor,
with Gordon McLeod as Inspector Verner, and Jean Simmons
as Eva Watkins. Meet Sexton Blake was reminiscent of
Sherlock Holmes and the Secret Weapon in that in both films
the Baker Street sleuths were taking on enemy agents who
were anxious to obtain important wartime inventions.

The next year Rathbone and Bruce made three more
Holmes films. The first, The House of Fear ("Walls of

Hate, Holding an Orgy of Murder--as Crime's Master Minds
Crack Their Weirdest Case!") was scripted by Roy Chanslor
and based on "The Five Orange Pips." One of the best in
the series, The House of Fear told the story of a unique club
known as "The Good Comrades," whose members lived in
voluntary seclusion at a rather mysterious looking Scottish
castle called Drearcliff House. The club members were
Ralph King (Dick Alexander), Stanley Raeburn (Cyril Delevanti), Guy Davies (Wilson Benge), Captain Simpson (Harry
Cording), Alan Cosgrave (Holmes Herbert), Simon Merrivale
(Paul Cavanagh), and Bruce Alastair (Aubrey Mather). Their
housekeeper was the grim-faced Mrs. Monteith (Sally Shepherd), and each of the Comrades carried a very large life
insurance policy, made out to the surviving members. Everything had been going along fine for the group, but when suddenly the Comrades started receiving strange messages one
by one and dying hideously shortly afterwards, it was time
for Holmes and Watson (and G. Lestrade) to step into the
case.

The messages that signaled doom came to the respective Comrades in the form of envelopes containing as many
orange pips as there were still Good Comrades alive. It
was all very perplexing, and frightening, but thanks to Holmes'
various deductions and a vital clue given Holmes by Watson
himself, the bizarre and compelling Adventure of the Good
Comrades of Drearcliff House was finally brought to a successful finish.

A non-Rathbone film, Pereda's Arsenio Lupin [Arsene
Lupin] was also released in 1945. Produced in Mexico, the
picture was based on the Arsene Lupin stories by Maurice
LeBlanc, including the story "Herlock Sholmes Comes Too
Late." In one segment Arsenio Lupin had Holmes arriving
at an estate where Lupin the thief was planning to steal the
valuables. The film has not been seen in years.

IN THE PERSON of Henry Daniell, Moriarty returned
to movie villainy in The Woman in Green, the second of the
1945 Rathbone-Bruce films. "Henry Daniell's masterly Moriarty," Rathbone had said of Daniell's performance. "There
were other Moriarty's, but none so delectably dangerous as
was that of Henry Daniell...."

Written by Bertram Millhauser, The Woman in Green
featured elements from "The Adventure of the Empty House"

--most notably the attempted assasination of Holmes from the
window of the house across the street from 221B--and saw
Daniell's fine Napoleon of Crime working in cahoots with
Lydia Marlowe (Hillary Brooke), beautiful and seductive hypnotist.   They were terrifying London with a crime wave the
newspapers were calling "The Finger Murders" because in
each case the victim was a young woman whose right thumb
had been hacked off.   The missing finger was part of a diabolical Moriarty-Marlowe plot to blackmail wealthy men.

        First the alluring Miss Marlowe would lure their po-
tential victim to her swank apartment, and then hypnotize the
man.   Then after she sent him out to commit murder while
in a trance, Moriarty would make sure to retrieve a thumb
from the unfortunate girl victim, and then plant that thumb
on their wealthy "client."   When he awoke the next morning,
lo and behold, there was someone's thumb in his pocket.
Then realizing he could remember nothing at all about what
happened the night before, he would hear there was a hor-
rible "Finger Murder" committed the night before, and putting two and two together would come to the conclusion that
he himself was the guilty party.   At this point enter Lydia
Marlowe again, though now with Professor Moriarty, and
promising an alibi for the hours in question (the time during
which the murder had been committed) in exchange for certain financial considerations.

        The climax had Lydia luring Sherlock Holmes himself
up to her swank penthouse apartment, where she apparently
hypnotized him.   Then Moriarty eased into view and ordered
Holmes to write a suicide note, put it in his pocket, and
then walk off the patio of the penthouse to certain death many
floors below.   But Holmes escaped the plot, and it was Moriarty himself who ended up taking the big plunge when he
tried getting away from Holmes, Watson, Inspector Gregson
(Matthew Boulton) and the London bobbies.

        Paul Cavanagh had the role of Sir George Fenwick,
one of Moriarty-Marlowe's wealthy clients, while Sally Shepherd (the eerie housekeeper in The House of Fear) returned
with another maid portrayal, that of Crandon, who was working for the beguiling lady hypnotist.   One particularly funny
sequence saw Holmes and Watson going to the Mesmer Club
where despite all his charges that hypnotism was a lot of tom-
foolery, and that it would never be put over on an intelligent
man, Watson was himself hypnotized and made to take off his
sock in public.

In The Woman in Green (Universal 1945), Professor Moriarty (Henry Daniell, left) and Lydia Marlowe (Hillary Brooke, right) force an apparently hypnotized Holmes (Rathbone) to write his own suicide note, as accomplices Crandon (Sally Shepherd) and Williams (Tom Bryson) look on. (Courtesy The Sherlock Company.)

Variety called the film "a creditable addition to Universal's 'Sherlock Holmes' series.... It carries plenty of suspense.... Hillary Brooke as the blonde menace does some worthy acting ... but she is plenty hypnotizing without even making the passes ..." (June 15, 1945). The Hollywood Reporter pointed out that "the art direction of John B. Goodman and Martin Obzina is painstaking ..." (June 15, 1945). And in The New York Herald-Tribune, besides also favorably reviewing the film as "one of the better Sherlock Holmes mystery thrillers," Otis L. Guernsey, Jr., said that "fortunately the picture isn't in too much of a hurry to show [Holmes] at home, with Watson, concentrating on logic and playing the violin, or to let [Holmes] exercise his sense of humor a little when he isn't foiling malevolent intent" (June 16, 1945). Guernsey felt that Rathbone came very close in spirit to the

Sir Arthur Conan Doyle original. He added that "Henry
Daniell makes a perfect Professor Moriarty--suave, self-
possessed and confronting Holmes in Baker Street in a cooly
audacious dual of wits."

The Woman in Green was Moriarty's second appearance in the Universal series, and though Universal destroyed
the professor rather effectively here, many hoped they would
return the criminal genius to life in other pictures. Moriarty
was certainly the most deadly, and most famous of all Holmes
villains, and Universal had done well by him in two films already; so even though Moriarty died (again) in this second adventure, audiences would have been glad to accept him alive
and back in full, evil harness again in other films. But Universal never did bring him back, although his shadow certainly loomed over the events in Terror by Night, released
the following year.

After The Woman in Green, Rathbone and Bruce made
Pursuit to Algiers. Scripted by Leonard Lee, the film was
based on a reference in "The Norwood Builder" story to "the
shocking affair of the Dutch steamship Friesland, which so
nearly cost us both our lives...." The picture had Holmes
and Watson agreeing to help the authorities of Rovenia, a
mythical European monarchy, after the King of Rovenia had
been assassinated. Their task was to insure the safe conduct
from London to Algiers of the King's young heir Nikolas (Leslie Vincent). Nearly the entire film, then, was spent aboard
the steamship Friesland that was taking Holmes, Watson and
Nikolas (disguised as Watson's nephew) to Algiers, where Ro-
venian dignitaries were going to meet Nikolas and take him
back to the home country. En route to the Mediterranean,
however, the expected trouble reared up when the ship was
boarded by three suspicious-looking characters with the
equally suspicious sounding names of Mirko, Gregor and Gu-
bec (Martin Kosleck, Rex Evans and Wee Willie Evans).
Later Holmes unmasked them as indeed being involved in a
plot against young Nikolas.

One other ship's passenger was outstanding: the attractive Sheila Woodbury (Marjorie Riordan). A red herring
in the story (audiences were supposed to think she was another
plotter), Holmes later revealed Sheila was simply the unwill-
ing agent for a jewel thief; and after Holmes finished trying
to help Sheila straighten out her life, there was a brief romantic interlude between them. Watson was astonished, but
Holmes enjoyed it; proving of course that no matter what kind

of a female-berater Holmes might appear to be at times, that beneath it all he was a regular ladies' man.

While Pursuit to Algiers wasn't one of the strongest films in the series, it did offer Nigel Bruce some memorable scenes: when he sang "Loch Lomond," when he told the story of "The Giant Rat of Sumatra" at a party on the ship, and the scene of his grim, even bitter-against-the-world reaction to hearing that Sherlock Holmes had been killed in an airplane crash. (This sequence took place before Holmes joined the Friesland.)

The year 1945 also saw the release of another new Sexton Blake exploit, and also radio's I Love a Mystery team of Jack Packard and Doc Long at last come to life on the screen.

British National-Strand's The Echo Murders returned David Farrar to the role of Sexton Blake. Also returning were John Varley as Tinker, and Kathleen Harrison as Mrs. Bardell, the Baker Street landlady. Written and directed by John Harlow, The Echo Murders featured Dennis Price, Pamela Stirling and Patric Curwen in a mystery-action film that saw Sexton Blake going undercover to trap a group of Nazis loose in England. Columbia's I Love a Mystery, on the other hand, was a moody, near-horror puzzler that had private investigators Jack Packard (Jim Bannon) and Doc Long (Barton Yarborough) going up against a weird Oriental cult that was anxious to get the head of the still-living millionaire Johnathan Monk (George Macready). Directed by Henry Levin, I Love a Mystery featured Nina Foch and Carole Matthews, and was based on the I Love a Mystery radio serial story, "The Decapitation of Jefferson Monk."

Probably the best mystery-adventure series ever heard on the air, Carleton E. Morse' I Love a Mystery unfortunately proved only mediocre fare when it came to the movies in 1945. On radio, Jack and Doc (with their friend Reggie York, an Englishman) braved thrilling and memorable adventures, but the film versions were extremely tame reminders of them. [4]

NOTES

[1] This special, explanatory prologue for updating the Holmes films has subsequently been cut from the television release prints of the Universal-Holmes pictures.

[2]Warner Baxter made 10 popular Crime Doctor films. All
produced by Columbia, the other films included The
Crime Doctor's Strangest Case (1943) with Reginald
Denny and Lynn Merrick; Shadows in the Night (1944)
with George Zucco, Minor Watson, Nina Foch and
Ben Wilson; The Crime Doctor's Warning (1944) di-
rected by William Castle, with Miles Mander and
John Abbott; The Crime Doctor's Courage (1945) with
Jerome Cowan and Hillary Brooke; The Crime Doc-
tor's Manhunt (1946) with William Frawley and Ellen
Drew; Just Before Dawn (1946) with Martin Koslech
and Mona Barrie; The Crime Doctor's Gamble (1947)
with Micheline Cheirel; The Millerson Case (1947)
with Paul Guilfoyle and Nancy Saunders; and The Crime
Doctor's Diary (1949) with Robert Armstrong, Adele
Jergens and Lois Maxwell.

[3]Basil Rathbone and Gale Sondergaard had previously worked
together in The Mark of Zorro (1940) with Tyrone
Power, and The Black Cat (1941) with Broderick
Crawford and Bela Lugosi. In both films they were
teamed for menace.

[4]There were three Columbia I Love a Mystery films in all,
and Jim Bannon and Barton Yarborough played Jack
and Doc in all of them. Yarborough had, in fact,
created the role of Doc Long on radio back in 1939.
The other two films were The Devil's Mask and The
Unknown, both released in 1946. Afterwards, Jim
Bannon became more famous in movies as Red Ryder
(in 1949), while Barton Yarborough went into television where he costarred with Jack Webb as Sergeant
Friday's sidekick in the very first television episodes
of Dragnet. Yarborough died while the series was in
production.

Nine

BAKER STREET:
TRANSITION TO TELEVISION

By 1946 Basil Rathbone had had it with Sherlock Holmes. He'd grown weary of the role and frustrated over his extreme identification with Holmes some time before, but he could not quit playing the detective because of long-term contracts with MGM (who loaned him out to Universal for the Holmes films) and the Music Corporation of America (with whom he'd signed years earlier for the Sherlock Holmes radio series). But in 1946 his contracts with MGM and MCA were both going to expire, and as he wasn't going to renew them, he saw this as the perfect opportunity to at last say goodbye to Sherlock Holmes.

Before he could vacate Baker Street, however, Rathbone had two more films to make, and also another season of Sherlock Holmes radio shows.

The first of the 1946 Holmes films was Terror by Night ("Starring Fiction's Mighty Men of Mystery--Basil Rathbone and Nigel Bruce!"). The picture was quite a bit like the previous year's Pursuit to Algiers in that the adventure took place away from London, this time aboard a train bound for Scotland. Written by mystery writer Frank Gruber, Terror by Night was partially based on "The Adventure of the Empty House" and saw Ronald Carstairs (Geoffrey Steele) commissioning Holmes to help him deliver the fabulous Star of Rhodesia diamond to Lady Margaret Carstairs. Watson and Lestrade (Dennis Hoey) were also aboard the train, as was an assorted gallery of passengers on their way to Scotland: Professor Kilbane (Frederick Worlock), Sands (Skelton Knaggs), Mrs. Shallcross (Janet Murdock), Vivian Vedder (Renee Godfrey), and Major Duncan-Bleek (Alan Mowbray), an old school chum of Watson's.

Despite the fact that Holmes, Watson and Lestrade

were all aboard the night train for Scotland, Ronald Carstairs, who was carrying the Star of Rhodesia, was nevertheless murdered, very mysteriously, and the diamond stolen from him. Later Holmes cleared up the strange death by showing that Carstairs had been killed with an air pistol (borrowed from "The Empty House" story) that fired a gelatin bullet that melted away once inside the body. And so the search for the murderer and the diamond got underway on the swiftly moving train.

Although it was strictly confined to the train and its various compartments, Terror by Night was still a better film than usually credited to be. Incidents and dialogue raced along well, and the effective use of many camera dissolves and shots of the train hurtling through the black night to Scotland helped greatly in keeping the pace humming. There was also at least one big surprise, when Holmes showed Watson and all concerned that Watson's old chum, Major Duncan-Bleek, was, in reality, none other than Colonel Sebastian Moran, Moriarty's righthand man; that the plot to steal the Star of Rhodesia was, in fact, hatched by the Moriarty gang.

"There's plenty of suspense and action," The Motion Picture Independent review said (February 2, 1946), "enough to hold any audience's attention. Sherlock Holmes fans will be especially pleased...."

The next adventure was Universal's Dressed to Kill, Basil Rathbone's final bow as Holmes on the movie screen. Fittingly though, it returned Rathbone and Bruce to London and Baker Street. Reviewer Jack D. Gant in The Hollywood Reporter said that the adventure "poses a puzzle worthy of the Doyle tradition and gives Dr. Watson a large, if unwitting share in pointing to the solution...." Rathbone and Bruce, Gant said, of course "account for smooth and practiced work" and the various situations in the film "are uniformly ingenious and will prove pleasing to the Baker Street Irregulars...." He said, "there are times when [director Roy William] Neill's pace is deliberately deliberate, but the production is in every respect tops, thanks to the photography by Maury Gertsman, art direction by Jack Otterson and Martin Obzina, and good music by Milton Rosen...." He thought Patricia Morison's portrayal of Hilda Courtney, the villainess, was "an attractive and engaging performance" and that "Carl Harbord and Tom Dillon are prominent as Scotland Yard men. There is simply a glimpse of Mary Gordon," he pointed out, "yet without her none of the Holmes adventures would be complete..." (May 16, 1946).

Dressed to Kill saw Holmes and Watson up against an alluring but highly unscrupulous and dangerous young woman, Miss Courtney. There was (according to Universal advertising) "A Price on Her Lovely Head, a Dare on Her Luscious Lips, Danger in Her Icy Heart ..." and she was the leader of a murder gang that was out to obtain three identical music boxes that had been made by a certain inmate at Dartmoor Prison. Miss Courtney's treacherous ensemble was composed of Colonel Cavanagh (Fredric Worlock) and Hamid (Harry Cording), and they were after the music boxes because together the boxes held the key to the hiding place of a stolen set of engraved Bank of England plates for five-pound notes. Holmes himself finally obtained one of the boxes, and then correctly decoded a message from its tune; a message that indicated the missing plates were hidden in the library of a certain "Doctor S...." But then Hilda Courtney cleverly stole that music box from Watson while Holmes was away from 221B. The scene was reminiscent of the scene in the story "A Scandal in Bohemia," wherein Holmes starts a phony fire to get Miss Irene Adler to show him where she had secreted a photograph he was after; except that in Dressed to Kill it was this scene in reverse: Miss Courtney started a fake fire to get Watson to show her where Holmes had hidden the music box at 221B. But now that she had all three music boxes, and could thus decode the entire message, it certainly looked like Sherlock Holmes was defeated. But then an unconscious suggestion from Watson (who was feeling terrible about having lost the box to the enterprising young villainess) gave Holmes the vital clue that saved the day.

Rushing to the historical home of Dr. Samuel Johnson, Sherlock Holmes trapped Miss Courtney and her gang in the very act of finding the hidden bank plates. Holmes, however, shrugged off credit for solving the case, and told Inspector Hopkins (Carl Harbord) and Detective Thompson (Tom P. Dillon) that all credit for cracking the mystery should go to Watson--who, surprised as he was by Holmes' quite unexpected and magnanimous gesture of praise, accepted the flattery and congratulations of the police with his usual blushing and harumph-umph-umphing speechlessness.

Opposite, left to right: Sherlock Holmes (Basil Rathbone), Inspector Lestrade (Dennis Hoey), train attendant (Billy Vevan), Colonel Sebastian Moran (Alan Mowbray), and Dr. Watson (Nigel Bruce) aboard the murder express in Terror by Night (Universal 1946). (Courtesy George Morgan Collection.)

Holmes and Watson with Mrs. Hudson (Mary Gordon) in
Dressed to Kill (Universal 1946).

Nigel Bruce, though, quite found his voice again when
his old friend Basil Rathbone shortly announced to one and
all that Dressed to Kill was his last Sherlock Holmes film.
That he was, in fact, going to quit playing Sherlock Holmes,
period.

Everybody--Rathbone's friends and associates alike--
told him he was mad. Quit Sherlock Holmes? It was un-
thinkable. It was absurd. And it was bad business too, they
said. The Universal Holmes films were all popular and profitable, as was the radio series, and Universal was very interested in making even more new Sherlock Holmes films
with Rathbone and Bruce. They had four more planned, in
fact. So Rathbone must go on playing Holmes, they argued.
Look at all the income he'd be losing.

    Rathbone stayed firm, saying he was quitting not only
Sherlock Holmes, but Hollywood too. He was going back to
New York City and the stage, where he believed he could
successfully shake the Holmesian typecasting that frustrated
him so much. Over the years his own identity had increasingly become so buried and lost beneath that of Holmes that
it had long ago even gotten to the point where people had
seriously begun addressing him as Mr. Holmes, or Sherlock;
and the actor in Rathbone could take it no longer. The actor
within him was crying out for new roles--fresh, stimulating
roles--the kind he wasn't getting in Hollywood anymore. In
Hollywood he was Sherlock Holmes, and the few films he did
make in between all the Holmes pictures could hardly be considered major triumphs that could in any way have furthered
his acting career. [1]

    So it was off to New York City then, where Rathbone
believed he could elude the Holmesian devil that pursued him;
where he could take up where he had left off as an actor before Sherlock Holmes came into his life. In New York City,
they never cared what you did in Hollywood. It only mattered
if you were a good actor, and Rathbone was.

    But while he was still in Hollywood, even Nigel Bruce
turned against him and would not speak to him for awhile.
Like everyone else, Bruce thought Rathbone was out of his
mind for wanting to quit Sherlock Holmes. Rathbone and
Bruce had been friends even before the Holmes films brought
them together professionally, and Bruce saw Rathbone's aban-
donment of Holmes (and all the employment that went with it)
as a preposterous thing, and a bad mistake.

    But not even his old friend Nigel Bruce could make
Rathbone change his mind. Universal Studios then decided
simply to stop making the Holmes films. They could have
continued the series with another actor in the role, but they
didn't want to. Rathbone was much too identified with the
part at that time, and it would have been much too soon after
his departure from the films to try to start breaking audiences into the idea of accepting someone else in the role.

    With or without Basil Rathbone, however, the Sherlock
Holmes radio series did continue. In the fall of 1946, Nigel
Bruce returned to the radio microphones with a new Holmes:
Tom Conway, who sounded something like Rathbone, and who
had also been linked with mystery films for some years then
because of his Falcon series. [2] So he was really quite a good

choice to take on the role of Sherlock Holmes at that time, in 39 new adventures broadcast from Hollywood. The next year, however, both Conway and Bruce left the series, which then continued through the years with John Stanley and Alfred Shirley (1947-1948), John Stanley and Ian Martin[3] (1948-1949), and finally Ben Wright and Eric Snowden (1949-1950).

GROWING A MOUSTACHE and leaving Hollywood in summer 1946, Basil Rathbone's escape to New York City proved ironical. Because despite the fact that he did manage effectively (if not totally) to break the Holmesian casting spell by now starring on stage in well-received plays like Obsession and The Heiress, and also by appearing in many different roles on television (whose home was New York in those days), Rathbone's old friend Sherlock Holmes nevertheless kept surfacing and when the offers to play Holmes again came his way, Rathbone didn't turn them down. The upshot of this was that Rathbone shortly became the first actor who could claim he'd played Holmes in films, on radio, television and also on the stage. Later he would even be able to add recordings to the list.

That Rathbone did not turn down these new Holmesian portrayals, however, was not so surprising. His complaint in Hollywood had been that Sherlock Holmes was virtually all he was doing. In New York, with his stage work and diversified television roles, Sherlock Holmes became merely just another in a long string of acting assignments.

Rathbone's first Holmes portrayal after vacating Hollywood was in a Chesterfield cigarette advertisement (see illustration) featured in newspapers and magazines in October 1946. The full-page, four-color ad showed Rathbone (but with moustache) wearing a Universal Holmes modern hat and coat, looking out at the reader, smiling, and lighting a Chesterfield. An inset at the top of the ad said: "BASIL RATH-BONE/ STAR OF/ 'DRESSED TO KILL'/ another of/ Universal's Sherlock Holmes Series."

In 1947 Rathbone was back to more detective work. In between his stage work he found time to star in a new weekly radio series called Scotland Yard's Inspector Burke, in which he had the title role. Then he guested as Sherlock Holmes on the George Burns & Gracie Allen radio show. It was a comedy sequence for Holmes, and one of the publicity photos for the program showed Rathbone in deerstalker and

Rathbone's Sherlockian advertisement for Liggett & Myers Tobacco Company appeared widely in 1946. (Courtesy Eddie Brandt's Saturday Matinee.)

Inverness cape, smoking a pipe. Burns and Allen were also
dressed up like Sherlock Holmes in the photo.   Perhaps the
most unusual Rathbone-Holmes event, however, was the short
story he wrote that year.   Published in the October 1947 issue of The Baker Street Journal, the official organ of the
Baker Street Irregulars, Rathbone's warm-hearted and nostalgic story "Daydream" told how while on a vacation in Sussex "he" chanced to meet the real Sherlock Holmes, who was
now living in retirement and keeping bees.   In "Daydream,"
Rathbone's first-person narrator identified himself to Holmes
as "an Inspector at Scotland Yard," and doubtless this was
Rathbone referring to his then-current role of Inspector Burke
on the Scotland Yard radio series.   Upon learning that his
visitor was connected with Scotland Yard, Holmes exclaimed,
"I thought so!", and then asked how were things down at the
Yard these days?   And judging by the story, Inspector Basil
Rathbone and Sherlock Holmes got along just fine.

Besides Rathbone-Burke meeting Holmes in print,
there was at least one other significant Holmesian event in
1948: the television broadcast of Teatime in Baker Street.
Although the show was only seen in Detroit, and was aired
to coincide with the annual meeting of the Amateur Mendicant
Society, Detroit's Sherlock Holmes club, the program was
nevertheless important because it was the first Holmes television story since the medium had started to catch on with
the public, and prosper.   The original Sherlock Holmes television program, NBC's The Three Garridebs in 1937 with
Louis Hector, was an experimental broadcast for a medium
that most people both in and out of show business really
didn't take seriously at the time, or at best thought would
be nothing much more than perhaps a novelty that would soon
fade away, like talking pictures.   The actual dating of television as a serious medium didn't begin until 1939, when
NBC announced publicly that it was indeed in the television
business.   But it still wasn't until around 1947 that television
really began making itself heard, and heard loudly, and so
it has always been from around this time that historians date
the popular birth of television.   So Teatime in Baker Street
became, then, the first Holmes TV program of the new era,
and the first of many Holmes television shows that were
shortly going to be coming into the nation's homes.

Produced by WWJ-TV in Detroit, and written by Russell McLauchlin, a prolific Holmes scholar, Teatime in Baker
Street was broadcast on March 12, 1948, and interestingly
enough Sherlock Holmes wasn't in it.   The scene of action

was Mrs. Hudson's rooms at Baker Street, where she was
seen first in conversation with Mrs. Wiggins and Mrs. Watson. Then Irene Adler showed up to return the photograph
Holmes had been after from her in the story "A Scandal in
Bohemia." Throughout the dialogue, the women kept referring to him, the man upstairs in 221B, usually with a glance
upwards or a crook of the thumb. Professor Moriarty was
also on hand, though. He showed up to destroy Holmes--
either that, or Holmes had to turn over the valuable gem,
the Blue Carbuncle, which Albert Wiggins (of Holmes' Baker
Street Irregulars) had lifted from the pocket of Moriarty himself when the professor was leaving the Northumberland Hotel
a few days earlier.

The climax of Teatime in Baker Street saw the women
all trouncing Moriarty, and tying him up for Holmes and the
police; all in all the show, tastefully and knowledgeably written, was charming. [4]

In 1949 Basil Rathbone's association with sleuthing
took another odd turn. Starting with The Pearl of Death film
in 1944, Universal Pictures had pretty much stopped advertising their Holmes films as such, announcing them as simply
new Basil Rathbone, Nigel Bruce mysteries, but Rathbone's
new radio series in 1949 went one step further. The show
was called Tales of Fatima (sponsored by Fatima cigarettes)
and many of the shows cast Rathbone as Basil Rathbone, the
famous actor-detective. The stories had Rathbone as Rathbone solving various baffling mysteries usually either before
or after he was finished appearing on stage in some play as
the actor he really was; and if anything, Rathbone's portrayal
here of "Basil Rathbone," sleuth-actor--the Rathbone most
people immediately thought of when they heard his name, or
saw his picture--was even more energetic than the Sherlock
Holmes roles he'd played for so many years before.

To say the least it was a most unusual series for
Rathbone, one that could easily have plunged into self-parody
and satire. But instead it was good fun and showed remarkably well what a sense of humor Rathbone really had about
himself, and his strong actor's identification with detective
roles.

ON TELEVISION IN 1966 the distinguished character
actor Alan Napier became famous for playing Bruce Wayne's
erudite and well mannered butler Alfred on ABC-TV's Batman

series, but it was years earlier when Alan Napier first gained
recognition on television for playing a famous fictional mystery character: Sherlock Holmes himself.

Filmed in Hollywood by ZIV Television and Marshall
Grant-Realm TV, NBC's Story Theatre in 1949 each week
broadcast a famous short story by a famous writer, and that
year presented a half-hour adaptation of Conan Doyle's The
Adventure of the Speckled Band.   Alan Napier played Holmes
as a seasoned investigator, while Melville Cooper's Watson
was closer to the Watson of the original stories than the Watson made so famous by Nigel Bruce.   The adaptation was directed by Sobey Martin and written by Walter Doniger and it
was quite a decent show that stuck closely to its source.
The Speckled Band here even included the famous scene at
Baker Street when Dr. Grimesby Roylott angrily bends the
fire poker out of shape to show Holmes he's not a man to
be taken lightly, and then Holmes bends the iron back into
shape again, showing he's also not to be dismissed so easily.
The television program was also effectively lit for an overall
brooding, Gothic mystery mood, and the sequences at Stoke
Moran, Roylott's home in Surrey, were properly foreboding
with expectant menace.

At the time it was thought that Story Theatre would
perhaps adapt even other Sherlock Holmes stories to its format (The Speckled Band with Napier and Cooper had received
favorable reviews), but this wasn't to be. 5   The idea for putting Sherlock Holmes regularly on national television did,
however, apparently take root with NBC because according
to certain accounts the next year NBC broadcast a Holmes
TV pilot on their Showcase series.   This pilot show is said
to have starred Basil Rathbone, whose 1939 The Hound of
the Baskervilles film was being reissued to theatres then;
but to date research has failed to turn up this reputed Holmes
TV pilot.   Possibly this NBC Rathbone program has for some
reason been confused with NBC's Alan Napier show, which
in fact was rerun by NBC in 1950.   At any rate, there was
a Holmes TV pilot in 1951.

Produced by Rudolph Carter in England, The Man
with the Twisted Lip starred John Longden as Holmes, Campbell Singer as Watson, and Hector Ross as the mysterious
Neville St. Clair.   Directed by Richard M. Grey, the 35-
minute film was based on the Conan Doyle story, and featured Beryl Baxter as Doreen St. Clair, and Walter Gotell
as Luzatto.   But it met with little enthusiasm and The

Monthly Film Bulletin's review of it was typical of the reaction it got: "A three-reeler which is directed and acted in
a rather shoddy manner; the plot development moves at some
points at the most startling speed ..." (April, 1951).

The Man with the Twisted Lip never was broadcast,
but a few months later Holmes did make it to British television. This was a "live" half-hour adaptation of The Adventure of the Mazarin Stone, with Andrew Osborne as Holmes,
and Philip King as Watson. Broadcast by the BBC on July
29, 1951, the teleplay received very favorable notices and so
the BBC was urged shortly to begin a regularly-scheduled,
weekly series of Holmes television adventures: the first such
series ever broadcast.

Produced by Ian Atkin, BBC-TV's Sherlock Holmes
series starred Alan Wheatley as Holmes, Raymond Francis
as Watson, Bill Owen as Lestrade, and Iris Vandeleur as
Mrs. Hudson. Adapted faithfully from the Conan Doyle
stories by C. A. Lejeune, the half-dozen weekly exploits
were set in period and debuted on "live" television with The
Adventure of The Empty House on October 20, 1951. The
episode featured Eric Maturin as Colonel Sebastian Moran;
and the following weeks' stories included A Scandal in Bohemia (October 27, 1951) with Alan Judd as the King of Bohemia and Olga Edwards as Irene Adler, "the woman"; The
Dying Detective (November 3, 1951) with Henry Oscar as
Culverton Smith;[6] The Reigate Squires (November 17, 1951)
with Thomas Heathcote as Alec Cunningham, and Beckett
Gould as the elder Cunningham; The Red-Headed League
(November 24, 1951) with the now-famous Sebastian Cabot
as Jabez Wilson, and Martin Starkle as Mr. Spaulding; and
The Second Stain (December 1, 1951) with John Robinson as
Trelawney Hope, Alvys Maben as his wife, and John Le
Mesurier as Lucas.

Only seen in England, Alan Wheatley's series seemed
to have generally been panned although Wheatley himself, and
Raymond Francis as Watson, seemed to satisfy. Those of
us living in America and not having had the opportunity to
see any of the six adventures can only judge the show, then,
by various publicity photos that have survived, but by those
photos, especially as they reveal the excellent sets, the
Wheatley series did seem at any rate to have adapted the
stories rather faithfully, presenting Holmes and Watson and
the goings-on at Baker Street in a much more Doylesque
light than usually was the case.

The first Sherlock Holmes television series, called simply
<u>Sherlock Holmes</u>.   Here are Raymond Francis (left, as Wat-
son) and Alan Wheatley (as Holmes) in episode number five,
"The Red-Headed League" (BBC, November 24, 1951).

That same year the Sherlock Holmes Society of London produced their own Holmes film, The Sage of Baker Street, a documentary showing photos, memorabilia and London street scenes; while back in America comedians Bud Abbott and Lou Costello lampooned the Holmesian world to some extent in Abbott and Costello Meet the Invisible Man. A Universal film that costarred Arthur Franz as a boxer who became the Invisible Man, Abbott and Costello played detectives complete with deerstalkers, Invernesses, and pipes.

America's scientific Sherlock Holmes, Craig Kennedy, also became a television star in television's early days. In 1952 Craig Kennedy, Criminologist comprised 26 half-hour adventures starring Donald Woods, an actor who earlier had played Earl Stanley Gardner's Perry Mason in The Case of the Stuttering Bishop, a 1937 Warner Bros. feature.[7] The Holmesian highlight of the 1952 winter season was, however, an event that was something unique: the publication in Life Magazine of a brand new Sherlock Holmes short story, "The Adventure of the Seven Clocks," written by Sir Arthur Conan Doyle's son, Adrian Conan Doyle, and that noted mystery writer and Doyle biographer, John Dickson Carr. Publicity had it that Adrian Conan Doyle had worked on the story using the. very same desk his father had used when writing the original Holmes adventures.

Published in the December 29, 1952, issue of Life, "The Adventure of the Seven Clocks" was illustrated by Adolf Hallman and based on a reference Watson had made to a case in "A Scandal in Bohemia." The new exploit was certainly an interesting and entertaining enough puzzler, about a certain Mr. Charles Hendon who was inexplicably going around smashing clocks, but the writing style itself was not quite the perfect duplication of Sir Arthur's style that the writers had hoped to achieve. Regardless, "The Adventure of the Seven Clocks" was well received by the readers, and the story itself was doubtless the prime factor in a new birth of public interest in Holmes, Watson, and the life and times at Baker Street. During the very next year Sherlock Holmes certainly did rise up again on a new wave of popularity and activity, a wave that was immeasurably helped along by the publication of further new Holmes stories by Adrian Conan Doyle and John Dickson Carr. And as with all success stories, whether for the first time around or not, there came with this new interest in Holmes the inevitable comedies, most notably Professor Lightfoot and Dr. Twiddle, two sleuths who were not portrayed by human actors, but chimpanzees.

Carleton Hobbs (right) remains the most famous Holmes of British radio; here he and Norman Shelley, England's most famous radio Watson, pose in a replica of Holmes' study at the Sherlock Holmes Hotel, London, in 1958, at a time when their BBC serial, "The Hound of the Baskervilles," was on the air.

Produced, written and directed by Jerry Courneya, the 1953 Professor Lightfoot and Dr. Twiddle was an outrageous CBC television program starring a bevy of trained chimps. With voices provided by Paul Frees and Daws Butler, the two chimps playing the Holmes and Watson characters came complete with their Baker Street-type apartment, deerstalkers, magnifying glasses, and even violins. There were thirteen 15-minute adventures in all, and they couldn't help but be funny. As the advertising itself promised, when you saw the show you'd go bananas over it.

Originally producer Courneya was simply going to call his program Sherlock Holmes, or at least Chimplock Holmes, but when the Conan Doyle estate threatened to make trouble, he changed the title and lead characters to Professor Lightfoot and Dr. Twiddle. It was absolutely weird, but funny

seeing a chimp walking around his apartment with a deerstalker on his head and playing a violin, while another chimp
sat in an armchair reading a newspaper and in voice-over
narration started telling you about one of their adventures;
but you really can't appreciate the full impact all this kind
of monkeyshines can have until you've actually seen such a
parody for yourself.

Generally speaking the 13 adventures were clever and
laugh-getting. They spanned the globe and included The
Haunted House, Mix-Up in Mexico, Terror by Train, A-
Feudin' and a-Fightin', Inside India, Trapped in a Trunk,
The Hatchet Man, Net of Fate, Out West, A Case of Hypnosis, Darkest Africa, Room for a Night, and Thief in the
Night. The adventures had been shot in color, but weren't
broadcast in color. And a popular series, there would have
been even more chimp shenanigans at Baker Street, and other
points of the compass, had not a fire broken out in the mon-
keyhouse where Courneya's chimps were living, and destroyed
them.

BEGINNING WITH the May 23, 1953, issue of Collier's
magazine, Adrian Conan Doyle and John Dickson Carr's new
adventures of Sherlock Holmes short stories began appearing
on a regular basis. That issue published the first one, "The
Adventure of the Black Baronet," and then brought readers
ten more new exploits over the next five months. Each story
was beautifully illustrated in four colors by Robert Fawcett:
"The Gold Hunter," The Highgate Miracle," "The Sealed
Room," and "The Wax Gamblers." Then John Dickson Carr
bowed out of the series because of illness and Adrian Conan
Doyle wrote the remaining adventures himself: "The Foulkes
Rath," "The Demon Angels," "The Abbas Ruby," "The Two
Women," "The Deptford Horror," and finally "The Red Wid-
ow." And just as had been done with the very first new
Doyle-Carr story, "The Adventure of The Seven Clocks" in
Life Magazine, the Collier's stories were also based on ref-
erences made by Watson to unchronicled exploits, and they
were all worth reading.

One of the new stories, "The Adventure of the Black
Baronet," was adapted to a television play and was, in fact,
broadcast exactly three days after its publication in Collier's
magazine. The issue was dated May 23, 1953, and the television show was broadcast May 26, 1953. Collier's even
made sure to call the reader's attention to the television show

by a special announcement that accompanied the published
story.   Even more interesting, the television program starred Basil Rathbone.

Broadcast on CBS-TV's popular and famous Suspense
show, a half-hour mystery anthology series which went back
to radio days, The Adventure of the Black Baronet starred
Basil Rathbone as Sherlock Holmes, Martyn Green as Watson, and was properly set in period.   The story had Holmes
and Watson traveling to Kent to solve the curious stabbing
murder of Colonel Jocelyn Dalcy, a guest at the ancestral
home of Sir Reginald Lavington.   Actually, Nigel Bruce had
been contacted back at his home in Santa Monica, California
(Suspense came "Live" from New York), about playing Watson in the new adventure, but unfortunately Bruce had to turn
it down on doctor's orders, as he had recently suffered a
heart attack.

Rathbone himself had especially been keen to have
Bruce do the Suspense show because he thought it would also
be good publicity for one of his own new projects: a Sherlock Holmes stageplay his wife Ouida was writing which he
wanted to do with Bruce playing Watson again.   The Black
Baronet television show, he thought, would be an excellent
opportunity to reacquaint national audiences with the Holmes
and Watson characters they'd played years before in films
and radio.   At that time (1953) their Universal pictures had
not yet been released to television, although some of the
films were still playing around the country in third- and
fourth-run houses, and so Rathbone really wasn't quite sure
how many people if any remembered them as having been
Holmes and Watson.

But Nigel Bruce had to turn down both the Suspense
television program and the forthcoming stageplay, and so Rathbone went ahead and did the TV show with Martyn Green.
Not only was it a very decent television version of the Doyle-
Carr short story, The Black Baronet also evoked the kind of
publicity Rathbone was looking for.   The episode brought the
names of Rathbone and Holmes back together again, and cou-
pled with the fact that The Black Baronet came from a series
of new Holmes stories that were going to be published in
Collier's right on through the next October, when his stageplay about Holmes was scheduled to open, Rathbone was
feeling extremely optimistic about the chances of success for
his play.   To further publicize his play, though, he even
agreed to guest star as Holmes on NBC's Texaco Star Theatre,

starring Mr. Television, Milton Berle. Rathbone appeared
on the show in September 1953, one month before his play
was to open in tryouts in Boston.   Complete with deerstalker,
Inverness and magnifying glass (although sporting a moustache
again), Rathbone as Holmes burst into a Milton Berle murder
mystery comedy sketch that really didn't seem very funny.
As Holmes he quickly stalked the stage looking for clues, and
then was gone.   Thankfully, it had been a brief appearance.
But unfortunately, his stageplay also had a brief life.

Rathbone had been thinking about playing Sherlock
Holmes on stage even when he was back at Universal in
Hollywood and making the Holmes films.   And now in 1953,
with the script written by his wife, he was at last making it
happen.   But afterwards he remembered it only as pretty
much of a nightmare.

Based on various of the Conan Doyle stories, Sherlock
Holmes opened at the Majestic Theatre in Boston on October
10, 1953.   Jack Raine played Watson, Bryan Herbert was
Lestrade, Thomas Gomez was Moriarty, and Elwyn Harvey
was Mrs Hudson; others in the cast included Jarmilla Novot-
na as Irene Adler, Richard Wendeley as Cadogan West, Greg-
ory Morton as Lucas, John Dodsworth as Trelawney Hope,
Mary Orr as Alice Dunbar, and Arthur Stenning as Inspector
Gregson.   The basic storyline had Moriarty plotting the theft
of top secret government plans, and after being pursued by
Holmes, meeting the sleuth for their famous encounter at the
Reichenback Falls.   The play was in period, but later even
Rathbone said the story was not quite up to snuff.   They also
had many production problems, and while it was something
Rathbone had wanted to do for a long time, he admitted that
when he finally played Holmes on stage, his heart wasn't in
it.   His performance suffered and it was Thomas Gomez as
Moriarty who actually walked away with the best reviews.
In Holmesian context, they had first worked together in Universal's 1942 Sherlock Holmes and the Voice of Terror,
where Gomez had played Meade, the head of a gang working
for the Nazis.

Rathbone's Sherlock Holmes play ran three weeks in
Boston and then on October 30, 1953, opened at the New Century Theatre in New York City, where it lasted only three performances.   What doubtless did not help Rathbone's mental
attitude about playing Holmes at this time was also the sad
fact that only two days before the play opened in Boston,
Nigel Bruce died in California.   Born in Ensenada, Mexico,

in 1895, Bruce was actually three years younger than Rathbone, a fact most people never realized because Bruce had
always seemed years older.   But Rathbone and the old veteran had been friends and working associates for many years.
Having to play Holmes again so soon upon his former partner's death could not have been for Rathbone very auspicious.

NOTES

[1] Between Sherlock Holmes and The Voice of Terror, the first
    Universal Holmes film in 1942, and Dressed to Kill,
    his last in 1946, Rathbone was cast in only four other
    films: Above Suspicion (1943), Bathing Beauty (1944),
    Frenchman's Creek (1944), and Heartbeat (1946).

[2] Tom Conway inherited the Falcon film series from his real-
    life brother, George Sanders. Created by Michael
    Arlen, Gay Falcon was a free-lance, adventuring in-
    vestigator with an eye for the ladies, and he debuted
    on screen in RKO's The Gay Falcon (1941).   George
    Sanders was the star, and he continued the popular
    role with A Date with the Falcon (also 1941) and The
    Falcon Takes Over (1942).   Then Sanders wanted out
    of the series, and in the next film, The Falcon's
    Brother (1942), the writers cleverly introduced Gay
    Falcon's brother Tom, played by Tom Conway.   To-
    gether, the Falcon brothers waged war on a Nazi spy
    ring, but in the process Gay Falcon was killed.   Tom
    Falcon, however, vowed to continue fighting the crim-
    inal element, and proceeded to do exactly that in nine
    more films: The Falcon Strikes Back, The Falcon
    and the Co-Eds, and The Falcon in Danger (1943);
    The Falcon Out West, The Falcon in Mexico, and The
    Falcon in Hollywood (1944); The Falcon in San Fran-
    cisco (1945); and finally The Falcon's Adventure and
    The Falcon's Alibi (1946).   Then, after playing Sher-
    lock Holmes on radio with Nigel Bruce in 1946-1947,
    Tom Conway once again returned to mystery films,
    now as the new Bulldog Drummond, in RKO's The
    Challenge and then Thirteen Lead Soldiers, a nifty
    puzzler released in 1948.

[3] Besides continuing with various acting assignments on both
    television and in the theatre--and in keeping with his
    (one-season) role of Watson on radio--Ian Martin has
    been one of the frequent writers of CBS Radio's

Mystery Theatre series, which debuted in 1974 and is
heard each night over the CBS Radio Network.   Martin has also acted on many of these mystery and suspense programs.

[4]Russell McLauchlin's script for Teatime in Baker Street
was published in The Baker Street Journal, July 1948,
and then reprinted in Ellery Queen's Mystery Magazine, February 1972.

[5]Other famous stories seen on Story Theatre included de
Maupassant's The Diamond Necklace, Frank R. Stock-
ton's The Lady or the Tiger?, Robert Louis Stevenson's The Sire De Maltroit's Door, Mark Twain's
Million Pound Bank Note, de Coster's Mysterious Picture, Gautier's The Mummy's Foot, and others of this
calibre.

[6]In 1922 Henry Oscar had played Sherlock Holmes on stage
in Conan Doyle's The Speckled Band: An Adventure
of Sherlock Holmes, which toured England and France.

[7]After completing the Craig Kennedy television series, Donald
Woods starred as Inspector Mark Saber on ABC-TV's
Mystery Theatre series.   The role of Saber was first
played, however, by Tom Conway, who thus continued
his association with detective characters begun with
the Falcon, Sherlock Holmes, and then Bulldog Drummond.

[8]In 1954 Random House (New York) collected all 12 adventures and published them in hardcover under the title
The Exploits of Sherlock Holmes.   In London that
same year, John Murray also brought out a hardcover
edition, while Ace Books (New York) then brought out
a paperback version which they called The New Exploits of Sherlock Holmes.   More recently Pocket
Books (New York) has issued a brand new 1976 paperback of the Adrian Conan Doyle-Carr stories, calling
it by the original title.   Pocket Book's edition marked
the first mass-market, English language edition of
these stories since 1954.

Ten

"YOU HAVE BEEN IN
AFGHANISTAN, I PERCEIVE..."

Rowland Bartrop holds a unique distinction in the history of film: whether he knows it or not, he's still the only actor who can claim the distinctive honor of having once introduced Sherlock Holmes to Dr. Watson in front of the cameras. The momentous occasion of this first meeting between Holmes and Watson took place in the opening show of The New Adventures of Sherlock Holmes television series in 1954.

Produced for American television by Sheldon Reynolds, The New Adventures of Sherlock Holmes starred Ronald Howard and H. Marion Crawford, two Englishmen, and was filmed in France. The series consisted of 39 half-hour episodes broadcast over NBC, and while it was never quite the smashing success of the Basil Rathbone-Nigel Bruce films, The New Adventures of Sherlock Holmes was still a very popular series that today is still successfully being syndicated to television stations across the country. (Under the title Sherlock Holmes, the series is, in 1976-1977, being syndicated by Prime TV Films, Inc., of New York City.) The Howard-Crawford shows, though, were not allowed to play in England because they were an unauthorized series.

The son of the noted actor Leslie Howard,[1] Ronald Howard played a young Sherlock Holmes at the very beginnings of his career. Indeed the opening adventures stressed this point: that the show was starting at the beginning of the life and times of Sherlock Holmes, sleuth, and thus pretty much portraying the detective's early, formative years. Yet for all that, Howard's Sherlock Holmes seemed a rather casual Holmes, perhaps too casual and light, and he really came off as being more along the line of the seasoned investigator as played by Basil Rathbone, particularly in the later Universal films when Rathbone had grown so accustomed to the role

Ronald Howard starred in television's <u>The New Adventures of Sherlock Holmes</u> series (Motion Pictures for Television-NBC 1954). (Courtesy Prime TV Films, Inc.)

he could have done it in his sleep.   H. Marion's Crawford's
Watson, however, was anything but reminiscent of the Watson
created by Nigel Bruce.

Crawford's association with Sherlock Holmes went back
to 1948 when he played Holmes on BBC Radio's half-hour
adaptation of "The Speckled Band" (December 27, 1948), and
his Watson now was much more in keeping with the Watson
of the original stories: a younger Watson with an eye for
the ladies; a Watson who many times throughout the series
was absolutely astounded by his new friend's powers of deduction.   Unfortunately though, his Watson would often as not be
astounded to the extent that he'd leap out of his seat, bound
all over the place, and sputter off too many loud-voiced ex-
clamations of surprise, amazement, perplexity and bafflement.
Certainly the Watson of the stories--at least in the early years
of his association with Mr. Holmes--was continually amazed
by the detective's various pronouncements, but Crawford's
portrayal of this kind of Watson did often irritate the ear of
at least this one viewer.

Filmed in France for economic reasons, The New Adventures of Sherlock Holmes was set in period, and was
mostly a series of original exploits, although now and then
it did borrow from the Conan Doyle stories.   The opening
show, The Case of the Cunningham Heritage (broadcast over
NBC on October 18, 1954), for example, used the very first
meeting of Holmes and Watson from the novel A Study in
Scarlet as one of its main ingredients.   Written by producer
Sheldon Reynolds himself and directed by Jack Gage, the show
had opened with Watson returning to London from medical
service in Afghanistan.   He was looking for lodgings, and
ran into an old friend of his, Stamford (Rowland Bartrop),
who told him that he just happened to know of someone else
who was also looking for suitable lodgings.   This other man,
Sherlock Holmes, had in fact located a good place on Baker
Street and was hoping to meet someone compatible with whom
he could share the rent.   Watson was interested of course,
and went with Stamford to St. Bartholomew's Hospital, where
Holmes was working out a problem in chemistry: trying to
find an infallible test for bloodstains.

Stamford introduced Watson to Holmes, who looked
back at the doctor and said, "You have been in Afghanistan,
I perceive...."   Watson was stunned that this man Sherlock
Holmes, whom he'd never set eyes on before, should have
pegged him so correctly.   But after Holmes explained how

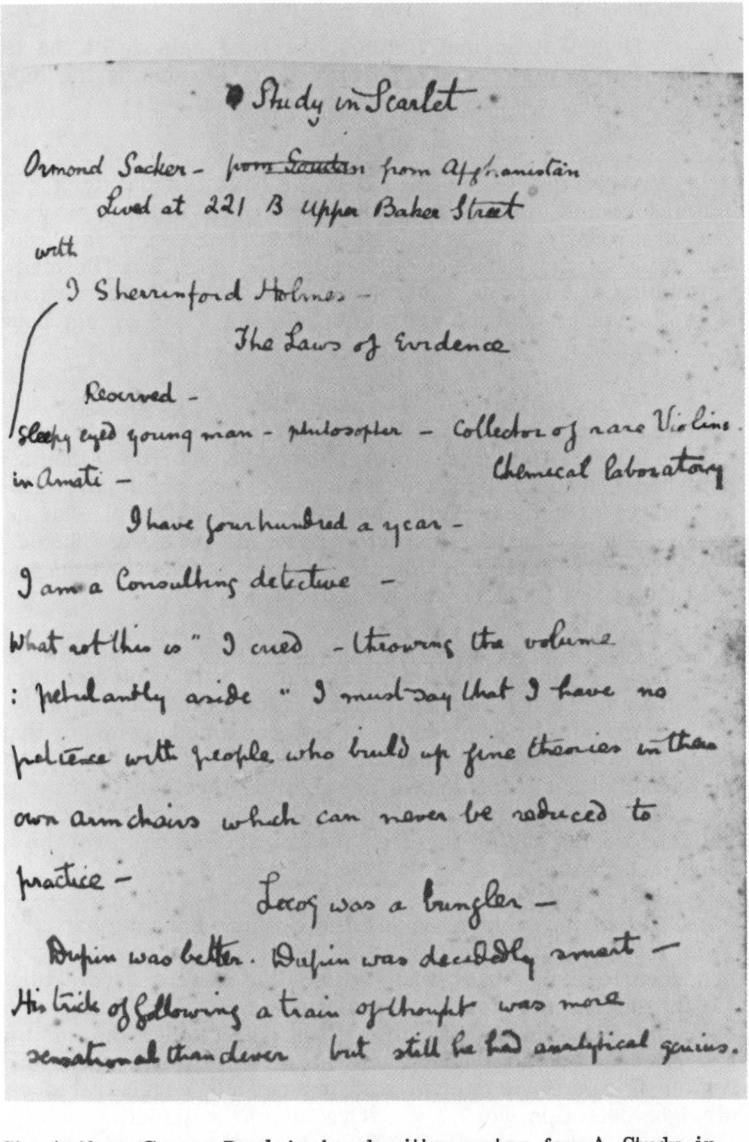

Study in Scarlet

Ormond Sacker - ~~from Soudan~~ from Afghanistan
    Lived at 221 B Upper Baker Street
with
    I Sherrinford Holmes -
            The Laws of Evidence

    Reserved -
sleepy eyed young man - philosopher - Collector of rare Violins.
in Amati -   Chemical Laboratory
        I have four hundred a year -

I am a Consulting detective -

What rot this is" I cried - throwing the volume
: petulantly aside " I must say that I have no
patience with people who build up fine theories in their
own armchairs which can never be reduced to
practice -
            Lecoq was a bungler -
    Dupin was better. Dupin was decidedly smart -
His trick of following a train of thought was more
sensational than clever but still he had analytical genius.

Sir Arthur Conan Doyle's handwritten notes for <u>A Study in Scarlet</u>, his first story, wherein Holmes and Watson meet for the first time. (Courtesy Cecil Ryder Collection.)

the trick was done--through observation and deduction--Watson agreed they should take a look at the rooms Holmes had found, and then ultimately take those rooms.

Thus Watson met Holmes; the first episode of the television New Adventures of Sherlock Holmes remains the only time the first meeting has even been filmed.

ACCORDING TO SHELDON REYNOLDS' Sherlock Holmes series, the first adventure to come Holmes' way after taking the rooms with Watson at 221B Baker Street was The Case of the Cunningham Heritage,[2] which saw Holmes unraveling the mystery surrounding the death of Cunningham, a gentleman of nobility whose fiancée was found by his body with a knife in her hand.

Vaguely based on "The Adventure of the Reigate Squires," the teleplay had Holmes investigating the murder and then ultimately (with Watson) sneaking into the Cunningham house to gain evidence against the real criminal.   This act nearly cost them their lives when the scoundrel shot at them.   But fortunately Inspector Lestrade (who was played throughout the series by Archie Duncan) arrived in time to help catch the fiend before he killed again.

The Case of the Cunningham Heritage was actually the pilot for the series; producer Reynolds wisely protected himself against its not selling by making certain that the next two scripts (for the intended series) contained elements that could tie all three half hours together.   That way the three individual stories could have been edited together to make one feature-length film.   But the television pilot episode did sell and so the edited-together theatrical feature never became necessary.

Chan in Variety thought the opening episode was a good one, and said, in fact, that as far as he was concerned producer Reynolds had "what seems like a sure syndication winner in this new telepix translation of Sherlock Holmes. Sheldon ('Foreign Intrigue') Reynolds has avoided the customary clichés that seem inevitable in any treatment of the Sir Arthur Conan Doyle stories and instead has concentrated on straight detection work...."   Overall, he called the show's production values excellent, from the costumes and sets to the music by Claude Durant, writing that producer Reynolds had dressed up the show with style and distinction, and that

director Jack Gage had kept everything moving quickly.   He
did point out, however, The Cunningham Heritage episode suffered because it was too simple.   "Of course, it's something
of an introductory pic, showing Holmes and Dr. Watson meeting, but the solution of the crime wasn't quite as elaborate
as most Holmes stories are...."   He liked Ronald Howard
as Holmes, though, and "bless him, he doesn't overplay.   H.
Marion Crawford is something new to a Dr. Watson, a com-
monplace type but by no means a buffoon.   Archie Duncan is
good as the blustering Inspector Lestrade ..." (October 20,
1954).

     The second adventure of the original three stories was
The Case of Lady Beryl, and it was properly broadcast by
NBC on October 25, 1954, as Holmes' second television exploit.   Guest-starring the well-known American actress Paulette Goddard as Lady Beryl herself, the story was again
written by Sheldon Reynolds and directed by Jack Gage.   It
opened as Watson arrived at Scotland Yard furious at Lestrade
over the press coverage given the previous Cunningham adventure; coverage that said it was Lestrade, not Sherlock
Holmes, who had solved the mystery.

     While there at Scotland Yard, however, Watson learned
about another murder, this one at the home of Lord Beryl
(Peter Copley) of the Foreign Office.   Returning to Baker
Street, Watson told Holmes he should investigate this case
because it was Lady Beryl herself who admitted being responsible for the deed.   At the moment Holmes was busy experi-
menting with poisons, but he took on the case anyway and
shortly proved that Lady Beryl had been lying about being the
murderer.   Then after carefully re-enacting the crime,
Holmes went on to show who the real culprit was and why
the distinguished Lady Beryl had tried to cover up.

     The third tie-in exploit was The Case of the Winthrop
Legend, but NBC didn't broadcast this story as the third
weekly Holmes adventure.   Instead, the network showed The
Case of the Pennsylvania Gun (on November 1, 1954), and
didn't broadcast The Case of the Winthrop Legend until the
seventh week (on November 29, 1954).

     Written by Harold J. Bloom, and directed by Jack
Gage, The Case of the Winthrop Legend tied into the first
two stories by opening with Watson's talking elatedly to
Holmes about his adventuresome new life in London (as
Holmes' partner).   Soon enough, though, the story involving

H. Marion Crawford starred as Watson in television's The
New Adventures of Sherlock Holmes (Motion Pictures for
Television--NBC 1954).   (Courtesy Prime TV Films, Inc.)

the Winthrop Legend arrived at Baker Street in the person
of Harvey Winthrop (Ivan Denny), a gentleman who believed
his brother John's life was in danger because of the infamous
Winthrop family legend.   Explaining it to Holmes and Watson,
Harvey Winthrop said the legend decreed that each member
of the family who was about to die violently would find silver
coins, and now brother John Winthrop (Peter Copley) had recently found just such silver coins.   The legend also told how
a gold doubloon would always be found by the dead body, and
this, Harvey Winthrop said, was exactly what happened when
their father had died violently 30 years earlier.

Intrigued by the case, Holmes with Watson left London and spent the weekend at the Winthrop estate in the company of Harvey Winthrop, his fiancée Peg (Guita Karen), brother John Winthrop, and John's blind wife Alice (Meg Lemonnier). In due course he uncovered a monstrous murder plot against John.

Directed by producer Reynolds,[3] and written by Henry Sandox, the fourth adventure was The Case of the Pennsylvania Gun (November 1, 1954). Based on the novel The Valley of Fear, the exploit saw Holmes investigating the murder of one John Douglas. At the scene of the crime (the Douglas castle, with its filled moat), Holmes and Watson met the local policeman (Frank Dexter) in charge of the case and also a man named Morelle (Emilio Carver), who had previously been involved with the slain Douglas in an American gold prospecting partnership some years before. Talking with Holmes, Morelle disclosed that both he and Douglas had recently been threatened by a third man, MacLeod (Russell Waters), their other partner in the gold prospecting enterprise.

Scouting the territory, Holmes shortly discovered a bloody footprint on the window of the room in the castle where Douglas had been murdered. Then he discovered there was a one-month-old spider's web beneath that window, and also that a dumbbell was missing from the room in question. This urged him to start a rumor that the castle's moat was going to be drained, and sure enough his ruse worked: he caught the murderer by surprise and revealed all the various aspects of the crime.

Up to this point Archie Duncan's Lestrade had established himself in the series by at least appearing in the first two adventures, but curiously enough Baker Street's good landlady, Mrs. Hudson, wasn't in the series at all. Also, the films had so far been dealt out in a rather straightforward, if sometimes lightly-handed manner (Ronald Howard's usually casual Holmes, or H. Marion Crawford's exuberant Watson), but starting with the fifth adventure, The Case of the Texas Cowgirl, an irritating kind of silliness began creeping in. This was unfortunate because for the most part the series had started out quite respectably. Not that each episode from The Case of the Texas Cowgirl onwards was silly or worthless--many of the future episodes were, in fact, good mysteries with sober performances--but silly characters and situations did seem to begin cropping up much too often after the adventure with the Western girl.

The Case of the Texas Cowgirl (November 8, 1954)
opened with an American cowgirl named Minnie coming to
Sherlock Holmes for help. She was in London with a traveling Wild West Show and had just discovered a dead man in
her hotel room, murdered with a tomahawk. But because
she was engaged to the dignified Lord Worcester, whom she'd
met only the week before, she wanted to know if Holmes could
hush up the matter?

Investigating, Holmes discovered that the dead man
was a burglar, and when Lestrade arrived on the scene
Holmes quickly hid the corpse in the adjoining hotel room,
which was occupied by a certain Mr. Honeywell, a rather
meek and nervous-appearing salesman. But you obviously
can't keep a good corpse down, so when Lestrade learned
there really was a murder at the hotel, he invited Holmes
into the case. Working officially now, Holmes continued his
discreet investigations, with the upshot that he interrogated
an Indian from the Wild West Show--an Indian who couldn't
speak English and who shortly put up his teepee right inside
Holmes' rooms at Baker Street.

Of course Holmes later correctly deduced the truth
behind the murder and also caught the killer and all, but
meanwhile the believability of the story had been stretched
beyond credibility, especially when that Indian put up that
tent.

The next adventure also had its somewhat silly moments, but overall it was a much more acceptable exploit.
Written by Charles M. Early, The Case of the Belligerent
Ghost (November 15, 1954) opened as Watson returned in a
fluster to Baker Street, where Holmes was working out another problem in chemistry. According to Watson, he'd been
coming back from his club when he aided a passerby in distress, a man who then died of a heart attack after Watson
got him to his house. Then after contacting the police to
take charge of the corpse, Watson stopped at a pub for a
much-needed drink. And then back on his way to 221B, he
told Holmes, he was suddenly hit right smack in the eye by
the dead man's ghost!

Visiting the morgue with Watson to examine the dead
man, Holmes met Lestrade there and the inspector dutifully
identified the dead man as Albert Higgins, an ex-counterfeiter
who'd recently been employed as a watchman at the Pembroke
Museum. This sent Holmes off on a fresh scent, and while

he was gone (to subsequently learn of the arrival at the museum of a special exhibition of Italian paintings, including a master-piece by Leonardo da Vinci), Watson went out walking again, and met up with the ghost again. This time the ghost pulled his nose.

Although Sherlock Holmes was actually too late to stop thieves from stealing the priceless Leonardo and substituting a fake, later with Watson in tow he did pay the museum's apartments a late-night call, and there he nabbed the gang behind the theft. And much to Watson's peace of mind, Holmes also triumphantly explained away the belligerent ghost of Albert Higgins.

THERE WERE FIVE MORE new Howard-Crawford tele-vision adventures of Sherlock Holmes broadcast in 1954. (The year also saw the release of another new Poe film based on the life and deductive times of Poe's sleuth, C. Auguste Du-pin.)

Written by Charles M. Early, The Case of the Shy Ballerina (November 22, 1954) once again saw Watson as the motivating factor.[4] This time Watson went to a restaurant where he'd accidentally taken the wrong coat when leaving. Meanwhile the other man had showed up with Watson's coat. The gentleman identified himself as Chelton (Geoffrey Addin-sell), but while he and Watson were exchanging coats, they mixed up their hats, with the result that Chelton walked off with the right coat but wrong hat. Later Watson realized the mistake and with Holmes went to Chelton's house to get his hat back.

At Chelton's home they met Mrs. Chelton (Natalie Schaffer), who thought Holmes had come there because her husband had consulted him on a professional basis. The rea-son she thought this was because Chelton had recently re-turned home to London from a post in St. Petersburg, where he had become involved with a ballerina named Olga (Martine Alexis), who was now blackmailing him. Olga'a ballet troupe was currently in London, and Mrs. Chelton was worried that her husband might try to do something rash to the girl. As it developed later though, Watson finally got back his hat-- from Lestrade, who had found it lying next to the body of Chelton, who had just been murdered. And so Holmes was off on another adventure.

Only incidentally based on "The Adventure of The
Gloria Scott," The Case of the Blind Man's Bluff (December
6, 1954) opened with the murder of a ship's chief petty officer named Jocko Farraday, and then went to Baker Street
where Lestrade was arriving in time to see Watson trying to
throw Holmes out the door.   Watson was doing this because
Holmes was in one of his masterful disguises and the good
doctor didn't recognize him.

With him Lestrade brought a chicken claw that was
found at the scene of the murder of Jocko Farraday.   Lestrade said, in fact, that this was the second murder-with-
chicken-claw in the past few days.   Holmes examined the
claw and told Lestrade it was a Caribbean death-threat sym-
bol.   Then after a Dr. Jonas of the Marine Hospital contacted Lestrade to tell him that he had also received a chicken
claw--he'd read about the two previous murders in the news-
papers--Holmes and Watson began checking official records,
where they learned that five years earlier Dr. Jonas, Chief
Petty Officer Farraday, and the first victim, a seaman, had
all been part of the crew of the ship Gloria Scott.   But when
they went to question Dr. Jonas about it, they found he had
already been murdered.

Holmes decided to check on a fourth man from the
Gloria Scott--the captain himself--and when he did, he discovered the captain was blind.   Over brandy however, Holmes
told the captain he knew who the murderer was, and that the
man had, in fact, committed a fourth murder.   Before a fifth
murder could happen, though, Holmes correctly deduced the
reason behind them and solved the case.

The next Ronald Howard adventure was inspired by a
real-life association.   Written by Harold J. Bloom, The Case
of Harry Crocker (December 13, 1954) had Holmes aiding a
flamboyant, world-renowned escape artist named Harry Crocker, who was based on the famous stage magician and escape
artist Harry Houdini.   In the 1920s Houdini and Holmes'
creator, Conan Doyle, had come to violent words with one
another over the subject of spiritualism, and it was a feud
that generally made the newspapers whenever one had something to say about the other.   A staunch believer in spiritualism, Conan Doyle was furious with Houdini's loudly proclaim-
ed opinion that spiritualism was nothing but the bunk, and that
he, Houdini, could duplicate (and duplicate even more effectively) any spirit manifestation conjured up by any of the numerous spiritualists and mediums who were so much in vogue

in those days. The Case of Harry Crocker didn't get into
spiritualism but in its own way did remind one that "Holmes"
and "Crocker" had a certain real-life connection.

The Case of Harry Crocker had Crocker (Eugene
Deckers) running to Sherlock Holmes for help. He was fleeing from the police because he had been charged with murdering a chorus girl at the London Music Hall, where he was
appearing. Shortly after Crocker arrived at Baker Street,
however, Lestrade showed up and Crocker had to pull one of
his famous disappearing acts. Later he returned to defend
himself, but after being taken into custody by Lestrade and
his men, he escaped again. But Holmes thought he knew
where he could find Crocker, and with Watson he went to the
Music Hall, where he located the elusive man and started investigating the murder.

Throughout the story--while Holmes looked into the
crime, talked with various performers like Zaza (Aka Yanai),
visited the morgue where the dead chorus girl lay, and eventually deduced the identity of the real murderer--Harry Crocker kept escaping from the hounding Lestrade, only to reappear again, and then escape again. But when Holmes finally
solved the murder mystery, Crocker turned up one last time
and then decided that since he was a free man again, he'd
confide all his escapes to the stage alone.

Written by Lou Morheim, The Mother Hubbard Case
(December 20, 1954) was a baffling little mystery involving
the disappearances of eight men. Events got underway at
Baker Street when Richard Trevor (William Millinship) arrived with his attractive daughter Margaret (Delphine Seyrig).
The father and the fiancé were supposed to have met at a
certain time the night before, but something had come up and
Margaret had sent a note delaying the meeting to her fiancé
via a little girl named Frances (Michele Wright), whom Margaret assumed was just one of the neighborhood children.
But now that her fiancé had disappeared, so had the little
girl. They couldn't find the girl anywhere.

The adventure led Holmes and Watson into an investigation that eventually uncovered the reason for the odd disappearance of not only Margaret Trevor's fiancé, but seven
other men as well.

The final show of the year was The Case of the Red-
Headed League (December 27, 1954). A faithful adaptation of

the Conan Doyle story by scripter Lou Morheim, The Red-
Headed League saw Holmes and Watson taking up the strange
business presented to them by their red-headed client, Jabez
Wilson (Alexander Gauge), and then discovering the daring
criminal undertaking of that remarkable "murderer, thief,
smasher, and forger," John Clay (Eugene Deckers).

Others in the cast of this most famous Sherlock Holmes
adventure were Michael Seyford as bank director Merryweather,
and Colin Drake as Duncan Ross.

The Phantom of the Rue Morgue was also released in
1954.   Based on Poe's "The Murders in the Rue Morgue,"
the Warner Bros. film was shot in color and Three Dimen-
sions, and returned Poe's Dupin to the screen.   Directed by
Roy Del Ruth, and written by Harold Medford and James
Webb, The Phantom of the Rue Morgue changed C. Auguste
Dupin's name to Paul Dupin, and instead of portraying him
as the reclusive dabbler in crime-solving, played him as a
young medical student.   Steve Forrest[5] had the role and he
turned in quite a decent job of it, in this well-made and often
exciting period thriller.

The story had zookeeper Karl Malden using his pet
ape (played by Charles Gemora, famous for such roles) to
maniacally murder various Parisian women.   Claude Dauphin
was very well cast as the police inspector investigating the
bizarre murders, and Patricia Medina played Paul Dupin's
girlfriend.   Others in the cast included Anthony Caruso as
the sailor who originally had brought the ape to Malden; Paul
Richards, Merv Griffin, and Erin O'Brien Moore.

NOTES

[1]In 1936 Leslie Howard had costarred with two Sherlock
      Holmeses of the screen when he made MGM's film of
      Shakespeare's Romeo and Juliet.   With Howard as
      Romeo, and Norma Shearer as Juliet, the classical
      production featured Basil Rathbone as Tybalt, and
      John Barrymore as Mercurio.   For his Tybalt, Rath-
      bone was also nominated for an Oscar as Best Sup-
      porting actor--in the very first year the Academy ever
      awarded Oscars for best supporting roles.

[2]Actually, Holmes' first case was "The Gloria Scott."

[3] Sheldon Reynolds directed all the remaining Howard television adventures except where noted.

[4] Although Watson was many times responsible for bringing cases to Holmes in the television series, in the original Conan Doyle stories Watson actually brought only a few cases to Holmes' attention.

[5] In 1975 Forrest continued fighting crime as the star of ABC-TV's S.W.A.T. series, leading his Los Angeles-based policemen of the Strategic Weapons and Tactical Division into various action-packed, cops and robbers stories.

Eleven

THE TELEVISION CASEBOOK
OF SHERLOCK HOLMES

It started out as a pleasant day in the country for
Holmes and Watson, but suddenly a very dishevelled young
man named Hatherley (Arnold Bell) came crashing out of the
woods carrying a frightened young woman in his arms, and
before the vacationing sleuth and doctor knew it, they were
plunged headlong into the first of their 1955 New Adventures
of Sherlock Holmes television exploits.

Written by Harold J. Bloom, The Case of the Shoeless Engineer (January 3, 1955) was adapted from "The Adventure of the Engineer's Thumb," and was the 12th adventure
taken on by Ronald Howard's Holmes, and H. Marion Crawford's Watson. After its startling opening, where Hatherley,
an engineer, told Holmes and Watson that he and the frightened girl were running because they were being pursued by two
violent men, the scene shifted back to Baker Street, where
Holmes learned from the young couple more about the circumstances surrounding that frantic dash through country woods
for freedom. He learned, in fact, that Hatherley had been
hired by one Colonel Stark to come to the man's home in the
country to inspect a hydraulic machine that had gone out of
whack. There Hatherley met the girl who was with him now
at Baker Street: a mute who served Stark as housekeeper.
Hatherley also met Colonel Stark's assistant, and after inspecting the machine and getting it working again, he had
been invited to stay the night. But during the night there
were attacks on his life and the servant girl had saved him
both times. Then in the morning they'd bolted for freedom,
with Stark and his assistant chasing them. In his haste to
get away from the house, Hatherley explained, he'd forgotten
to put on his shoes. Hence the title, The Shoeless Engineer.

Calling on Lestrade to accompany them back to the

184

country, Holmes and Watson journeyed to Colonel Stark's
home and there wrapped up the mystery.

The Case of the Split-Ticket (January 10, 1955) opened
humorously enough (though Watson was infuriated), with Holmes'
arrest by a policeman when the Great Detective saw a pick-
pocket at work, tried to right the wrong, and then got mistaken for the thief himself.   More shenanigans were on their
way in Lou Morheim's teleplay, though, when, after being
released by the bobby, Holmes returned with Watson to Baker
Street to find that someone had broken in and then had fallen
asleep on the couch.   Waking him up, Holmes learned the intruder was the exhausted and frantic Brian O'Casey (Harry
Tomb), a one-third owner of a sweepstakes ticket that had
won, but that would be void if not presented to the judges before midnight.   The problem was that each of the three part-
ners owned one-third portion of the ticket (it had been torn
in three), and now O'Casey could not find the third partner,
a man named Albert Snow (Colin Drake), who had apparently
disappeared.   Could Mr. Holmes please help him?

Holmes, Watson and the distraught Brian O'Casey later
met with the second partner at a pub in London.   She was
Miss Belle Rogers (Margaret Russell), a flirtatious little
thing who told them she'd just heard the terrible news that
Mr. Snow, the third partner, had commited suicide.   Therefore they couldn't get hold of his portion of the ticket, and
so their own two portions were worthless.   And so saying,
she took O'Casey's portion, and her own, and tossed them
into the fireplace at the pub.   But before this case was over,
Holmes proved that the hand is indeed quicker than the eye,
and that two heads are better than one only when the two are
not plotting the destruction of a man who also happened to be
one of Sherlock Holmes' clients.

The Case of the French Interpreter (January 17, 1955)
was the next adventure.   Written by Lou Morheim, the story
was based on "The Adventure of the Greek Interpreter" and
except for the fact that here on television Mr. Melas, the
Greek Interpreter, became Claude Dubec, the French Interpreter, and other names in the script were changed to French
names, the adaptation was quite a faithful one.   Unlike the
original story, however, Holmes was not introduced to the
exploit by his brother Mycroft.   It was Watson himself who
brought the matter of the worried interpreter to Holmes.
This happened when Watson burst into Holmes' club (apparently the same Diogenes Club so beloved by Mycroft Holmes)

and interrupted all the silence there to tell Holmes there was
a new client awaiting him at Baker Street.

The Case of the Singing Violin (January 24, 1955) was
a bit of a departure for the series in that it was Watson himself who saved the day, as well as the heroine's life. Holmes
was there at the scene of the intended, climactic crime, but
he was completely unable to come to the girl's rescue because
the villain of the piece had locked him in a closet.

The puzzler began when a young man named Guy Durham (Arnold Bell) arrived at Baker Street to see Holmes.
Durham never made it into the house, though, because he
died just outside. But a witness told Holmes that he'd heard
the words "singing violin" just before Durham died so inexplicably. So with Watson in tow Holmes went to see Durham's
employer (Ben Omanoff), who also happened to be the father
of the girl Durham was going to marry. But when Holmes
asked to see the girl Betty (Delphine Syrig) herself, he was
told she'd been sent away because she was suffering lately
from a great emotional strain brought on by ghostly visions
and haunting violin music. Investigating further, however,
Holmes learned of the strange death of Betty's mother 15
years before, and also that Betty was coming into a sizeable
inheritance. Then he managed to locate the mysterious in-
strument, "the singing violin," and went to the hospital where
the girl was being treated. He overheard a murder plot
against her, but unfortunately was locked in a closet by the
murderer before he could do anything about saving the helpless girl. Watson and the police, though, showed up in the
nick of time to catch the fiend and save the girl.

Based only superficially on "The Adventure of the
Musgrave Ritual," The Case of the Greystone Inscription
(January 31, 1955) brought Holmes and Watson to eerie Greystone Castle and to its equally mysterious owner, Sir Greystone (Eric Micklewood). What precipitated this trip was a
young woman (Martina Maye) who had come to Baker Street
because her fiancé had completely vanished. A scholar,
he'd told her only a few nights before of something he'd
found in his researches, something that would be of tremendous importance to both himself and the family of Greystone,
whom he was planning to visit the next day. But that, she
told Holmes, was the last time she'd seen him. When he
didn't return from Greystone Castle, she had of course gone
there herself, but Sir Greystone told her that her fiancé had
never been there. Leaving the castle, however, she dis-

covered a railroad timetable in the garden; her fiancé's notes
were written all over it.   He had been at the castle!

Holmes, Watson, Lestrade and the girl discovered
foul dealings at Greystone Castle and aided by her fiancé's
discovery (made while translating an ancient parchment), they
also uncovered a very old family treasure.   Before accomplishing this, however, they had to escape various death plots
against them.

Flavorfully, the adventure had opened at Baker Street
with Holmes using the wall for pistol shooting practice.

As in The Case of the Shoeless Engineer, which opened
the 1955 season, The Case of the Laughing Mummy (February
7, 1955) also turned up while he and Watson were on vacation.   This time, however, the new exploit popped up just
after they'd boarded the train in London that was to take them
out to the country.   Watson ran into an old school chum of
his, Reggie Taunton (Barry Mackay), who was en route to
his country estate.   Talking over old times, Reggie had mentioned a rather peculiar gift made to him by his archaeolo-
gist uncle, Professor Caulkins (Frederick O'Brady).   The
gift was an Egyptian mummy, and the odd thing about it was
that the mummy laughed at times!   Reggie said he himself
had heard the mummy laughing.   Now he invited Holmes to
come visit his estate, meet the mummy, and see if he could
clear up the mystery of what made it laugh.

Accepting the invitation, Holmes went to Taunton's
estate with Watson, and while at dinner with Taunton's fiancée Rowena (June Elliott), his obnoxious aunt Agatha (Lois
Perkins Marechal), and a Professor Caulkins, both Holmes
and Watson themselves heard the mummy laughing.   But ever
skeptical of the supernatural, Holmes investigated and finally
cleared up the mystery.

The Case of the Thistle Killer (February 14, 1955)
returned Holmes to sleuthing in London.   In this exploit he
was up against a maniacal murderer running loose in the
city, who had already killed six women in six days.   The
maniac left each of his victims with sprigs of thistle near
their corpses, and Scotland Yard was admittedly so baffled
by these seemingly insane crimes that the Superintendent
himself asked Sherlock Holmes to help.

Taking on the case (which bore some resemblance to

the Jack the Ripper murders in London's real-life 1890s),
and with no clues to go by except the sprigs of thistle found
at the scenes of the various horrendous crimes, Holmes used
a plotted map of London to deduce the game of the murderer
and trap him.   The capture was effected in foggy, late-night
London with the able assistance of a policewoman, who used
herself as a decoy for the strange killer of women.

IT WAS WATSON'S TURN to go sleuthing in The Case
of the Vanished Detective (February 21, 1955).   The vanished
detective was Sherlock Holmes himself.

At first Watson hadn't thought much about Holmes' being away from Baker Street for a few days, but then he began to worry, and finally he went to Lestrade.   Together
they tried using Holmes' own methods of deduction to find
the missing sleuth, and wonder of wonders, they did.   They
found him working in disguise at an old curiosity shop, where
he said he was busy tracking down a dangerous prison escapee who'd vowed revenge on the judge who'd sent him up.
Later, the escapee used a clever ruse to get by police who
were guarding the judge, but Holmes was on the job and
caught the man before he could kill both the judge and his
wife.

The day after NBC broadcast The Case of the Vanished
Detective, ABC Television broadcast The Sting of Death, a Mr.
Mycroft mystery starring Boris Karloff as the old sleuth. [1]
Shown on the Elgin Hour anthology series, The Sting of Death,
broadcast "live," was on H. F. Heard's novel A Taste for
Honey in which Mr. Mycroft found himself up against a bril-
liant but crazy murderer who was using killer bees to de-
stroy people he didn't like.

A retired bee-keeper living in Sussex, Mr. Mycroft
is really Sherlock Holmes and after debuting in A Taste for
Honey with his chronicler-associate Sydney Silchester, he appeared in two more Heard novels, Reply Paid and The Notched Hairpin.   A Taste for Honey was first published in 1941
and, ironically enough, featured a dust-jacket blurb from
Boris Karloff himself.   Karloff had thought the story was
"a triumph of ingenuity."   But while Mycroft (the name he
chose to call himself after retiring from London to keep bees
in Sussex) is Holmes in retirement, Mycroft's associate Silchester is not Watson.   Silchester is merely a Watson-type
who decided to live in the country because he liked the quiet,
and who then met this man named Mycroft.

In A Taste for Honey Silchester, in fact, tried to stay
away from Mycroft because the feisty old man was getting
him into an adventure he wanted no part of.   He'd come to
the country for peace and quiet, not excitement.

The Case of the Careless Suffragette (February 28,
1955) continued the new adventures of Sherlock Holmes on
television.   Directed by Jack Gage, and written by Joseph
and Charles M. Early, the story had Holmes and Watson
meeting a suffragette named Doreen (Dawn Addams), who'd
chained herself to a fence hoping to be jailed so she could
get publicity for her cause.   Over tea at Baker Street she
told Holmes that at the last meeting of her group, the League
of Women Voters, she had even been chosen to head their
next publicity project: tossing a bomb at a stone lion in
front of the museum, and exploding the lion.   But she got
no help from either Holmes or Watson when she asked if
they knew of anybody who could make the bomb for her?
Undaunted however, she placed an advertisement in the paper;
an ad that was shortly answered by a certain Mr. Boris Tur-
goff (Frederick O'Brady), an anarchist who specialized in
making bombs.   He made Doreen the bomb, but then when
her group's Master Plan went all wrong she called on Sherlock Holmes again.

What went wrong was that instead of going off where
it should have, and exploding the stone lion, somehow the
bomb (which was made in the shape of a croquet ball) ended
up on the lawn of Henry (David Thomson), a government man
who was opposed to women's getting the vote.   Playing croquet, Henry struck the ball with his mallet, and the bomb
exploded and killed him.   It was up to Holmes, then, to question everybody involved in the affair and figure out who was
the guilty one responsible for putting the bomb-ball on Henry's
lawn.

The Case of the Reluctant Carpenter (March 7, 1955)
saw Holmes tangling with an unknown fiend who was setting
fires around London and committing outright murder.   One of
the fires, a raging warehouse disaster that killed a foreman
and workmen, had in fact been set to cover a specific murder.   But the fire hadn't done the job expected on the previously murdered man, and when Scotland Yard investigated
the deaths at the warehouse they found one victim who had
died of knife wounds.   Lestrade and Sergeant Wilkins (Kenneth Richards) took a sample of the mud found on the murdered man's shoes to Holmes to analyze (because their own

lab at the Yard was painfully slow with analysis in those days), but when they arrived at Baker Street, Holmes wasn't there. Actually, Holmes was in the house across the street, watching his own quarters because he'd recently received a death threat.

Besides Lestrade and Wilkins, however, a chemist (Donald Kotite) also showed up at Baker Street now. He mistook Lestrade for Holmes and told him he knew when other fires were going to start. He wanted money for his information, and Lestrade pretended to play along with him, telling the chemist to come back later. When the man left, Watson followed him, and saw him murdered. Then when Holmes finally returned to 221B, he analyzed the mud found in the knifed man's shoes, and went on to trace the mud back to the person responsible for the fires and various murders.

Written by George and Gertrude Fass, The Case of the Deadly Prophecy (March 14, 1955) took on international scope as Holmes and Watson traveled to a small town in Belgium, and Watson later to Paris by himself to check out some information for Holmes. The story was about Antoine (Stephen Swarbrick), a student at an exclusive Belgian boys' school, who had already awakened in the middle of the night for four nights, each time going to a nearby church where he wrote the names of four different people on the steps. Each of these four people died shortly afterwards. But Antoine could never remember having made his prophetic, late-night walks.

Called into the mystery by the school's headmaster, Carolan (Yves Branville), Holmes and Watson went to Belgium where they met Carolan, Antoine, and Dr. Dimarche (Jacques François), the village doctor. Later they visited one Mme. Soule (Helena Manson), who had previously offered to sell good luck charms to the four people who were now dead. They also met Count Passevant (Maurice Teynac), the wealthiest man in town. After some sleuthing, Holmes not only shortly prevented the murder of a fifth victim, but gathering all the suspects together at the school at midnight, he also triumphantly named the unscrupulous wretch who was responsible for all the strange deaths by prophecy.

The next adventure, The Christmas Pudding (April 4, 1955), was also written by George and Gertrude Fass, though directed by Steve Previn. It opened in court during the Christmas season, where the judge had just sentenced mur-

derer John Norton (Eugene Deckers) to death. While being
led out of the courtroom, however, Norton first reminded his
wife (June Rodney) to be certain to bring him a Christmas
pudding in foil (it being the Season and all), and then because
Sherlock Holmes had been instrumental in capturing him, Norton told Holmes he was going to escape from prison and kill
him.

Holmes and the police thought Mrs. Norton might try
to sneak a file or something into her husband when she
brought him the Christmas pudding, but the pudding and its
package wrappings were carefully examined and found harm-
less. Regardless, it wasn't too long afterwards that the Gov-
ernor of Newgate (Richard Watson) came to Holmes and told
him that despite all precautions, Norton had still somehow
escaped and was now on the loose. Immediately the police
surrounded Baker Street to protect Holmes, but the clever
Norton disguised himself as one of the policemen and got
through the cordon. But his try at killing Holmes was unsuccessful, and after Holmes captured him again, he deduced
the solution to the real mystery in the case: exactly how
Norton had escaped from prison with the help of the innocent-
looking Christmas pudding.

The Night Train Riddle (April 11, 1955) had Holmes
solving the strange disappearance of a boy named Paul (Sonny
Doran). As with some of the other adventures in the series,
The Night Train Riddle also came Holmes' way when he and
Watson left London for a vacation.

Traveling by night train into the country, the first
hint that something was upwind for Holmes came when their
train lurched to a screeching halt. Then according to a frantic governess (Roberta Haynes), who shortly came to Holmes
when she heard he was aboard, the woman's young charge,
Paul, had vanished from the train. She'd been taking Paul
(who would someday fall heir to a vast fortune) to school,
and she told Holmes that Paul, in fact, had told her he'd
run away if he was sent off to school. Now, apparently,
he'd done just that. She begged Sherlock Holmes to find him.

Investigating, Holmes discovered not one, but two sets
of footprints outside the stopped train. One set belonged to
Paul, but whose was the other pair? The governess couldn't
imagine; and realizing now there was possibly much more to
Paul's disappearance than originally had been thought, Holmes
got busy tracking down the owners of both sets of prints, and
shortly uncovered an insidious murder plot.

The Case of the Violent Suitor (April 18, 1955) saw a
newspaper columnist named Alex Dugal coming to Holmes
with a black eye.   Dugal wrote a lovelorn column under the
name "Aunt Lotty," and recently he'd given an "S. D." advice
not to marry her fiancé, a man who'd shown violent tenden-
cies.   That the fiancé really was a violent type, though, was
shortly proven when a Mr. Murdock showed up at Dugal's
newspaper office and angrily punched him in the eye.   Murdock also threatened Dugal with even worse treatment if he
didn't go to see "S. D."--Miss Susan Dering--and take back
his advice about not marrying him.   Murdock also demanded
"Aunt Lotty" be the best man at the wedding.

Holmes asked to see a picture of Murdock (a picture
Dugal was going to run in the newspaper when the couple was
married).   He studied the picture, and then tying it to the
recent death of Susan Dering's father, he rushed off with
Lestrade and Watson to solve one murder and prevent another.

The next adventure had a silly situation: The Case of
the Baker Street Nursemaids (April 25, 1955) saw a messen-
ger leaving a baby at Baker Street.   With the baby came a
note from the mother, Mrs. Durand, asking Holmes to take
care of the child.   Then Lestrade turned up with the news
that a famous inventor named Professor Durand had just been
kidnapped.   Deciding they'd best visit the Durand home,
Holmes and Lestrade left Watson in charge of the baby, and
when they arrived at the Durand home they discovered that
Mrs. Durand had now also been kidnapped.

The exploit ended happily enough of course, with the
kidnappers caught and the Durand family once again reunited,
but in the meantime (particularly in some of the scenes where
Watson had to take care of the baby) there were some embar-
assingly weak moments.   The next adventure, The Case of
the Perfect Husband (May 2, 1955), was better.

A bluebeard caper, The Case of the Perfect Husband
saw the supposedly happily married Janet Partridge (Mary
Sinclair) running to Sherlock Holmes with the alarming news
that her husband of one year, Russell Partridge (Michael
Gough), was planning to kill her.   He'd just told her so himself, in fact.   The thing that really made all this so unbe-
lievable, however, was that everybody (including Janet Partridge) had always thought her husband was absolutely the
most attentive and considerate husband a girl could ever hope
to find.   But now he said he was going to kill her, just like

he'd killed seven other women in the past, and he said he was going to kill her the very next night.

Holmes believed the distraught young woman, and investigated the case. And besides saving Janet Partridge from being murdered by her "perfect husband," he also uncovered a secret hiding place in the house where he found the bodies of the man's seven other lady victims.

The Case of the Jolly Hangman (May 9, 1955) came into Holmes' life when a not very financially well off woman named Mrs. Hooper asked Holmes to look into her husband's suicide. Mr. Hooper was a salesman, and while it was true the firm he worked for was letting him go, Mrs. Hooper didn't believe her husband had hanged himself just because he was losing his job. The adventure took Holmes and Watson to Scotland, where Mr. Hooper had died in Edinburgh, and soon enough Holmes agreed with Mrs. Hooper that her husband had not committed suicide.

Tracking down further clues, Holmes eventually collared the real murderer, and saved Mrs. Hooper's own life in the process.

AN OFFBEAT, nearly tongue-in-cheek adventure, The Case of the Imposter Mystery (March 16, 1955) opened as both Lestrade and an irate client tore into Sherlock Holmes for having given them some bad advice. According to the client (whom Holmes said he'd never seen before), Holmes had told him to hide his family jewels in a cookie jar and they'd be safe. But the jewels were stolen anyway. And Lestrade said he was now in disgrace at Scotland Yard because he'd followed Holmes' (wrong) advice about a burglary case. But Holmes claimed he was innocent of both these charges, and that in fact he and Watson had been away from London at the times of these various consultations. And he decided, then, that someone had been impersonating him.

Planning to trap the rogue, Holmes and Watson went undercover. They appeared in the city as a Grand Vizier and the Maharajah of Gandor, respectively, and at their hotel held a press conference. The upshot was that one Mr. Bollingbrooke (Ronald Howard) fell under Holmes' suspicion, and to bait the man Holmes inquired if Bollingbrooke could possibly suggest someone who could discreetly investigate a certain young man who wanted to marry the Maharajah's daughter?

Bollingbrooke said Sherlock Holmes was the man for the job,
and that he himself would get in touch with Holmes.   Then,
briefly themselves again at Baker Street, Holmes and Watson
announced they were leaving London for a holiday in the country.   Returning to their guises as the Grand Vizier and the
Maharajah, at the hotel, they were shortly contacted by Bollingbrooke with the news that he'd made an appointment with
them to meet the private inquiry agent, Sherlock Holmes.
The climax of the story saw Holmes confronting "Holmes," at
Baker Street.

The 30th television adventure was The Case of the Eiffel Tower (May 23, 1955), an exploit that took Holmes, Watson and Lestrade to Paris.   Written by Roger E. Garris,
the tale began with the accidental death in London of the notorious criminal Frederick Martinez, on whose body police
had found a large amount of money, an odd French coin, and
a message written in code.   Holmes successfully broke the
code and learned that Martinez was supposed to have met
someone in Lambeth Square.   Curious about what the infamous Martinez might have been up to, Holmes kept the appointment himself, and received instructions for another meeting,
this one in Paris.

Going to Paris with Watson and Lestrade, Holmes
went to the Eiffel Tower, where he was supposed to make
his next contact.   But the other people involved had meanwhile learned of Martinez' death, and so they tried stealing
the French coin from Holmes.   But he tossed it over the
edge, and when it was picked up on the street by another of
the mystery gang, Lestrade followed the man.   This took
them to a pub, where they confronted a singer (Martine
Alexis), who knew exactly why the coin was so valuable and
why others were after it.

Written by Joseph and Charles M. Early, The Case
of the Exhumed Client (May 30, 1955) pitted Holmes against
supernatural elements when he was asked to investigate the
strange death of wealthy Sir Charles, who had defied a curse
on a dare, and spent the night up in his castle's legendary
haunted tower.   The odd thing about Holmes' being called in
to investigate Sir Charles' death, however, was that it was
Sir Charles himself who had requested Holmes.   This came
out after his burial, when the attorney was reading Sir
Charles' will to his family.   One of the provisions of the
will was that before his estate be divided, Sherlock
Holmes must investigate his death.

Arriving at the castle with Watson, Holmes learned
from the family the facts of the tower legend (that anyone
spending the night there would die), and then he had Sir
Charles' body exhumed. The autopsy showed the man had
died of arsenic poisoning--hardly the work of any ghosts.
Holmes then announced that he himself was going to spend
the night up in the tower, with the result that Holmes was
seriously poisoned that night, and saved from death only
through the timely intervention of Watson.

The climax of the story had Holmes conducting a seance up in the haunted tower, with all members of the family
present. The seance was a ruse to smoke out the murderer
of Sir Charles, and the would-be killer of Sherlock Holmes.

The Case of the Impromptu Performance (June 6, 1955)
was written by Joe Morhaim, and had an interesting hook. It
opened late at night with the chiming of Big Ben, while in
prison a mild-mannered bank clerk was made ready to be
hanged. He had been condemned to death for mudering his
wife of only some few months, and now in prison he was
asked to make his final request. Which he did. He asked
to see Sherlock Holmes.

When Holmes and Watson came to see the prisoner,
the man said Holmes was his last hope of being proved innocent of his wife's murder. Then he told them the entire
story of the night his wife had been killed, and while listening Holmes picked up a clue that led him back out into the
streets of London, and onto the track of the real murderer:
a killer he trapped and brought to justice barely in time to
save the doomed bank clerk.

Another weak and silly adventure, The Case of the
Baker Street Bachelors (June 20, 1955) saw Holmes and Watson going to a marriage bureau looking for wives. Written
by Joseph Victor, the story had Jeffrey Bourne, who was
running for Parliament, coming to Holmes to tell him that
he was about to be blackmailed. Bourne's wife had died a
few years earlier, and feeling lonely he'd gone to a marriage
bureau, where he was now going to publicly claim that he'd
beaten and otherwise mistreated her. There wasn't an ounce
of truth in the charges, Bourne insisted, but the scandal
would certainly result in his public disgrace, and cost him
his run for Parliament. The woman said she would keep
mum, however, if Bourne paid her off.

Taking on the case, Holmes went to the marriage bureau with Watson and they became clients looking for wives. In turn they were introduced to two women, but after a violent scene at a tea shop with the <u>husband</u> of one of the women, Holmes was thrown in jail. That left Watson, and Lestrade, to continue working on the affair, but ultimately both Watson and Lestrade were taken prisoner by the racketeer who was running the bureau, and they had to be rescued by police.

The wrapup saw Holmes himself ending the blackmailers' schemes, and saving Jeffrey Bourne's political career.

Directed by Steve Previn, and written by Joseph and Charles M. Early, <u>The Case of the Royal Murder</u> (June 27, 1955) saw Holmes preventing a war between two Balkan countries. The conflict broke out when Prince Stefan (Maurice Teynac) died while visiting the estate of neighboring King Conrad (Jacques Decqumine). As it happened, Holmes was at King Conrad's estate with Watson for a hunting party after Holmes had solved a case for the king that involved the theft of valuable state documents. And now that Prince Stefan's father, King Johann (Jacques François), was threatening to make war with King Conrad's country, Holmes was once again plunged into adventure.

Investigating the prince's odd death (which happened during a toast to King Conrad, and also involved a gypsy woman's refusing to read the prince's future), Holmes uncovered the grim truth: someone at King Conrad's own estate had murdered Prince Stefan in a desire to see war break out between the countries to satisfy his own ends.

<u>The Case of the Haunted Gainsborough</u> (July 4, 1955) again put Sherlock Holmes up against superstition and ghosts. Also directed by Steve Previn and written by Joseph and Charles M. Early, the Gainsborough affair took Holmes and Watson to a Scottish castle where they investigated the ghost of the long-dead Heather MacGregor (Cleo Rose). The ancestress of their frantic client Malcolm MacGregor, Heather's ghost had been appearing to MacGregor and warning him not to sell a valuable Gainsborough that she once owned. MacGregor had been wanting to sell the painting because he desperately needed money to pay the castle mortgage, which was due shortly.

At the castle Holmes and Watson saw the ghost themselves. But after Sam Scott (Roger Garris), and American

interested in buying the Gainsborough, also showed up at the
castle, the painting mysteriously disappeared, and Malcolm
MacGregor became more desparate than ever.   Using ancient
plans of the castle, however, Holmes discovered a conspiracy
against the worried Scotsman, and finally cornered the people
behind the ghost masquerade.   Holmes' investigations also revealed a vast treasure hidden in one of the castle's secret
rooms.

The Case of the Neurotic Detective (July 11, 1955)
cast Holmes himself as the chief suspect in a series of stu-
pendous London crimes that involved the thefts of state documents, gold seals, and even crown jewels.   The mastermind
behind these crimes was, in fact, so highly regarded as an
enemy of England that the Commissioner of Scotland Yard
(Seymour Green) finally harassed Lestrade into humbling himself (for having failed to catch the super-villain) and going to
Sherlock Holmes to beg for help.   But Holmes, oddly enough,
refused to help Lestrade; he said he had no wish to become
involved.   Watson and Lestrade both thought this was a very
peculiar attitude, and later after Watson thought he saw a
diamond necklace hidden in Holmes' tobacco humidor, he followed Holmes when his friend went out.   But Holmes caught
him.   The next time, though, Watson disguised himself as a
cabby, and had better luck following Holmes: he saw Holmes
meeting with what appeared to be a gang of men.   And as
written by Joe Morhaim, Watson's next piece of action in this
adventure fully anticipated the very much troubled Dr. Watson
who twenty years later was going to appear in Nicholas Meyer's best-selling Sherlock Holmes novel, The Seven-Per-Cent
Solution.

Thinking his friend Sherlock Holmes had become a
neurotic because of overwork (why else would Holmes become
the leader of a criminal gang?), Watson went to visit Dr.
Fishblade (Eugene Deckers), who was a disciple of Sigmund
Freud.   Together they talked over Holmes' problem, and decided the sleuth should be put away for his own good.   But
Holmes foiled their plans and the next evening, elegantly
dressed, he escorted Miss Jennifer Ames (June Crawford)
to a fabulous reception at the Foreign Embassy.   Watson and
Lestrade secretly watched Holmes from the garden, and when
they later saw him emerging from a vault hidden behind a
bookcase in the library, they believed they had discovered
the Holmes gang's hideout.   But then the Commissioner of
Scotland Yard himself appeared with the gang, and at last
Watson and Lestrade learned what was happening: that Holmes,

far from going crazy and turning crooked, was in fact working with a "gang" of secret service men to test various national security measures.   The thefts of state documents and
crown jewels had all figured into this test, of which Lestrade
had necessarily to be kept in the dark so that he and his men
could try to crack the case on their own.

Another adventure written by Joe Morhaim was The
Case of the Unlucky Gambler (July 18, 1955).   This one had
Holmes helping a boy named Andy (Richard O'Sullivan) to locate his missing father, Jack Driscoll (Duncan Elliott).   Andy
told Holmes his mother was home sick in bed and that his
father had been gone three weeks now.   His father would often leave home for days on end, but this time, Andy thought,
something must have happened to him.

While talking with Andy, Holmes learned the boy's
father often used aliases, and shortly Holmes deduced the
man was a gambler.   Taking to the streets of London then,
visiting various pubs and meeting with members of the city's
boxing world, Holmes successfully established not only the
missing man's whereabouts but also thwarted a crime in the
making.

The next Ronald Howard adventure wasn't broadcast
for two months.   Meanwhile however, the series did not go
off the air.   During the interim NBC played repeats of episodes like The Case of the Blind Man's Bluff, The Case of
the Red-Headed League, and The Case of the Laughing Mummy, among others.

The next new exploit was The Case of the Diamond
Tooth (September 19, 1955), which started when Watson was
strolling along the bank of the Thames River and found a peculiar yellow diamond tooth.   He advertised for the owner in
the Lost and Found section of the newspaper, and a few days
later a clerk arrived at Baker Street claiming he was the
owner of the tooth.   Lestrade came right on the man's heels,
though, with the news that they had just found a body floating
in the Thames; a body with nearly every bone broken.   While
Lestrade told Holmes about this murder, the clerk tried to
steal the diamond tooth.   But he was unsuccessful, and he
fled Baker Street emptyhanded.

Holmes traced the diamond tooth back to a Portuguese
dentist, where he learned that the owner of the tooth and the
dead man found floating in the Thames were one and the same.

Ronald Howard (left, as Holmes) and H. Marion Crawford (as Watson) disguised as sailors in "The Case of the Diamond Tooth" on The New Adventures of Sherlock Holmes (Motion Pictures for Television on NBC 1955). (Courtesy Prime TV Films, Inc.)

Then he and Watson disguised themselves as sailors, and visited a dockside pub where they heard about a ship that was sailing for Brazil. They went aboard, but were trapped in the hold, and before Holmes managed to clear up the case, he and Watson very nearly met the same fate as the man who'd been found dead in the Thames.

This adventure of the diamond tooth was followed on

NBC by more repeats of previously broadcast episodes, so it wasn't until a month later that the very last of <u>The New Adventures of Sherlock Holmes</u> was shown. This was <u>The Case of the Tyrant's Daughter</u> (October 17, 1955), on the air almost exactly one year to the day after the series began.

As the story opened, a bobby walking his beat, looked through a window and saw a dead man crumpled over his desk. The case shortly brought the dead man's housekeeper, Mary Dugan, to Baker Street looking for help. The dead man was Mr. Hemingway, whose daughter Janet's fiancé was now being held by Lestrade for the murder. Lestrade made the arrest based on testimony from the elderly housekeeper herself, but she told Holmes she did not believe Janet's fiancé was guilty. Would Mr. Holmes please look into the matter?

Holmes did, and discovered that Hemingway had been at odds with a chemist named Vernon. Then after examining Hemingway's corpse at the morgue, Holmes found the clues that led him into direct confrontation with the real murderer.

And thus the series ended. Afterwards it went into syndication, where it remains healthily alive to this very day. It is interesting to note that during the show's original run (39 episodes), Ronald Howard and Marion Crawford played Holmes and Watson (counting the repeats sandwiched in between the new episodes) almost every week on television for one solid year. (A very few weeks of that year, October 19, 1954, to October 17, 1955, saw the Holmes program preempted for some special broadcast.)

SHERLOCK HOLMES NEXT FIGURED in a film that really had nothing to do with him except in its locale. Released by 20th Century-Fox in 1956, <u>23 Paces to Baker Street</u> was directed by Henry Hathaway and starred Van Johnson, Vera Miles, and Cecil Parker in a mystery exploit based on the novel <u>Warrant for X</u> by Philip MacDonald. In the film Johnson played a blind American playwright who took on a gang of criminals, and according to a newspaper item of the time both director Hathaway and actor Johnson were given honorary memberships in the London Sherlock Holmes Society while they were in England filming the picture. They were given their memberships partly because of the film's title, and partly because the society felt that "the film's plot reflects the same meticulous criminal detection as was incorporated in Sir Arthur's works." The article also said that

Hathaway and Johnson now joined two other Hollywoodites, "Basil Rathbone and Nigel Bruce, who were made honorary members in absentia for their portrayals of Holmes and Dr. Watson on the screen, radio and television."

Two years later Universal released their 12 Rathbone-Bruce Sherlock Holmes pictures to television. As if recognizing a good thing in the Holmes shows' regular exposure (as evidenced by the popular success of the 39 weekly Ronald Howard adventures), the 12 Universal films were packaged as one unit and it was suggested that stations buying the package program the films to play once each week on a regular basis, exactly like a television show. Many stations found the Rathbone films so popular with viewers, however, that even after playing the films once, twice or even three times through, they simply kept on playing them, week in, week out, over and over and over again.

That same year (1958) Basil Rathbone returned to Holmes with a brand new production: a special long-playing record for Audio Books. Titled The Adventures of Sherlock Holmes, the recording featured Rathbone reading four complete tales from the Conan Doyle book of the same name: "A Scandal in Bohemia," "The Red-Headed League," "The Adventure of the Blue Carbuncle," and "The Adventure of the Speckled Band."

At about this time there was also a Solar Pons television pilot. In the immortal words of Vicent Starrett, "Solar Pons is not a caricature of Sherlock Holmes. He is, rather, a clever impersonator, with a twinkle in his eye, which tells us that he knows he is not Sherlock Holmes, and he knows that we know it, but that he hopes we will like him anyway for what he symbolizes."

Created by August Derleth, Solar Pons, the masterful sleuth of 7B Praed Street, London, and his chronicler-associate Dr. Lyndon Parker first appeared on the scene in 1929 in the story "The Adventure of the Black Narcissus," published in The Dragnet magazine. A longtime admirer of the Holmes stories, Derleth had written Conan Doyle after the publication of The Casebook of Sherlock Holmes (the 1927 short-story collection that turned out to be the last Conan Doyle book about Holmes ever published) and asked him if he was going to write any more Holmes adventures. Conan Doyle said he was not, and so Derleth sat down and wrote some of his own. Shortly thereafter, Derleth decided to

change Holmes' name to Solar Pons--and so made the character his own.   The stories, however, are pure Holmes-type
exploits, and have been published in the books "In Re: Sherlock Holmes"--The Adventures of Solar Pons (1945), The
Memoirs of Solar Pons (1951), The Return of Solar Pons
(1958), The Reminiscences of Solar Pons (1961), The Casebook of Solar Pons (1965), Solar Pons: Mr. Fairlie's Final
Journey (1968), and The Chronicles of Solar Pons (1973).
(In 1974, Pinnacle Books of New York began publishing all
the Solar Pons books in a brand-new paperback format.)
They are really very clever tales and have gathered Pons
quite a following.   In 1956 Luther Norris, renowned Baker
Street Irregular and Holmes portrayer himself, even started
The Praed Street Irregulars, a society devoted exclusively
to Pons. [2]

The Solar Pons television pilot, however, seems tem-
porarily lost to the ages.   It was a half-hour filmed program
based on one of Derleth's stories, and broadcast on one of
CBS-TV's various anthology shows, like The General Electric
Theatre or Schlitz Playhouse, but it's never been seen again.
Even historians and collectors have run up against a stone
wall trying to track it down.

1958 also saw some Holmesian shenanigans on screen
when Huntz Hall and the Bowery Boys tackled London crime
in the Allied Artists comedy In the Money.   Directed by William Beaudine, the film costarred Patricia Donahue and featured Huntz Hall (in Holmesian wardrobe at times) inheriting
a fortune, traveling to England to collect it, and then encoun-
tering various hassles in the castle he now owned.   Paul
Cavanagh was also in the film; he had appeared in many of
the Basil Rathbone-Sherlock Holmes adventures at Universal.

NOTES

[1] Boris Karloff's first role as a television sleuth was starring
as Colonel March of Scotland Yard.   Created by John
Dickson Carr, Colonel March investigated murders
and baffling crimes in 26 half-hour episodes broadcast
during the 1954-1955 season.   Colonel March was
filmed in England.

[2] Information regarding membership in the Praed Street Irregulars (and the Baker Street Irregulars as well) may be
obtained by sending a self-addressed, stamped envelope
to Luther Norris, PO Box 261, Culver City, CA 90230.

Twelve

PETER CUSHING AND CHRISTOPHER LEE
AT BAKER STREET

When Peter Cushing and Andre Morell starred as
Holmes and Watson in the British Hammer Films' The Hound
of the Baskervilles in 1959, they kicked off a new era in
Baker Street sleuthing. Directed by Terence Fisher from a
screenplay by Peter Bryan, Hammer's The Hound of the Baskervilles was not only the first new Sherlock Holmes feature
film in more than a dozen years, but it was also the first
made in color.

A nicely mounted, interesting enough adaptation of the
Conan Doyle novel about the spectral Hound of Devonshire,
the Hammer Films remake, distributed by United Artists,
was highlighted by Peter Cushing's excellent performance as
Sherlock Holmes; a performance that immediately ranked
Cushing's Holmes right up there along with the immortal
characterizations of the sleuth by Basil Rathbone, William
Gillette, and Arthur Wontner. In fact, when producer James
Nederlander was preparing to bring the Royal Shakespeare
Company's production of Gillette's Sherlock Holmes stageplay
to New York City in 1975 (it had opened in London in 1974
with John Wood as Holmes), Nederlander had asked Cushing
if he would like to return to Holmes again and play the part
on stage. Cushing unfortunately had previous commitments.

Everybody, it seemed, praised Cushing's work in The
Hound of the Baskervilles. "This latest ... movie revival
of the hair-raising Arthur Conan Doyle classic has among its
distinctions actor Peter Cushing, who seems likely to strike
many oldsters as the best Sherlock Holmes yet," Newsweek
said. Their review continued, "Tense and taut, with a steely
glint on his close-shaven cheekbones, even-voiced, Cushing
is the epitome of the classical detective: Pipe-smoking, ir-
ritable, witty, dry-humored. His deerstalker cap and tweedy

The new, color <u>The Hound of the Baskervilles</u> (Hammer-United Artists 1959) starred Peter Cushing (right) as Sherlock Holmes and Andre Morrell as Dr. Watson. (Courtesy John Robert Christopher Collection.)

cloak are the genuine nineteenth-century article.   He is a
living, breathing Holmes ..." (June 8, 1959).

Rich, in Variety, said that "although every patron will
have his own idea of Sherlock Holmes, it is difficult to fault
the performance of Peter Cushing, who looks, talks and be-
haves precisely the way approved by the Sherlock Holmes Society" (April 1, 1959); and Film Daily said, "Peter Cushing
gives a tantalizing performance ..." (June 16, 1959).

Many also liked Andre Morell's Watson, but there was
never any real camaraderie between Cushing's Holmes and
Morell's Watson in their many film scenes.   If anything,
Morell's doctor seemed much too intelligent a man to have
to play sidekick to a man like Sherlock Holmes.   He seldom
seemed astonished, or even impressed with any of Holmes'
various deductions, and actually gave one the distinct impression that he might easily have solved the mystery of the Baskervilles phantom himself.   At other times he even seemed
mildly amused at Holmes.   His Watson was not effective.

But that Andre Morell should seem capable of solving
crimes himself was probably to be expected because in 1938
he had, in fact, starred in his very own mystery movie series.
Released by Century Films in England, the On Top of the Underworld films were produced by Charles Leeds, and directed
by Mickey Delamar and Denis Kavanagh.   The series was
based on the true crime book by ex-Detective Inspector Leach
of Scotland Yard, and starred Morell as Inspector Simmonds
of the Yard, the lead character.   There were five adventures
in all, each a two-reeler and scripted by Rupert Downing:
The Murdered Constable, The Confidence Tricksters, The
Receivers, Criminals Always Blunder, and The Kite Mob. [1]

Playing Sir Henry Baskerville in Hammer's new Hound
was Christopher Lee, always a fine actor who once again
turned in another good performance even though he had comparatively little to do in the film.   Previously Cushing and
Lee had starred together in other famous Hammer films--
such as Curse of Frankenstein (1957) with Cushing as Victor
Frankenstein, Lee as the Monster, and Hazel Court as Elizabeth; The Horror of Dracula (1958) with Cushing as Van Hel-
sing, the vampire hunter, and Lee as Count Dracula; and The
Mummy (1959) with Cushing as John Banning, Egyptian ar-
chaeologist, and Lee stalking the countryside as Kharis, the
living mummy.   They'd become a famous movie team within
only a few short years, and certainly two of Hammer's best-
known players.

What was strikingly odd about Cushing and Lee in the
Sherlock Holmes film, however, was that Cushing was, relative to the others in the cast, a rather short man and when
his Holmes stood alongside the towering Lee, playing Sir Henry, he seemed even smaller in height.   Perhaps Hammer
should have cast Lee as Holmes, and Cushing in another part,
although by that time Cushing was the studio's major star
and had successfully established himself in protagonist roles,
while Lee had always been seen (in films with Cushing) in
roles of mystery, like Count Dracula or the cursed Mummy.
The role of Sir Henry did fit Lee well, because although Sir
Henry was introduced in the story in a sympathetic light, he
certainly could not entirely be ruled out as a suspect.

But regardless of the handicap in height that Cushing
had to labor under as Sherlock Holmes, he turned in a truly
fine performance.   One interesting scene out on the moors
between Lee and Andre Morell, however, offered the opportunity to at least get the glimmer of an idea of what Christopher
Lee as Holmes might have been like.   Crying out "Watson!,"
Lee pointed out some fact or other to Morell, and for a moment there it was Holmes and Watson on screen.   The impression was strong.

Others in the cast also turned in generally good performances.   They were Francis De Wolff as Dr. Mortimer,
Ewen Solon as Stapleton, Marla Landi as Cecile Stapleton,
John Le Mesurier as Barrymore the butler, Helen Goss as
the butler's wife, and Miles Malleson as Bishop Frankland.
In the recounting of the Baskerville legend itself, David Oxley played Sir Hugo Baskerville.

ORIGINALLY HAMMER FILMS had thought The Hound
of the Baskervilles was going to be the first in a whole series
of Sherlock Holmes films they would make, like the various
series they'd already begun with Frankenstein, Dracula and
the Mummy.   But the generally lukewarm reception given
their Holmes film by audiences dashed those hopes.[2]   The
Hound of the Baskervilles was a decent enough film, but for
Hammer, a studio that was increasingly gaining a reputation
for producing colorful shock and scream thrillers, their version of The Hound was a rather mild entry.   Objectively,
the film really couldn't seem to make up its mind whether
to favor horror more (the Hound) or detective mystery
(Holmes and Watson).   Too, while the market for a horror
film was a good one at that time, the market for a new

Holmes film was not particularly strong, at least in America.
The Basil Rathbone films were on television, along with reruns of the Ronald Howard series, and what mostly did appeal to American audiences about Hammer was their skill
with out-and-out horror stories.   In fact, in America The
Hound of the Baskervilles was not especially advertised as
being a new Sherlock Holmes adventure.   The studio, probably
realizing better than anyone else the horror trend then ram-
pant in the country, advertised the film as more or less a
new chiller from Hammer; a film that was based on the famous novel by Sir Arthur Conan Doyle.

Newspaper and trade magazine reviewers were generally very favorable towards the film, but a few like L.E.R.
of the Hollywood Citizen-News identified some reasons why
the film never quite made it.

" 'The Hound of the Baskervilles,' one of Sir Arthur
Conan Doyle's best-known thrillers," L.E.R. said, "is a tale
calculated to make your hair stand on end when the hound on
the moors emits his terrifying howl.   Yet, in this British
screen version, there is nothing of a terrifying nature at all.
True, the howls are heard; ultimately you see the fearful
hound attacking a victim, but so leisurely paced is this film,
so matter-of-fact in its presentation, so indifferently directed,
that all of it seems nothing at the fadeout.... You've simply
seen a celluloid version of the noted book, and aside from the
colorful settings, filmed in color, there is little to shout
about ..." (Hollywood Citizen-News, July 3, 1959).

Margaret Harford of the Los Angeles Mirror News
was another who saw the film for what it was: picturesque
but dull.   "Starring Peter Cushing as the detective, Sherlock
Holmes," Miss Harford said, "the film invokes some splendid
pictorial images (in color) but has little more life than a
chestful of Victorian costumes....   Blame it on a lack of any
real spirit in the script which seems entirely too calculated
and sauntering to fool even the obtuse Dr. Watson.... Perhaps it is just over-familiarity with the subject matter, but I
found myself dozing fairly often throughout....

"The kids liked it.   When the sound went off temporar-
ily, they were delighted to fill in with their own version of
the hound's eerie howl.   I doubt if the producers ever realized
the audience participation possibilities of their picture ..."
(July 2, 1959).

But with Cushing's <u>The Hound of the Baskervilles</u> the
die had been cast. It opened up the doors after 13 years
for the making of new Sherlock Holmes feature pictures.

<u>A Baker Street By-Way</u> was also released in 1959.
This was a documentary film produced by the Sherlock Holmes
Society of London, and showed famous real-life streets and
scenes from the Holmes stories.   There was also a new Sexton Blake film that year; the first new one in 14 years.

Produced and directed by Francis Searle, <u>Murder at
Site Three</u> starred Geoffrey Toone as Baker Street's second
most famous detective, with Richard Burrell as Tinker,
Blake's assistant, and John Warwick as Commander Chambers.
Others in the cast included Barbara Shelley as Susan Dane,
and Jill Melford as her sister Paula.   Based on the novel
<u>Crime Is My Business</u> by W. Howard Baker, the film was
written by Manning O'Brien and saw the intrepid Sexton Blake
battling spies and other evildoers in a nuclear-age thriller in
which Blake eventually used a truth serum to help unmask
the culprits.

Then as he did with 1956's <u>23 Paces to Baker Street</u>,
Sherlock Holmes next figured into the promotion of two 1960
films in singular fashion.   The pictures were Paramount-
Embassy's <u>Jack the Ripper</u>, and 20th Century-Fox's <u>The Lost
World.</u>

Presented by that master of publicity, Joseph E. Levine, <u>Jack the Ripper</u> was produced and directed by Robert
S. Baker and Monty Berman, and was a period film about
the horrendous harlot slayer of 1890's London.   Written by
Jimmy Sangster, one of Hammer Films' top hands, <u>Jack the
Ripper</u> not only told the story of the maniac slasher, but also
offered a possible solution to the identity of the killer.   Nicely
done, the film starred Eddie Byrne as Scotland Yard's Inspector O'Neill, who was in charge of the case, and also
Lee Patterson, John Le Mesurier, Ewen Solon, George Rose,
and Betty McDowall.   And where Sherlock Holmes, even Conan Doyle, came into the picture was in Levine's showman-
ship promotion campaign.

First of all, Levine created a Panel of Crime Connois-
seurs to look at the film, and then pass judgment on it.   Levine said the members of his panel were all experts in the
mystery field: Gypsy Rose Lee ("who writes 'em")[3]; Peter
Lorre ("who slays 'em"); and Basil Rathbone ("who solves

'em"). And as might be expected, all three experts found the film to their liking. Basil Rathbone's comments were particularly interesting, though.

"If Sherlock Holmes had been a real man instead of Conan Doyle's brainchild," Rathbone said, "he probably would have run Jack the Ripper down and delivered him up to jus- tice. Unfortunately, Scotland Yard never could get to the bottom of that terrible series of murders. As an amateur detective, soaked in the Sherlock Holmes tradition, I think this picture is definitely on the right track in its probing of the mystery. I say this with a slight blush, as the final revelation of Jack's identity took me completely by surprise. Every connoisseur of crime, I am sure, will thoroughly en- joy Jack the Ripper" (Jack the Ripper, Paramount Pictures Press Release, 1960).

Levine's promotion for the film also included a news- paper story titled "Could Television 'Private Eyes' Catch Jack the Ripper Today?," an item that pointed out how some of the sleuths currently on television might have handled the mystery of Jack the Ripper.

"Sherlock Holmes," the article said, "the master sleuth of them all (played so many times by Embassy Pictures' own mystery expert, Basil Rathbone, and now interpreted by Ronald Howard on TV), really owes some of his fame to 'The Ripper.' A. Conan Doyle was still an obscure physician when the Whitechapel slasher's exploits prompted him to advance a theory as to the medical background of the killer. Holmes, if on the 'Ripper' case, might utilize his famed Baker Street Irregulars, a motley but efficient gang of investigators which foreshadowed our modern technique of massive investigation in depth."

Other television sleuths, the article went on, might use other methods to catch the Ripper. Mickey Spillane's Mike Hammer (Darren McGavin) might crack the case by a lot of legwork. Markham (Ray Milland), the suave interna- tional private eye, might take an approach to the case through some lofty underworld figure, a man whose net of contacts could locate the Ripper without Markham's having to do the legwork of Mike Hammer. Elliot Ness (Robert Stack) of The Untouchables might, on the other hand, apply the main crime detection instruments of the 1920s (a hatchet, and a La Salle touring car) and could be imagined racing around London from one likely hideout to another, roaring to a screeching halt,

smashing in the door with his axe and leading out Jack in
chains.   Frontier marshall Wyatt Earp (Hugh O'Brien) though,
used to direct if violent methods, would probably shoot it out
with the Ripper in an English equivalent of the old corral.

For good measure, Levine also threw in Raymond
Chandler's Philip Marlowe, even though Marlowe wasn't on
television except in reruns of old feature films with Humphrey
Bogart, Dick Powell, and George Montgomery.   Working on
the case of The Ripper, Marlowe might first head to a likely
bar to think things out.   While there he'd be sure to run into
a beautiful girl who, solely for love of the hero, would set
herself up as a decoy to catch the Ripper in action.   Of
course this would be tough on the girl, but since Marlowe
usually got his man, she probably really wouldn't have much
to worry about when Jack lunged at her in the night.

Levine also had a newspaper tie-in feature about how
Conan Doyle was himself baffled by the Ripper mystery; a
story that told how Doyle had written to Scotland Yard recom-
mending the use of the Bertillon fingerprint system, which
was new.   Conan Doyle believed the killer was a physician
or medical man.

There were also ads for Jack the Ripper that used
Conan Doyle's name, as well as the names of George Ber-
nard Shaw and Robert Louis Stevenson: "Even Arthur Conan
Doyle [George Bernard Shaw/Robert Louis Stevenson] was
Confounded by the Most Ingenious Murderer in All the Annals
of Crime...."

The other 1960 film using Sherlock Holmes for pro-
motion purposes was 20th Century-Fox's The Lost World,
produced and directed by Irwin Allen.   A full color treatment
of Conan Doyle's famous adventure novel, The Lost World
was written by Irwin Allen and Charles Bennett, and starred
Claude Rains as Professor Challenger, Michael Rennie as
Lord John Roxton, David Hedison as reporter Edward Malone,
Richard Haydn as Professor Summerlee, Fernando Lamas as
Gomez, who pilots the expedition to the lost plateau in South
America, and Jill St. John as Jennifer Holmes.

Not quite the exciting spectacular that the 1925 Lost
World, with Wallace Beery as Challenger, was, Allen's updated version still had its moments with 60-foot dinosaurs
battling to their deaths, a 70-foot Brontosaurus ramming the
Challenger helicopter, 10-foot spiders and long leafy vines

attacking the safari, and more. The prehistoric monsters in the new film were not animated models, though, as in the original film, but live animals, desert lizards and such, made to look huge on the screen by trick photography.

The part Jill St. John played in the film was entirely original to the story, and had been written in simply because (according to an unwritten law in horror and monster films) no movie thriller like this one could possibly be complete without at least one attractive girl in it. Her name of Jennifer Holmes in the picture was also the inspiration of producer Allen. He said he believed that because of Conan Doyle's world-famous association in the public's mind with Sherlock Holmes, that people who went to see The Lost World would be looking for a character named Holmes. So while the sleuth himself doesn't appear in the film, a leading lady named Holmes does, along with her father Stuart Holmes (John Graham), who financed Challenger's expedition, and Jennifer's brother David Holmes (Ray Stricklyn), who went with Jennifer and Challenger's party on their perilous trek through the South American jungles.

The year 1960 also saw the Sherlock Holmes Society of London producing two more Holmes documentaries, The World of Sherlock Holmes, and Return to Hampstead, using footage of London and photographs from Holmes movies to further scholarly explore the detective's life and times.

In 1961 producer Jack H. Harris planned to film The Scarab, which featured Holmes and Watson, but the picture was never made. Written by Jim Harmon from Harris' own idea, The Scarab was a turn-of-the-century horror thriller with a stellar cast of characters. The story had an unknown murderer running loose in London, and among the suspects were Dr. Frankenstein, Dr. Jekyll, and Jack the Ripper. Working to crack the case and bring the fiend to justice were Sherlock Holmes, Dr. Watson, Lestrade, Jules Verne, Mark Twain, and even Buffalo Bill Cody.

Harris wanted Basil Rathbone to play Holmes, Herbert Marshall for Watson, and Sir Cedric Hardwicke as Lestrade. But the film never materialized.

THE IDEA FIRST brought to mind in Hammer's The Hound of the Baskervilles, that Christopher Lee might well have made an excellent choice to play Holmes, came to life

Christopher Lee as Conan Doyle's celebrated sleuth in Sherlock Holmes and the Deadly Necklace (Constantin 1962).
(Courtesy Christopher Lee.)

---

in 1962 when Lee took on the role of the Baker Street sleuth
for Sherlock Holmes and the Deadly Necklace.

Made in Germany by Constantin Film Verleib, Sherlock Holmes and the Deadly Necklace was produced by Artur
Barumer, directed by Terence Fisher, and costarred Thorley

Walters as Watson. A black-and-white period film, the adventure was based on Conan Doyle's novel The Valley of Fear
and was written by Curt Siodmak, the best horror-thriller
film writer ever to sit down at a typewriter. Siodmak had
created Lawrence Talbot, the Wolf Man, for Universal's 1941
horror film on the same name, and if for no other reason
than this, Siodmak's name belongs right up there with Mary
Shelley and Bram Stoker.[4] Unfortunately however, Sherlock
Holmes and the Deadly Necklace never quite lived up to the
high expectations everyone had for it. There are several
reasons for the let-down.

     For one thing, while Christopher Lee turned in a fine
visual performance as Sherlock Holmes, his sleuth can never
properly be judged because Lee's voice is not on the soundtrack. When the film was dubbed into English, some other
actor gave Holmes his voice. Also, Curt Siodmak's original
script had been rewritten by the German production team,
and although the story as filmed did have its moments, it
wasn't exactly what it had started out to be. The picture
also seemed technically crude, hardly of the level of professional slickness that American or British films achieved.
The pacing of the story was very European too--that is, rather slow and tedious at times. But to make matters worse,
when the film was dubbed (and an inferior job was done) and
scored, added to the film (at least in America) was, of all
things, a modern jazz score.

     "On the face of it, Christopher Lee and Thorley Wal-
ters ought to make a fine Holmes and Watson," The Monthly
Film Bulletin reported, "but their performances here are
swamped by abysmal dubbing. The photography has an occasional grainy look, rather reminiscent of an early German
silent film; and apart from some startling anachronisms the
period detail is on the whole nicely done (in particular the
snake motif of Moriarty's apartment). But the film itself,
feebly directed by Terence Fisher, is plodding and colourless
..." (March 28, 1968).

     As seen, the exploit featured Hans Sohnker as Profes-
sor Moriarty, Hans Neilsen as Inspector Cooper of Scotland
Yard, Edith Schultze-Westrum as Mrs. Hudson, Ivan Denny
as Paul King, Senta Berger as Ellen Blackburn, and Wolfgang
Lukschy as Peter Blackburn; and had Moriarty battling Holmes
for possession of a priceless Egyptian necklace that had been
taken from a recently excavated Pharaoh's tomb. Actually
the necklace was reportedly Cleopatra's own, and Moriarty

had gotten his hands on it by murder most foul.   Then an in-
former turned up at Baker Street, to tell Holmes about Moriarty and the necklace: the man got out but one word before
he was killed.   At the time Holmes was looking into various
murders committed in London, believing they were the work
of his old archenemy, and he now decided to follow up on the
clue of the spoken word from the dying man's lips.   Inspector
Cooper advised Holmes to stay out of it, but it did no good.

The dying man's clue led Holmes and Watson to a pub,
the Hare and the Eagle, where Holmes picked up some more
clues and realized that not only was Moriarty behind the murders, but that an Egyptian necklace was also involved.   Then
with Watson he broke into Moriarty's home, and found the
necklace.   One of the various quaint little death traps the
professor had waiting around his apartment for unwelcome
visitors was a glass Egyptian display case that when opened
spewed forth a poisonous gas.   But as soon as Moriarty realized Holmes had the necklace now, the game between them
was afoot once again.   The struggle ended with Moriarty's
never having won the necklace, but at least escaping capture
by Holmes.

"I've always regarded it as something of a tragedy
that a film with such an excellent cast and so many convincing sets should have been virtually ruined by a lamentable
lack of knowledge on the production side," Christopher Lee
said (Letter to the author, dated London, February 26, 1976).
"The script, to say the least, was inadequate.   The story
was supposed to be that of The Valley of Fear but eventually
bore no resemblance to that story whatsoever.   As you rightly
point out, the music was ludicrous and the result was something of a travesty.   I even discovered subsequently that when
the film was released, the voice of Sherlock Holmes was not
mine, although I had indeed shot the film in English.   I can
only assume that when the post-synchronization had to be
done, I was not available and the voice of another actor was
used.   And that is, perhaps, being over-charitable.

"At least I can claim to have come close to Conan
Doyle's conception of Holmes, both physically and professionally.   And as you know, I am the only actor who has ever
played both brothers...."[5]

Because of the poor dubbing work, Thorley Walters'
Watson also cannot be properly judged, although Walters'
doctor seemed a good enough job of it.   Interestingly enough,

in 1966 Walters went on to play the doctorish sidekick to another famous movie Holmes, Peter Cushing. The film was
Hammer's Frankenstein Created Woman and featured Cushing
as Frankenstein, and Walters as Dr. Hertz, Frankenstein's
laboratory assistant and chief source of income (Hertz was
paying all of Frankenstein's bills for experiments, housing
and food). Then in 1969 Walters again appeared with Cushing in a Frankenstein thriller, this one Frankenstein Must
Be Destroyed. Here Walters had the role of Inspector Frisch,
a policeman tracking down Frankenstein and trying to get to
the bottom of a series of brutal murders. Norman Shelley
was also in the film. At that time Shelley was playing Watson on BBC Radio in a Holmes series that will be discussed
shortly.

     In 1962 while Christopher Lee was playing Holmes on
screen, Basil Rathbone was again returning to the sleuth, on
television. This time Rathbone flew to Chicago, where for
WGN-TV he taped a series of introductions to the Universal-
Holmes films he had made with Nigel Bruce. Called The
Basil Rathbone Mystery Theatre, each program opened on
Rathbone sitting in a comfortable armchair (presumably at
Baker Street), welcoming the viewer, and then introducing
that evening's Sherlock Holmes movie. Rathbone reappeared
during some of the breaks in the films, and also at the closing. His remarks were generally directed towards recalling
the particular film exploit the station was broadcasting that
night, although now and again he might comment on his old
friend Nigel Bruce, and about the making of the film(s).

     But so far as can be determined, this special series
of Basil Rathbone introductions to his Sherlock Holmes films
has been broadcast only by WGN in Chicago, which continued
playing them even after Rathbone's death in 1967. For national release, however, in 1963 Rathbone recorded another
Sherlock Holmes album: Caedmon Records' The Stories of
Sherlock Holmes, Volume 1, which featured readings of Conan
Doyle's "The Adventure of the Speckled Band," and "The Final Problem." The liner notes were written by Rex Stout,
creator of Nero Wolfe.

     The next year in England the BBC also returned to
Sherlock Holmes, this time with a 50-minute television version of the "Speckled Band" story. Broadcast on May 18,
1964, BBC-2 Television Service's The Speckled Band adventure was directed by Robin Midgley and adapted by Giles
Cooper. Douglas Wilmer starred as Sherlock Holmes, Nigel

Stock played Watson, and others in the cast included Mary
Holder as Mrs. Hudson, Liane Aukin as Helen Stone, Felix
Felton as Grimesby Roylott, and Marian Diamond as Julia
Stoner, the doomed woman.

Wilmer's Holmes was not a particularly energetic
sleuth, but he came off well. The show, in fact, received
a very favorable reaction and the following year sired a whole
new BBC series of Holmes adventures, also with Wilmer and
Stock, a modestly engratiating Watson. In the new series of
12 exploits Peter Madden had the recurring role of Lestrade,
Enid Lindsey was Mrs. Hudson, and Jimmy Ashton played
Billy, the Baker Street pageboy.

Produced for the BBC by David Goddard, the Douglas
Wilmer series of 50-minute, closely-adapted adventures opened with The Illustrious Client (February 20, 1965), directed
by Peter Sasdy, written by Giles Cooper, with Ballard Berkeley as Sir James Damery ("a man of the world with a natural turn for diplomacy ... a household word in society ...
a reputation for arranging delicate matters which are to be
kept out of the papers..."); Peter Syngarde as Baron Gruner,
and Rosemary Leach as Kitty Winter.

"A satisfying initialler indicates that this skein ...
will attract kudos and audiences to BBC-1, despite stiff Saturday competition from the commercial web," Otta said in Variety. "David Goddard's production, helped by largely convincing sets from Roy Oxley, showed admirable fidelity to
Conan Doyle's original descriptions of background and character, and the scripting by Giles Cooper also captured the true
flavor. ... Peter Sasdy's direction got the balance between
detail and pace. In fact, the skein promises to combine nos-
talgia with well-mannered excitement in a pleasing mixture...."

Douglas Wilmer and Nigel Stock also came in for good
notice. Besides the fact that Wilmer looked like the Sherlock
Holmes from the famous illustrations, Otta thought Wilmer
"struck the right note of cool and probing composure" and
didn't overuse familiar Baker Street mainstays like deerstalker
and pipe. Nigel Stock's Watson was also likable, "a loyal,
slower witted helpmate to the 'tec but dodging the peril of
seeming too stupid ..." (March 3, 1965).

Opposite: Douglas Wilmer as Holmes and Nigel Stock as
Watson on BBC-TV's The Speckled Band (1964).

The opening adventure of The Illustrious Client was
followed a week later by The Devil's Foot (February 27, 1965)
directed by Max Varnel and written by Giles Cooper again,
with Frank Cranshaw as Owen Tregennis, Derek Birch as
George Tregennis, and Camilla Hasse as Brenda Tregennis.
Then came The Copper Beeches (March 6, 1965), directed by
Gareth Davies and adapted by Vincent Tisley, with Patrick
Wymark as Jephro Ruscastle, Althea Charlton as Mrs. Ru-
castle, and Paul Harris as Mr. Fowler; The Red-Headed
League (March 13, 1965) directed by Peter Duguid and writ-
ten by Anthony Read, with Toke Townley as Jabez Wilson,
David Andrews as Vincent Spaulding, Trevor Martin as Dun-
can Ross, John Barcroft as Inspector Hopkins, and Geoffrey
Wincott as Mr. Merryweather of the bank; and The Abbey
Grange (March 20, 1965) directed by Peter Cregeen, written
by Clifford Witting, with Michael Grover as Sir Eustace
Brackenstall, Nyrea Dawn Porter as Lady Brackenstall, and
David Harrison as William Randall.

The other Wilmer adventures were The Six Napoleons
(March 27, 1965), directed by Gareth Davies, written by Giles
Cooper, with James Bree as Dr. Barnicott ("an enthusiastic
admirer of Napoleon ... his house is full of books, pictures,
and relics of the French Emporer..."), Terry Leigh as Ve-
nucci, and Andreas Marko as Beppo; The Man with the Twisted
Lip (April 3, 1965), directed by Eric Taylor and written by
Ian Read, with Victor Brooks as Inspector Bradsheet, Anna
Cropper as Mrs. Neville St. Clair, and Anton Rodgers as
Hugh Boone; The Beryl Coronet (April 10, 1965), directed by
Max Varnel and written by Nicholas Palmer, with David Burke
as Sir George Burnwell, Sandra Hampton as Lucy Parr, and
Leonard Sachs as Holder; The Bruce-Partington Plans (April
17, 1965), directed by Shawn Sutton and written by Giles
Cooper, with Derek Francis as Mycroft Holmes ("Brother
Mycroft is coming round....   Mycroft has his rails and he
runs on them....   Once, and only once, has he been here;
what upheaval can possibly have derailed him?"), Allan Cuthbertson as Colonel Valentine Walter, and Sandra Payne as
Violet Westbury; Charles Augustus Milverton (April 24, 1965)
directed by Philip Dudley and written by Clifford Witting,
with Barry Jones as the evil Milverton, and Penelope Horner

Opposite: Douglas Wilmer (center as Sherlock Holmes), Derek
Francis (left, as Sherlock's brother Mycroft Holmes), and
Nigel Stock (as Watson) in "The Bruce-Partington Plans"
(BBC-TV 1965), part of the BBC Sherlock Holmes series.

as Lady Eva Brackwell; The Retired Colourman (May 1, 1965),
directed by Michael Haues and written by Ian Read, with Maurice Denham as Josiah Amberley, William Wilde as Dr. Ernest, and Leslie Seward as Ellen Amberley; and then Lady
Frances Carfax (May 8, 1965), directed by Shawn Sutton and
written by Vincent Tisley, with Ronald Radd as Dr. Shlessinger, Sheila Gibbs as Lady Frances, Joss Acklund as the
Honourable Philip Green, and Diane King as Mrs. Shlessinger.

After hanging up his BBC deerstalker, Douglas Wilmer
went to work in a new Fu Manchu feature film series being
produced in England and Italy by Harry Alan Towers.   In
1954 producer Towers had headed a BBC Radio series of 12
Sherlock Holmes stories with Sir John Geilgud and Ralph
Richardson. [6] Besides featuring Douglas Wilmer, however,
Towers' Fu Manchu films were not without other Holmesian
overtones.

In all, Harry Alan Towers produced five Fu Manchu
films in color, and they all starred Christopher Lee as the
devil doctor and H. Marion Crawford as Dr. Petrie.   Crawford, of course, had played Holmes on radio in 1948, and
then Watson on television's The New Adventures of Sherlock
Holmes in 1954.   The first film, The Face of Fu Manchu
(1965), also starred Nigel Green as Fu Manchu's enemy,
Nayland Smith, but when Douglas Wilmer took over the role
of Smith in the second film, The Brides of Fu Manchu (1966),
Towers' films really took on a Holmesian look.

Wilmer stayed with the series through the third film,
The Vengeance of Fu Manchu (1967), but then left for other
acting assignments.   Taking his place as Nayland Smith in
the fourth film, however, was none other than Richard Greene,
who'd played Sir Henry Baskerville in 1939's The Hound of
the Baskervilles with Basil Rathbone.   Greene debuted as
Nayland Smith in the 1968 The Blood of Fu Manchu (also
called Kiss and Kill), and then finished out the series with
The Castle of Fu Manchu (1970).

The year (1965) also saw the production of a film
called The I. B. M. Puppet Shows, featuring Sherlock Holmes.
At the New York World's Fair that year Charles and Ray
Eames had been entertaining visitors with their clever little
puppet programs, and one of their shows was a Holmes and
Watson sketch called "Sherlock Holmes in the Singular Case
of the Plural Green Moustache." Later it was filmed, and
made up one-half of The I. B. M. Puppet Shows, a nine-

minute picture in color that was filled out with another of
their skits, "Computer Day at Midvale." The Eames film
was never distributed nationally, however, and so has been
seen by only a few people.

NOTES

[1] In 1938 Morell also starred with Arthur Wontner in 13 Men
and a Gun, a British-Italian coproduction. Directed
by Mario Zampi, the war film was set in 1914 Austria;
it also featured H. Marion Crawford in the cast of
players.

[2] In 1961 Hammer did reunite Cushing and Morell though. Directed by Quentin Lawrence, Cash on Demand saw
Morell forcing Cushing to help him in robbing the bank
where Cushing was employed as manager. If Cushing
didn't agree to go along with Morell on this project,
then Morell swore that Cushing's wife and son were
going to come to a sorry end. Cash on Demand was
hardly a Holmes-Watson-type association for either of
them.

[3] In 1941, Gypsy Rose Lee, who was always more famous as
one of the top strippers in the world, wrote (with mystery writer Craig Rice) The G-String Murders, and
the next year (also with Rice) a second mystery novel,
Mother Finds a Body. In 1943, The G-String Murders
was purchased for whodunit filming, and released under the title Lady of Burlesque, starring Barbara
Stanwyck.

[4] Among many other memorable films, Siodmak also wrote
Frankenstein Meets the Wolf Man (1943), in which
Dennis Hoey's "Lestrade" made his cameo appearance.

[5] Lee played Sherlock Holmes' brother Mycroft in The Private
Life of Sherlock Holmes (1970). See Chapter Fourteen.

[6] BBC Radio's 1954 Adventures of Sherlock Holmes series was
adapted from the Conan Doyle tales by John Keir Cross,
who was in reality John Dickson Carr. The last episode of the series, The Final Problem, starred Orson
Welles as Moriarty. Earlier though (on September 25,
1938), Welles had played Holmes himself on radio, in
an hour-long Mercury Theatre on the Air production of
William Gillette's play. Welles had also written the
radio version, which costarred Ray Collins as Watson.

Thirteen

JACK AND THE DEERSTALKER

A foggy night in 1890's London. A woman walks the streets. There's a sudden blur of movement from the shadows, and ... Jack the Ripper ....

Released in late 1965, Columbia's A Study in Terror was based on the very same premise that Paramount Pictures five years earlier had used in promoting Joseph E. Levine's Jack the Ripper; a premise that has in fact often been discussed by Holmes scholars through the years: how would Sherlock Holmes have tracked down Jack the Ripper had he gone to work on the case? Would Holmes have triumphed over the fiend, or would he have been outsmarted?

Produced by Henry E. Lester and directed by James Hill, A Study in Terror starred John Neville as Holmes, Donald Houston as Watson, Robert Morley as Mycroft Holmes, Frank Finlay as Lestrade, and Barbara Leake as Mrs. Hudson. The thriller was filmed in England in color, and told exactly what would have happened had Sherlock Holmes ever taken on the Ripper: he'd have caught him; no doubt about it.

An entertaining, well-produced Victorian adventure, A Study in Terror was written by Donald and Derek Ford,[1] and saw the British Government asking Holmes to investigate the current Jack the Ripper murders. This request for help came to Holmes through his brother Mycroft (famously played by Robert Morley), and although the Ripper concentrated on streetwalkers operating in London's dismal East End section, Holmes' inquiries into the matter led him first to the aristocratic Osborne family, headed by the Duke of Shires (Barry Jones). The Duke's youngest son, Lord Carfax (John Fraser), confirmed to Holmes that his brother Michael (John Cairney), now missing, had been disowned by the family because he'd married a prostitute, Angela (Andrienne Corri). Then as the

Ripper struck twice more, Holmes went to the East End where
he confronted a surgeon, Dr. Murray (Anthony Quayle), who
worked there. Investigating even further, Holmes went to see
the prostitute Angela herself; her face, he discovered, was
badly scarred from acid, thrown on her during a fight between
her husband, the missing Michael Osborne, and East End pub
owner Max Steiner (Peter Carsten); a fight that erupted when
the bully Steiner tried to involve Osborne in a blackmail plot.

As Holmes had suspected, the Ripper rampage was in-
delibly linked to Angela, and the climax of A Study in Terror
saw Sherlock Holmes awaiting the Ripper's arrival at Angela's
bedside in her room above a Whitechapel tavern. Facing the
Ripper himself now, Holmes revealed the man's true identity,
and then they started battling away in a fight to the death.
In the midst of their frantic struggling, a lamp was knocked
over, a fire quickly broke out, it spread into a roaring holo-
caust, and it was only Holmes who managed to escape.

The inferno swallowed up the Ripper--whose identity
Holmes decided he was going to keep secret forever.

"A fine production ...."; that's what Sy Oshinsky called
A Study in Terror in Motion Picture Herald. "The color
photography does an excellent job of transporting the viewer
into old England ... [and] the disreputable 'red light' district
of London, and the brawdy flavor of the area comes through
strongly. One is also indebted to an original story and
screenplay by Donald and Derek Ford, who have created an
intelligent and exciting vehicle for the return of Sherlock
Holmes ..." (April 27, 1966).

Other reviews of the film were equally flattering, with
Kevin Thomas calling it simply "art without artiness ..."
(The Los Angeles Times, January 25, 1967). John Neville
as Sherlock Holmes also came in for well deserved mention.
Rich in Variety, for example, said that "Neville gives a stylish performance in full keeping with the Holmesian tradition
..." (November 24, 1965), while Time magazine said, "Under [James Hill's wry direction, John Neville and Donald
Houston play Holmes and Watson with a quaint and slightly
stilted charm that defines them as exactly what they are: impressive pieces of Victorian bric-a-bric ..." (November 25,
1966).

When interviewed recently, Herman Cohen, [2] the executive producer of A Study in Terror, said he still gets letters

and hears from Holmes fans everywhere around the world
that A Study in Terror is the best Sherlock Holmes film ever
made.   Cohen also said they think John Neville's portrayal
of Holmes is absolutely great.   Cohen said, in fact, that after
theatrical producer James Nederlander saw the film, he immediately wanted Neville to play Sherlock Holmes in the Royal
Shakespeare Company's stage production of William Gillette's
Sherlock Holmes when it opened in New York in 1974.   As
it turned out, Neville accepted that offer and so went on to
do the role in a play that was a big hit.

Henry E. Lester, the producer of the film, had been
trying to lure John Neville into playing Holmes for at least
a year before he finally got him to play Holmes in A Study
in Terror.   Originally Lester had wanted Neville to play
Holmes in the musical play Baker Street in America in 1964,[3]
but tied up as he was with his Nottingham Playhouse reper-
tory work in England, Neville had had to decline.

"As the script [for the film] took shape it became
more tempting all the time," Neville said later.   "I'd only
hesitated because of my commitment to Nottingham Playhouse
and my work there as actor-manager, but everyone bent back-
wards to allow me to do it" (A Study in Terror, Columbia
Pictures Press Interview, 1966).

"Neville made the film while at the same time appearing each night on stage at the Nottingham Playhouse in Vol-
pone.   A standby airplane flew him back and forth, from the
studio to the theatre, again and again.

Donald Houston's Watson, on the other hand, was another of the unfortunate impersonations given the doctor whenever an actor heartily announces that he is going to do his
damndest not to play Watson as Nigel Bruce, for example,
had.   Houston's Watson was another explosive characterization, constantly over-amazed by Holmes and chockful of over-
reacting at other times too.   In the beginning, though, there'd
been good high hopes for Houston's Watson.   "So completely,
utterly right for the part," Adrian Conan Doyle had said when
he'd met Houston.   "At last Dr. Watson will appear as a

Opposite: John Neville as Holmes, Donald Houston (left) as
Watson, and Peter Carsten as the villainous pub keeper Max
Steiner, in Herman Cohen's well-received A Study in Terror
(Columbia 1966).   (Courtesy Herman Cohen.)

character in his own right. I've always felt until now that the poor chap had been rather badly done by."

Houston himself said that he was indeed going to show Watson in a new light: as a man capable of assessing evidence, intelligent and alert.

"Sherlock Holmes' genius would dwarf any normal intelligence," Houston said, "but that's no reason for imagining that Watson should always be treated as a bumbling, doddering idiot. While he might not match Holmes' brilliance, he was certainly no fool. After all, Holmes and Watson shared a flat as well as their working lives. How could Holmes have borne it if he had lived in close proximity with an idiot?"

The advertising for A Study in Terror was certainly ridiculous. A well-produced, straightforward thriller, the film had been made during the height of popularity of the campy Batman television series, and so the studio thought they could cash in on the "camp craze" by selling their new Holmes film now as perhaps the campiest hero film of them all.

HOLY TERROR! IT'S SHERLOCK HOLMES
AGAINST JACK THE RIPPER

That was one of the more subtle catchlines and blurbs used to promote the picture. But other gems were quick in coming.

FLY AWAY BATMAN! HERE COMES
THE ORIGINAL CAMP-COUNSELLOR-IN-A-CAPE!
(AIEEE! CRUNCH! POW! BIFF!)

FASTER THAN A SPEEDING COMPUTER!
ABLE TO LEAP TALL TALES IN A SINGLE
STROKE OF GENIUS! IT'S SHERLOCK HOLMES!
THAT BRILLIANT BLOODHOUND OF BAKER
STREET TRACKING THE FEROCIOUS FIEND
JACK THE RIPPER!

HE'S JAMES BOND IN A CAPE!
HE'S BATMAN WITH BRAINS!
HE'S SHERLOCK HOLMES AGAINST
JACK THE RIPPER!

SHERLOCK HOLMES IS THE HERO (CHEER!)
JACK THE RIPPER IS THE VILLAIN (HISS!)
AND THE 'FLICK' IS A STUDY IN SUSPENSE
A STUDY IN SHOCK!

Really the most flavorful one of all, and actually appropriate
for the film if you would take your Holmes with even a slight
grain of salt, was:

> GRAB YOUR HOUNDSTOOTH CAPE
> AND YOUR DEERSTALKER CAP!
> GET YOUR MEERSCHAUM PIPE
> AND YOUR MAGNIFYING GLASS!
> SHERLOCK HOLMES IS BACK --
> AND JACK THE RIPPER'S GOT 'IM!

Besides its being a much applauded Holmes film though,
Herman Cohen's A Study in Terror can also claim at least
one other important distinction. In 1966 famed mystery writer Ellery Queen (who's been called "the logical successor to
Sherlock Holmes" for years) took the script of the film and
turned it into a uniquely clever Lancer paperback novel (also
called A Study in Terror) in which both Holmes and Queen,
working in their own respective areas, fathom the very same,
ageless mystery of Jack the Ripper. (In 1967 Victor Gollancz
(London) published the Queen novel under the title Sherlock
Holmes vs Jack the Ripper.)

In 1966 Basil Rathbone once again returned to Sherlock
Holmes, with another new Caedmon record album. The
Stories of Sherlock Holmes, Volume 2 had Rathbone reading
Conan Doyle's "The Red-Headed League," with liner notes
written by the noted Sherlockian, Christopher Morley. The
next year, however, there were two new Rathbone-Holmes
records. The Stories of Sherlock Holmes, Volume 3 featured
"A Scandal in Bohemia," with the liner notes written by Rath-
bone himself, and The Stories of Sherlock Holmes, Volume 4
featured "Silver Blaze," with liner notes by Robert N. Brodie.
The year also saw the BBC in England producing a new Conan
Doyle television series.

FIFTY MINUTES in length, The Stories of Sir Arthur
Conan Doyle comprised ten weekly television adaptations of
various Doyle stories that were now cleverly reworked to
make them vehicles for a regular set of continuing characters: Tom Crabbe (Keith Buckley), Vicky Heald (Michele
Dotrice), Monkhouse Lee (Christopher Matthews), and Philip
Hardacre (Michael Latimer). Conan Doyle characters all,
the boys were shown at the outset of the series as under-
graduate students at Oxford University, with Tom Crabbe
actually the main character and star of the programs. He
was studying to be a doctor, and in the opening episodes

Vicky Heald was his girlfriend.   By the fifth story, however, they were married.

The BBC's The Stories of Sir Arthur Conan Doyle was an admirable series of taped teleplays set in period, and the sets and costuming were very well handled.   The programs began[4] with Lot 249 (January 15, 1967), a tale of mystery and horror that took place at Oxford University where the three undergraduates--Tom Crabbe, Monkhouse Lee and Philip Hardacre--encountered horrific doings when a fourth student, Bellingham (Philip Mankum), started examining a mummy. The following week, The Croxley Master (January 22, 1967) saw Tom Crabbe enter the prizefighting ring in hopes of winning money to further his medical ambitions.   The Chemistry of Love (February 5, 1967) was a romantic story and The Lift (February 12, 1967) took Crabbe to the fashionable Paris of the 1890s for a holiday.   There he ran into trouble at the Eiffel Tower when his elevator jammed and refused to take him back down to street level.

Crabbe's Practice (February 19, 1967) saw Tom Crabbe now a fully qualified doctor, married to Vicky Heald, and setting up practice in Brisport.   Crabbe's only real problem (not unlike Conan Doyle's own real-life problem when he first set up practice as a doctor) was that he had no patients. The Willow House School (February 26, 1967) focused mainly on Crabbe's friend Monkhouse Lee, though, and Lee's visit to a school where he found great personal danger awaiting him.   The next story, The Mystery of Cader Ifan (March 12, 1967), pretty much established Crabbe as making a go of his practice and settling down to married life with Vicky, so the tale centered around Crabbe's other friend, Philip Hardacre, who in this mystery story befriended a strange old hermit of the hills.   The New Catacombs (March 19, 1967) was also a mystery, this one featuring Monkhouse Lee and the Honorable Hugo Danvers (Barry Justice) investigating new and strange catacombs findings in England.   Other mystery stories then closed out the series: Red Handed (March 26, 1967), about the murder of Lord Mannering (Kenneth Benda) at his estate, and The Black Doctor (April 2, 1967), about Inspector Lavendar's (John Stratton) solving of another murder case.

The feature film The Deadly Bees was also released in 1967.   Written by Robert Bloch and Anthony Marriott, The Deadly Bees was based on H. F. Heard's novel A Taste for Honey, featuring Mr. Mycroft of Sussex.   The Paramount film, however, did not likewise feature the indomitable Mycroft, although his shadow (at least) was very much in view.

Produced by Max J. Rosenberg and Milton Subotsky, who've gained a great reputation for their many horror films, [5] The Deadly Bees was filmed in England in color. Directed by Freddie Francis, the story had a comely young woman named Vicky Robbins (Suzanna Leigh), suffering from over-work and a nervous breakdown, arrive on Sea Gull Island for some peace and quiet. In the Heard novel, it was Mr. My-croft's eventual "Watson," Sydney Silchester, arriving in Sus-sex for peace and quiet. Once she came to Sea Gull Island, however, Vicky Robbins did virtually take up the position of Silchester from the book, and the menace of the murderous bees of bee-keeper Hargrove (Guy Doleman) also remained intact in the film. Mr. Mycroft's name was changed to Man-fred, though. Ironically, he was played by Frank Finlay, who'd played Inspector Lestrade in Herman Cohen's A Study in Terror.

"I had always admired Heard's novel," Robert Bloch said (letter to the author, dated October 20, 1976), "and when asked to adapt it for the screen I was quite pleased. Although I introduced the obligatory heroine as a central char-acter, I did my best to preserve the basic premise and sub-stance of the book. I thought it might be interesting to write the two principal roles for Boris Karloff and Christopher Lee --putting Karloff in a wheelchair and using Lee as the active antagonist.

"Well, a funny thing happened on the way to the shoot-ing-stage; exactly what, I don't know. Apparently the budget wouldn't stretch far enough to include the fees for such stars, so somebody decided their roles would have to be rewritten. Unfortunately the rewriting didn't end there--the heroine's part and the plot were both 'improved' and all that was re-tained of my script were certain structured shock-sequences. I've read and been told several versions of what then occurred --that the producers weren't on hand when the changes were made and were unhappy about the extent of the alterations; but faced with a shooting schedule deadline, they couldn't re-vert back to my original script and concept, etc.

"At any rate, what finally emerged didn't really re-flect Heard's book or my adaptation. And with all due re-spect to those responsible, the result was a 'Bee' picture..."

There was tragedy that year: on July 21, 1967, at his apartment in New York City, Basil Rathbone died. The man who was and who always will be Sherlock Holmes to most of the world was only 75 years young. Rathbone had

always held a sentimental attachment for the character that
had brought him so much acclaim over the years, even when
he was dissatisfied with the type-casting it meant for him; in
truth he never forgot Mr. Sherlock Holmes.

ANOTHER CONAN DOYLE television series returned
in 1968 to the BBC in England: Sherlock Holmes, starring
Peter Cushing and Nigel Stock.

Quoting from BBC's production notes, which accompanied the release of various publicity photos at the time,
what was novel about their new series of 15 Holmes adventures was the basic approach, "a daring realization of the
lurking horror and callous savagery of Victorian crime, especially sexual crime." The new exploits were going to recreate "the Victorian half-world of brutal males and the fur-
tive innocents they dominate." They were going to show the
"evil-hearted servants scheming and embracing below stairs."
There would be "murder, mayhem and the macabre as the
hansom cab once again sets out with Dr. Watson and his debonair, eccentric and uncannily observant friend--Mr. Sherlock
Holmes."

It all rather sounded like Hammer Films had invaded
television, and according to British reviewers like Michael
Pointer the series did indeed play up the sex and violence.
Because of all his Hammer pictures, Peter Cushing, of
course, would have been right at home with monstrously evil
goings-on, though Nigel Stock (who three years earlier had
played Watson to Douglas Wilmer's Holmes on BBC Television) might have been a bit surprised at the new treatment
of the famous stories. Regardless, the new series was popular fare, and with Cushing and Stock on hand must also
have been good Holmesian fare too. But unfortunately, only
those living in Great Britain will ever, it seems, have the
opportunity to see the Cushing television series. An attempt
by the present writer to get the shows to America got as far
as an enthusiastic reception from the Eastern Educational
Television Network (PBS), but on further investigation it was
learned to the dismay of all concerned that there were insur-
mountable clearance problems with the Conan Doyle estate;
clearance problems the BBC just could not overcome so they

Opposite: Peter Cushing (left) and Nigel Stock as Holmes
and Watson on the BBC-TV series Sherlock Holmes (1968).

could then distribute the Cushing series in America. In fact,
it was learned that all BBC Sherlock Holmes productions were
mired down in clearance problems.   There was a report that
the Cushing series might just have been wiped clean off the
tapes as well; and if this is true all that remains of this very
recent series (besides the memories of British viewers) are
various publicity photos which some of us have managed to
secure.

The Cushing series may have been very good entertainment, or it may have been poor material, or anywhere
in between, but Cushing has always been regarded as one of
the best Sherlock Holmes ever to slap on a deerstalker, and
the television series would be eagerly greeted by his many
fans in America.

Be that as it may, the series was produced for the
BBC-1 Television Service by William Sterling and there were
15 programs in all.   Fifty minutes each, the series debuted
with The Second Stain (September 9, 1968), directed by Henri
Saffan and written by Jennifer Stuart, and featuring Daniel
Massey as "the Right Honourable Trelawney Hope, Secretary
for European Affairs, and the most rising statesman in the
country"; Cecil Parker as "the illustrious Lord Bellinger,
twice Premier of Britain"; Alica Deane as Madame Fournaye,
and Penelope Horner as Lady Hilda.   William Lucas played
Lestrade throughout the 15 stories, with Grace Arnold as
Mrs. Hudson, and George A. Cooper in the recurring role
of Inspector Gregson.

The second Cushing television adventure was A Study
in Scarlet (September 16, 1968), directed by Henri Safran
and written by Hugh Leonard, with Larry Cross as Jefferson
Hope, Craig Hunter as Enoch Drebber, Edward Bishop as
Joseph Strangerson, Edina Ronay as Alice Charpentier, and
Tony McLaren as Wiggins, the leader of the ragamuffin Baker
Street Irregulars.   Safran also directed the third show, The
Dancing Men (September 23, 1968), which was written by
Michael and Mollie Hardwick, with Maxwell Reed as Hilton
Cubitt of Riding Thorpe Manor, Richardson Morgan as In-
spector Martin, and Judee Morton as Elsie Cubitt.   Then
came The Hound of the Baskervilles, which was broadcast in
two parts (September 30 and October 7, 1968).   This gave
Peter Cushing the distinction of having played Sherlock Holmes
in that story both in film and on television.

Directed by Graham Evans, the Hound teleplay was

written by Hugh Leonard, and featured Gary Raymond as Sir
Henry Baskerville, David Leland as Dr. Mortimer, Philip
Bond as Stapleton of Merripit House, Gabriella Licundi as
Beryl Stapleton, Christopher Burgess as Barrymore the butler, June Watson as the butler's wife, and Tony Rohr as Selden, an escaped convict living out on the bleak and desolate
moors.

     The next ten shows were The Boscombe Valley Mys-
tery (October 14, 1968), directed by Viktors Ritelis and written by Bruce Stewart, with Nick Tate as James McCarthy
and John Tate as Turner; The Greek Interpreter (October 21,
1968), directed by David Saire and written by John Gould,
with Clive Cazes as Melas the interpreter, Ronald Adam as
Mycroft Holmes, and Peter Woodthorpe as Wilson Kemp; The
Naval Treaty (October 28, 1968), directed by Anthony Kearney and written by John Gould again, with Corin Redgrave as
Percy Phelps, Dennis Price as Lord Holdhurst, and Robin
Wentworth as Mrs. Tangey; The Mystery of Thor Bridge (November 4, 1968), directed by Anthony Kearney and written
by Harry Moore, with Juliet Miles as Grace Dunbar, "the
best woman God ever made"; Grant Taylor as J. Neil Gibson,
and Willoughby Gray as Sergeant Coventry; The Musgrave
Ritual (November 11, 1968), directed by Viktors Ritellis and
written by Alexander Baron, with Norman Woodland as Sir
Reginald Musgrave, Brian Jackson as Brunton the butler, and
Georgia Brown as Rachel the housemaid; and Black Peter
(November 18, 1968--originally scheduled to be episode two),
directed by Anthony Kearney and written by Richard Harris,
with James Kenney as Inspector Hopkins, John Tate as Captain Peter Carey, and Ilona Florence as Mrs. Carey.

     There was Wisteria Lodge (November 25, 1968), di-
rected by Roger Jenkins and written by Alexander Baron,
with Derek Francis as Scott Eccles, who had just had the
"most incredible and grotesque experience"; Carlos Pierre
as Garcia, and Christopher Carlos as Lucas; Shoscombe Old
Place (December 2, 1968), directed by William Bain and
written by Donald Tosh, with Nigel Green as Sir Robert Nor-
bertson, Peter Miles as Sam Brewer, and Kevin Lindsay as
George Nortlett; The Solitary Cyclist (December 9, 1968), directed by Viktors Ritelis and written by Stanley Miller, with
Carole Porter as Miss Violet Smith, and Charles Tingwell
as Mr. Carruthers; and The Sign of the Four (December 16,
1968), directed by William Sterling and written by Michael
and Mollie Hardwick, with John Stratton as Inspector Athelney
Jones, Paul Daneman as Bartholomew Sholto, Howard Goorney

Captain Peter Carey (John Tate) meets his fate in "Black
Peter," part of the BBC-TV series Sherlock Holmes (1968).

---

as Johnathan Small, Sydney Conabere as McMurdo, Ann Bell
as Miss Mary Morstan, and Zen Keller as Tonga the treacherous pygmy.

The last Cushing adventure was The Blue Carbuncle
(December 23, 1968), directed by William Bain and written
by Stanley Miller, with James Beck as James Ryder, Frank
Middlemass as Petersen, and Neil Fitzpatrick as John Horner, the plumber who "was brought up upon the charge of
having ... abstracted from the jewel case of the Countess of
Morcar [Madge Ryan] the valuable gem known as the blue
carbuncle...." Then Peter Cushing went back to work in
more horror films.

Nigel Stock and occasional scripters Michael and
Mollie Hardwick, however, shortly thereafter continued their

association with Sherlock Holmes.   Actually, the Hardwicks
had been adapting Holmes stories for BBC's Sherlock Holmes
radio series with Carleton Hobbs and Norman Shelley ever
since 1959.   The year after the Cushing television series,
however, they teamed up with Nigel Stock again, for a 15-
part BBC Radio broadcast of The Hound of the Baskervilles.
Starting October 20, 1969, the program had Stock as Watson
reading the original novel to listeners.   In 1970 Stock and
the Hardwicks united once more, this time to produce four
long-playing, record-album adventures of Sherlock Holmes.
With Robert Hardy as Holmes, these albums were released
in England by Discourses and included Charles Augustus Milverton and Black Peter (1970); The Speckled Band and The
Blue Carbuncle (1970); The Norwood Builder and The Disappearance of Lady Frances Carfax (1971); and Shoscombe Old
Place and The Illustrious Client (also in 1971).

There were also two Holmes films, and two Holmes
documentaries made the year Peter Cushing did the BBC
television series.   The features were The Hound of the Baskervilles and The Valley of Fear, both made in Italy with
Nando Gazzolo as Holmes, and the documentaries were The
Life of Sherlock Holmes and In the Footsteps of Sherlock
Holmes.

Both documentaries were produced by the Sherlock
Holmes Society of London, and featured Holmes in photos
and art illustrations, and scenes of Baker Street.

NOTES

[1]In 1966 Roulette Records (U.S.) issued an album of the
    soundtrack to A Study in Terror, while Springbook
    Editions (also U.S.) produced a new Holmes jigsaw
    puzzle that advertised the film.   The puzzle was
    called Silver Blaze--From the Memoirs of Sherlock
    Holmes.

[2]Known primarily by his many horror films, Herman Cohen
    also produced I Was a Teen Age Werewolf (1957), I
    Was a Teen Age Frankenstein (1957), Blood of Dra-
    cula (1957), How to Make a Monster (1988), The Head-
    less Ghost (1959), Horrors of the Black Museum
    (1959), Circus of Horrors (1960), Konga (1961), and
    Trog (1970), among others.

[3]When Baker Street: A Musical Adventure of Sherlock Holmes
     opened at Boston's Shubert Theatre on December 28,
     1964, Fritz Weaver played the role of Holmes; Peter
     Sallis was Watson.

[4]To get audiences primed for the Conan Doyle series, the
     BBC broadcast 20th Century-Fox's 1960 film The Lost
     World a week before Lot 249.

[5]Under their Amicus banner, Rosenberg and Subotsky have
     produced Dr. Terror's House of Horrors (1964), The
     Skull (1965), Dr. Who and the Daleks (1965), Torture
     Garden (1968), The House That Dripped Blood (1970),
     Tales from the Crypt (1971), and Asylum (1972).
     Peter Cushing and Christopher Lee have starred in
     many of the Amicus films, while The Skull, Torture
     Garden, The House That Dripped Blood, and Asylum
     were all based on stories by Robert Bloch, who also
     scripted many of these fine horror entertainments.

Fourteen

THE MILLION DOLLAR SLEUTH

How was it that a beautiful woman came to spend the night in Sherlock Holmes' bed, and what were the circumstances that led him to battle the infamous Loch Ness Monster? Why did Holmes, with the greatest mind in England, depend on drugs, and why did he start a rumor that he and Watson were more than just good friends? How was he taken in by a German spy?

These were some of the provocative questions raised by producer-director-writer Billy Wilder, and then explored in his 1970 film The Private Life of Sherlock Holmes, at that time the most elaborate and costly Holmes picture ever made. Wilder seemingly spared no expense (it was a million-dollar thriller) in bringing his "exposé" tale concerning "matters of a delicate and sometimes scandalous nature," to the screen. For all his efforts, though, The Private Life of Sherlock Holmes turned out to be a very big public loser: audiences stayed away in droves, and the film quickly disappeared from circulation.

Released by United Artists, The Private Life of Sherlock Holmes was an ambitious project starring Robert Stephens as Holmes, Colin Blakely as Watson, Christopher Lee as Mycroft Holmes, George Benson as Lestrade, and Irene Handl as Mrs. Hudson. [1] Wilder had written the script with I. A. L. Diamond, and the story began with the opening after all these years of Watson's black dispatch box at a bank in London. Inside lay Holmes' pipe, magnifying glass, deerstalker, and hypodermic syringe; various faded photographs of Holmes, Watson, and Holmes' brother Mycroft; a sheet of music that was inscribed "For Ilse Von H., by S. H."--and Watson's manuscript for an unpublished story about Holmes. Wilder's film then went on to dramatize the events as related in this manuscript; events of a "sometimes scandalous nature."

237

The Private Life showed various incidents in Holmes'
life before actually getting into a Holmesian adventure.   Of
these incidents, perhaps the most striking was the one in
which Madame Petrova (Tamara Toumanova), a Russian ballet
star, wanted Holmes to mate with her so they could produce
a superior child.   Holmes was flattered, but graciously de-
clined her invitation.   But the lady persisted, and despite his
other (diplomatically engineered) refusals, he could see it
was not going to be so easy to get out of the situation.   So
he tried yet another ploy: he hinted to Madame Petrova that
such a mating would be entirely out of the question because
his sexual persuasions happened to be like those of Tschaikow-
sky; that he was, in fact, not a free man; and that he had
been living with another man (Watson) for five very happy
years.   And this, finally, turned the tide--and turned Madame
Petrova off cold.   The upshot of this delicate conversation,
however, was that word of it quickly spread around a cele-
bration party the cast was enjoying after the performance of
Swan Lake that evening.   Watson was there too, having a rio-
tous good time dancing with various girls from the troupe.
But as word of the Petrova-Holmes conversation spread, Watson suddenly found himself dancing with a group of limp-
wristed dancers who giggled knowingly.   When Watson learned
about Holmes' conversation with Madame Petrova, he exploded
with rage.

Dashing back to Baker Street, Watson angrily confronted
Holmes.   He called him a wretch and a monster for having
started such a rumor.   Holmes managed to quiet him down,
though, by explaining his reasons.   Still, Watson felt a scandal was in the making and said he could find women on three
different continents who would vouch for him; that no doubt
Holmes could also produce evidence on his own behalf?   He
had no wish to pry into Holmes' personal life, of course, and
he wanted to assure Holmes that the matter held no concern for
him; just that there might be a possibility of legal action
against those who would use Holmes' conversation with Madame Petrova to sully their names now.

"I must beg you to forgive the presumption," Watson
said, "and ask you straightforwardly.   Have there been wom-
en in your life?" Holmes replied, "The answer is yes, Watson ... I will forgive your presumption...." And so Holmes
never did answer the question, leaving Watson (and the movie
audience) to wonder about him.

The Holmesian adventure got underway shortly afterwards

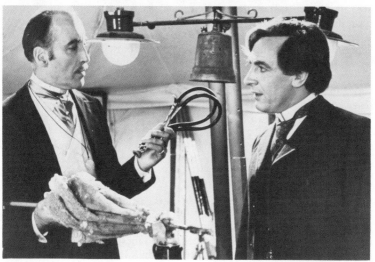

Stills from The Private Life of Sherlock Holmes (United Artists 1970). Top: Robert Stephens as Holmes, Colin Blakely as Watson, and Genevieve Page as Gabrielle Valladon. (Courtesy Bond Street Books.) Bottom: Christopher Lee (left) as Mycroft Holmes and Stephens. (Courtesy Eddie Brandt's Saturday Matinee.)

with the arrival at Baker Street of Gabrielle Valladon (Genevieve Page), an amnesia victim who had just tried to commit
suicide by throwing herself off Westminster Bridge.   Subsequently she spent the night in Holmes' bed, but it was never
made clear whether or not Holmes spent the night there with
her.   The next day, however, after Holmes and Watson snap-
ped her out of her amnesia, they learned she was desperately
looking for her husband, who was missing.   Thus the game
was afoot: a thrilling enough, well-plotted Holmes adventure
that eventually brought the Great Detective face to face with
the legendary Loch Ness Monster in Scotland.   But as Holmes
had cleverly deduced, the Monster was not a monster at all
but "an underwater vessel, disguised as a monster to mis-
lead the gullible."   A submarine, "an experimental model,
operated by a crew of midgets."

Besides the Loch Ness "monster," Holmes and Watson
also met Holmes' brother Mycroft in Scotland.   In London,
Mycroft had tried to keep Holmes from tracking down Gabrielle Valladon's missing husband, but had been unsuccessful.
Now that Holmes' search had led him to the Loch Ness "monster," Mycroft took Holmes and Watson on a tour of the submarine and revealed exactly what it was: the H. M. S. Jonah,
a new invention being secretly tested in the Loch Ness by the
British Government under Mycroft's supervision.   The vessel
was also the prey of unscrupulous German spies, and their
leader, Mycroft told Holmes, was none other than Gabrielle
Valladon--in reality, Mycroft said, the notorious German spy,
Ilse von Hoffmannsthal.   Therefore, Mycroft concluded, it
was none other than his brilliant brother Sherlock himself
who had successfully led the German spies directly to Britain's
top secret.   Ilse von Hoffmansthal was captured by Mycroft's
agents and sent back to her home country in exchange for a
captured British spy.

The truth of how he had been taken in was a blow to
Holmes and he requested that Watson never write up this adventure for his readers!   The ending of the film, however,
was a romantic one that left little doubt that during the exploit Holmes and Ilse von Hoffmansthal had fallen in love.
Holmes learned from his brother sometime later that she had
been sent out on another assignment by her superiors in Germany, and subsequently had been arrested in Japan; that she
had, in fact, been summarily executed by a Japanese firing
squad.   Mycroft added that it might also interest Holmes to
know that she had been living in Japan as a Mrs. Ashdown--
the name she and Holmes had used when they registered as

husband and wife (with Watson as valet) at the Loch Ness hotel, when they first arrived in Scotland searching for her
"missing husband."

Hearing this news about her death, Sherlock Holmes
then quietly retired to his room.   Watson, in a brilliantly
warm-hearted and nostalgic scene in the Baker Street sitting
room--alone amidst the sudden sad silence that enveloped
221B now--thought for a moment, and then began writing this
narrative. [2]

PROBABLY THERE WAS not one but many factors responsible for the sudden boxoffice death of The Private Life
of Sherlock Holmes.   Some have said, for example, that it
was simply the wrong time for such a grandiose Sherlock
Holmes film, that it was ahead of its time.   But closer to
the truth might be that right from the start it did not really
sound like a very appealing film.   It was touted pretty much
as an "exposé" of Sherlock Holmes and some of the advertising reminded one of the suggestive blurbs used by romance
or Hollywood gossip magazines to lure readers.   The film
did not sound like a fun-type Sherlock Holmes adventure.
One wondered, for instance, what the otherwise esteemed
producer Billy Wilder was trying to do here?   Turn Sherlock
Holmes into a sensationalistic gimmick?   Put him down ma-
levolently?

"Whilst the idea is interesting," Margaret Tarratt
said (in Films & Filming, January 1971), "the film fails to
live up to it.   The early sequences are very slow.... A
more basic weakness is that Robert Stephens and Genevieve
Page fail to convey the growing intensity of the relationship
silently developing between them.   Wilder is mostly successful in the middle scenes, featuring Holmes' detective work....
[But] the film remains very much at the level of an incipient
idea rather than of a carefully developed work...."

Larry Cohen, in The Hollywood Reporter, said "the
picture is affectionate in its treatment of the relationship between Holmes and Dr. John H. Watson, lovely, and even
lyrical....   It's an old-fashioned, even quaint picture, strong
on recreative atmosphere, mood and feeling ..." (October 22,
1970).   Rich, however, in The Motion Picture Exhibitor
pointed out that while "the film evokes another more glamor-
ous era ... it has a curious coldness which might thwart
audience involvement.   Lacking the astringency and bite of

the Basil Rathbone prototypes, it never captures that brandy,
coffee and cigars English club atmosphere which so enthralled
viewers of the 30s and 40s.   The script ... takes half running time to get off the ground ..." (December 23, 1970).

    Billy Wilder's choice to play Sherlock Holmes, and
how Robert Stephens should have played the part[3] has also
come in for criticism.   For the most part, Stephens' Holmes
was a rather limp-wristed type of sleuth, while Colin Blakely's
Watson was again generally the irritating, oftimes loud-voiced
and over-reacting kind of Watson seen in some other films.

    "Stephens plays Sherlock in rather gay fashion under
Wilder's tongue-in-cheek direction...," Gene in Variety said
(October 22, 1970).   "Robert Stephens does give Holmes a
certain dash and aristocratic panache," Alex Keneas wrote
in Newsweek, "and Colin Blakely's Watson is youthful and
less fusty.   But the pair don't come up to the dynamic duo
of Basil Rathbone and Nigel Bruce.   Still, the pace is smooth,
a few offbeat wrinkles keep the whole thing moving along, and
the color footage nicely shows off the area around Inverness,
all of which make the film pleasant in a rather elementary
way ..." (November 2, 1970).

    Actually, besides the wonderful sets and photography
and more than capable performances by others in the cast,
the real star of the film was Christopher Lee.   While hardly
the visual recreation of Mycroft Holmes from the Conan Doyle
stories, Lee's Mycroft was nevertheless a strong character,
purposeful and dominating; the kind of man one would think of
more as Sherlock, not the otherwise lazy and over-indulgent
Mycroft.   It was one of Lee's best roles in films of any kind.

    But, as most everybody has agreed, the adventure it-
self--with Sherlock Holmes following clues that eventually lead
him to Loch Ness and its giant monster--was very good.   But
most people simply didn't bother going to see the movie.   Had
it been played up perhaps as simply another Holmes exploit
(albeit lavishly produced) it might have done better. [4]

    "The picture played at the Radio City Music Hall, NYC,
in October [1970] where its gross was disappointing despite
fine critical reception in the press," The Motion Picture Exhibitor reported.   'It was the first pre-Xmas booking in
RCMH history to have been yanked prior to Thanksgiving Day.
Just one of those things ..." (December 23, 1970).

In all fairness to Billy Wilder, though, the version of
The Private Life of Sherlock Holmes that was released was
not the complete film.   For one thing, various opening sequences showing Holmes solving cases like a murder in a re-
volving room were cut from the release print because the
film was running too long.   A later flashback sequence that
was also cut showed how Holmes had come to distrust women.
This sequence was actually very important to that scene in
Baker Street when Watson asks Holmes about other women in
his life.   As seen, the ending of the Baker Street sequence
left one wondering about Holmes, but had the flashback scene
been left in the film, everything would have been cleared up:
the flashback showed that Holmes had come to distrust women
(in general) because once he'd fallen in love with a (specific)
girl who then badly jilted him.   It was therefore a time in
his life that he simply did not care to ever discuss with anyone, even Watson.   Eliminating this scene, however, gave
the Baker Street sequence after the Madame Petrova incident
an entirely different meaning.

        THE NEXT SHERLOCK HOLMES film was also an
unusual entry, though strictly speaking it was not a Holmes
film.   Released by Universal Pictures in 1971, Newman-Fore-
man's production of They Might Be Giants starred George C.
Scott and Joanne Woodward and was based on James Goldman's
1961 stageplay of the same name. [5]   The big budget Universal
film was adapted by Goldman himself.

        Directed by Anthony Harvey, They Might Be Giants
told the intriguing, at times funny, and well-played story of
a highly respected and successful criminal lawyer named Jus-
tin Playfair (George C. Scott), who after suffering a nervous
breakdown believed he was Sherlock Holmes.   Dressing up
like Holmes in a deerstalker and Inverness, smoking a pipe,
deducing like Holmes, and in general acting like Holmes in
every manner possible, Playfair in fact metamorphosed into
Sherlock Holmes.   Then he met a lady psychiatrist named Dr.
Mildred Watson (Joanne Woodward).   Playfair's family (Lester
Rawlins, Rue McClenahan) had consulted her because they
were concerned about Playfair's mental well-being.   But meeting his "Watson" now, Playfair's belief that he was Sherlock
Holmes was even more strongly reinforced.

        Fascinated by Playfair's fixation that he was Sherlock
Holmes, Dr. Mildred Watson began following Playfair-Holmes
all around New York City while he tracked down (in a series

of deductions that were impeccably Sherlockian) his archenemy, Professor Moriarty.   After a while even Dr. Watson began accepting Playfair as Holmes.   The climax saw Holmes
preparing to meet Moriarty in Central Park: an encounter
from which he believed neither of them would come out alive.

All in all, George C. Scott's portrayal of Holmes was
one of the better characterizations ever given the sleuth, and
the film itself was entertaining, if whacky. [6]   One amusing
scene had Holmes and Watson running into a policeman, who,
seeing Playfair-Holmes' deerstalker and Inverness outfit, mistook him for Basil Rathbone.

That same year (1971) a new, legitimate Sherlock
Holmes film was also produced.   Made in Czechoslovakia,
The Longing of Sherlock Holmes starred Randovan Lukavsky
as Holmes, Vaclaw Voska as Watson, and Vlasta Fialova as
Lady Abraham, the sleuth's desire.   Another "untold tale,"
The Longing of Sherlock Holmes also claimed the distinction
of featuring none other than Sir Arthur Conan Doyle himself
in the cast of characters.   Joseph Patocka played Doyle.

Mr. Sherlock Holmes of London was also produced in
1971.   Another of the scholarly documentaries produced by
the Sherlock Holmes Society of London, the 43-minute film
saw the noted Holmes scholar and lecturer Anthony D. Howlett following the footsteps of Holmes and Watson to many of
the famous London locales written about in the original stories.
Other noted Holmesians such as Guy Warrick, Dr. Maurice
Campbell, George Roberts, and Bernard Davies were also in
the film.

At the Hollywood Film Festival that year, Mr. Sherlock Holmes of London won second prize honors in the documentary field.

IN 1972 UNIVERSAL PICTURES and ABC Television
combined to produce The Hound of the Baskervilles for the
home screen, a rather mild-mannered, even unconcerned
Stewart Granger ineptly cast as Holmes.   The telefilm was
produced by Stanley Kallis, directed by Barry Crane, and

Opposite: Director Anthony Harvey (left), George C. Scott
as Holmes, and Joanne Woodward as Dr. Mildred Watson
in They Might Be Giants (Universal 1971).

scripted from the Conan Doyle novel by Robert E. Thompson.
Filmed in England in color, the new Hound adventure costar-
red Bernard Fox as Watson, Alan Caillou as Lestrade, Ian
Ireland as Sir Henry Baskerville, Anthony Zerbe as Dr. Mor-
timer, William Shatner as Stapleton, Jane Merrow as Beryl
Stapleton, Brendan Dillon as Barrymore the butler, Arline
Anderson as Mrs. Barrymore, and Sally Anne Howes as
Laura Lyond.

This television version of The Hound (shown on February 12, 1972) was actually the pilot for an ABC-Universal
television mystery series that each week would have featured
a famous detective. The series had been designed to show
the exploits of early sleuths and besides Sherlock Holmes
would have included the adventures of Nick Carter and Hercule Poirot. ABC did film Nick Carter starring Robert Conrad, placing America's master detective properly at the turn-
of-the-century, but they never did get around to Poirot. The
Nick Carter television film rated fairly well, but The Hound
of the Baskervilles with Sherlock Holmes was generally considered too unexciting--even plain dull--and was not received
well at all. So Universal and ABC abandoned their plans for
a classic detective series; a worthwhile, interesting idea
nevertheless.

Holmes and Watson next appeared as cartoon characters in The Case of the Metal-Sheathed Elements. Produced
by the Larkins Studios in London in 1972, the animated film
was an educational film designed strictly for use by the electric company, and basically showed Holmes instructing Watson (and therefore the audience) how to use electricity more
efficiently. Then in 1973 England's BBC produced another
Holmes television show. Elementary, My Dear Watson (January 18, 1973) starred John Clese and William Rushton in a
light-hearted look at Baker Street that went over about as
well as ABC-TV's The Hound of the Baskervilles the year
before. (Not well.) Like the ABC show, Elementary, My
Dear Watson was also a pilot program and had the comedy
succeeded would have been a regularly scheduled series of at
least five more episodes. Much more successful on all counts
was the British Masterpiece Theatre's television production of
The Edwardians: Conan Doyle.

A 50-minute taped teleplay, the Conan Doyle installment of The Edwardians series[7] was broadcast in America
over the Public Broadcasting System on July 28, 1974. Nigel
Davenport starred as Conan Doyle, Maria Aitken was Lady

Jean Conan Doyle, and Sam Dastor played the unfortunate Mr.
George Edalji. The story was based on Conan Doyle's real-
life 1906-1907 sleuthing to clear Edalji, a Birmingham soli-
citor, of the charge of hideous animal maiming, for which
Edalji had already served some three years in prison. Conan
Doyle's detective work in the Edalji case was straight out of
Sherlock Holmes and was certainly more important and difficult because real lives and reputations were hanging in the
balance. In Masterpiece Theater's fine presentation of the
story, Preston Lockwood played Mr. R. D. Yelverton, a
former Chief Justice of the Bahamas, who fought constantly
to show the court the circumstantial case they were trying
to pin on his friend Edalji; and John Nettleton had the role
of Major Alfred Wood, Ret; Conan Doyle's secretary.

     That same year French television broadcast their own
Holmes show. Based on the novel The Sign of the Four, the
hour-long adventure was called Monsieur Sherlock Holmes,
and starred Rolf Becker as Holmes and Roger Lumont as
Watson.

     A NEW HOLMES FEATURE, Murder in Northumber-
land, was also made in 1974. Produced and directed by Paul
Roach of West End Productions in England, it starred Keith
McConnell as Sherlock Holmes and Anthony Seerl as Dr. Watson. The story had Holmes and Watson traveling up into the
North country, around York, where they cracked a baffling
murder mystery involving a family of distinction. Murder
in Northumberland was not, however, the first time Keith
McConnell ever played Sherlock Holmes. It was actually his
fourth such portrayal.

     The first time McConnell donned a deerstalker was in
October 1973, when he filmed a Schlitz Malt Liquor commercial for American television; a commercial that saw Holmes
and Watson (played by Lorie Maine) investigating an odd murder in which Holmes deduced that a mysteriously murdered
victim was fond of drinking Schlitz Malt Liquor. But though
friends and associates had for years been telling him he looked like Sherlock Holmes, McConnell said he got the role quite
by chance.

     "I'd had a number of publicity photos taken in color,"
McConnell recalled (in "Keith McConnell at Baker Street,"
by Ron Haydock, Sherlock Holmes [E-Go Collectors Series
3] July 1976), "and actually I'm rather light haired. But

Keith McConnell (right) and Lorie Maine as Holmes and Watson in their famous Schlitz television commercial (Victor Haboush Pictures 1974).   (Courtesy Keith McConnell.)

when I had black and white photos made from the color trans-
parancies, my hair turned very dark in the pictures. Victor
Haboush of Haboush Pictures, who make commercial films,
saw these photos and said, 'He looks like Sherlock Holmes!'
It turned out they were looking for Holmes for a commercial,
and there I was. But when I did the Schlitz Malt Liquor
film ... they darkened my hair so much that I looked like a
bloody vampire, Bela Lugosi!"

          After the Schlitz film McConnell played Holmes in
television commercials for Harris & Frank (Cricketeer
Clothes) and the Abco-Financial Services; and around July
1974 producer Gene Wilder called McConnell about playing
Holmes in Sherlock Holmes' Smarter Brother, a multi-mil-
lion-dollar comedy Wilder was then writing. Both Wilder
and his producer-associate, Richard Roth, were eager for
McConnell to take the part, and said shooting would begin at
Fox Studios in Hollywood in May 1975. McConnell accepted,
but when Wilder made the film McConnell wasn't in it. What
happened was that in March 1975 McConnell went to work
with a small part in the film version of Alistair MacLean's
Breakheart Pass, with Charles Bronson, which started shooting in Idaho. The work was supposed to be only for a few
weeks, so McConnell would be sure to be free for the Holmes
role in the Wilder film, but it stretched on and on. Regardless, McConnell would still have been available for the Holmes
role by the first of May, except that in the meantime Wilder
and Roth moved up the starting date for Sherlock Holmes'
Smarter Brother to the first of April. (Wilder had also decided to shoot the film in London, instead of Hollywood, but
McConnell had known about that and it would not have affected
his work schedule.) The moving up of one month did mean
that McConnell was not available. McConnell also said that
the original script for the Smarter Brother film (the script
Wilder had planned with McConnell in mind) had much more
Sherlock Holmes in it than did the version released in December 1975. McConnell said Wilder and Roth had also
wanted Lorie Maine (Watson in McConnell's Schlitz commercial) to recreate the role in Smarter Brother, but unfortunately, as things worked out, neither McConnell nor Maine
appeared in the film.

          McConnell has also played Holmes in Neil Simon's
Murder by Death feature (see the next chapter) and also on
radio, in a pilot show produced by Greg Burson and directed
by Joel Rosenzweig. Based on Conan Doyle's story, the
radio show was The Speckled Band, featuring Ivor Barry as

Watson. McConnell's first association with Sherlock Holmes,
however, goes back to the late 1940s when in England he met
and became a close friend of Adrian Conan Doyle, Sir Arthur's son.   He also got to know Denis Conan Doyle, the son
who was then in charge of the Doyle Estate.

"At that time," McConnell said, "Denis was married
to Princess Nina Midivani, whose brother David I knew very
well. As a matter of fact, David lives here in Hollywood
now, and since Denis' death Princess Nina has assumed control of the Doyle estate.   She wrote me a letter just a short
while ago, recalling the years we have known each other,
and how that now I've come into the family, so to speak, as
Sherlock Holmes, how she would like to know all that is happening and would be delighted to help me in any way possible
with Holmes."

NOTES

[1]Noel Johnson was also in the film. In 1957 on BBC Radio
     Johnson had played Watson in a reading of The Hound
     of the Baskervilles, and in 1958 again was Watson in
     The Blue Carbuncle, another BBC reading. In The
     Private Life of Sherlock Holmes, Johnson had the role
     of a boat captain.

[2]Mayflower Books (England) published a novelization of the
     film, written by Michael and Mollie Hardwick. In
     1971 Bantam Books (New York) published it in paper-
     back.

[3]In 1975 Stephens again played Sherlock Holmes, this time on
     stage in America in the Royal Shakespeare Company's
     production of William Gillette's Sherlock Holmes play.

[4]Besides novelizations of the script, other promotional tie-
     ins for the film included a Sherlock Holmes Detective
     Kit, from Gemini Ltd. (London), and a Sherlock
     Holmes "Follow the Clues" Jigsaw Puzzle from Multi
     Media Promotions (also in London).

[5]Goldman's play of They Might Be Giants opened at the The-
     atre Royal in London on June 28, 1961. The leads
     were played by Harry H. Corbett, and Avis Bunnage.

[6]In 1970 Lancer Books (New York) published a paperback of

They Might Be Giants, featuring a special photo section of scenes from the movie.

[7] In the _Edward VII_ episode of _The Edwardians_ series, Thorley Walters (Dr. Watson of _Sherlock Holmes and the
Deadly Necklace_) had the title role.

Fifteen

THE RIVALS OF SHERLOCK HOLMES

Based on anthologies edited by Sir Hugh Greene, British Thames Television's The Rivals of Sherlock Holmes series was a flavorful and entertaining series of 13 one-hour Victorian detective adventures featuring sleuths who had immediately followed in the footsteps of Sherlock Holmes. Some of the actors playing these rivals of Sherlock Holmes were, in fact, former Holmeses of the screen themselves.

Thames' The Rivals of Sherlock Holmes programs were distributed in America by the Eastern Educational Television Network, and broadcast over the Public Broadcasting System. The official release date for the series was May 23, 1975, and Thames had even suggested a specific order in which the individual tales should be broadcast, but various local PBS stations shortly made up their own schedules and airdates, and then played episodes as they saw fit. Then later, after September 4, 1975, when a second series of 13 Rivals episodes was released, some stations, not having finished playing the first set one time through began inserting some of the second cycle stories into the original set, and since the PBS stations across the country were running the respective shows (from whichever cycle) at their own discretion, it is virtually impossible to specify an exact first-showing air date in the United States for any of the stories. Suffice it to say that after May 23, 1975, and then September 4, 1975, the PBS stations ran the entire series of 26 episodes at least once during the calendar year 1975.

A well-produced, Victorian-era mystery series of charm and deduction, The Rivals of Sherlock Holmes is still a favorite series that continually plays in America. Its popularity, in fact, can be likened somewhat to the longevity of the Basil Rathbone and Nigel Bruce series of Sherlock Holmes films: it seems no one gets tired of watching them. New viewers and fans are always being added to the audience.

252

The Rivals series was produced for Thames Television by Jonathan Alwyn and Robert Love, who did a crackerjack job of it, as did the various writers and directors who also captured well the Victorian era of Holmes and those sleuths who directly followed in his tradition. The stories themselves were taken from Hugh Greene's book anthologies--The Rivals of Sherlock Holmes (1970), Cosmopolitan Crimes: The Foreign Rivals of Sherlock Holmes (1971), and The Further Rivals of Sherlock Holmes (1973)--collections of early detective stories (published in paperback in the U. S. by Penguin Books) that were as well presented as the television series itself. Now and then a story not in any of the three books would be adapted to the home screen; these new stories, however, were also written by Greene.

Among the former Sherlock Holmeses of films, stage and television who went on to star in various episodes of the Rivals series were John Neville, Douglas Wilmer, and Robert Stephens. Neville played Dr. John Thorndyke, the famous medical sleuth; Wilmer played Professor S. F. X. Van Dusen, better known to all as the Thinking Machine; and Stephens played Max Carrados, the blind detective. Charles Gray, who earlier (in 1973) had played Ernst Stavro Blofeld, James Bond's archenemy in Diamonds Are Forever--and who in 1976 would play Sherlock Holmes' brother Mycroft in the film version of The Seven-Per-Cent Solution--also appeared in the Rivals series. He played Monsieur Valmont, France's greatest amateur detective.

Released May 23, 1976, the first cycle of 13 Rivals programs included The Duchess of Wiltshire's Diamonds by Guy Boothby, directed by Kim Mills and adapted by Anthony Steven, with Roy Dotrice as Simon Karne, alias Klimo, the man of mystery; A Message from the Deep Sea by R. Austin Freeman, directed by James Goddard, with John Neville as Dr. John Thorndyke, and James Cossins as Dr. Jervis, Thorndyke's partner; The Mysterious Death on the Underground Railway by Baroness Orczy, with Judy Geeson as Fleet Street reporter Polly Burton and Richard Beckinsale as her police sergeant boyfriend; The House of the Invisible by William Hope Hodgson, directed by Alan Cooke, with Donald Pleasence as Carnacki, the world-renowned ghost hunter; The Affair of the Tortoise by Arthur Morrison, directed by Bill Bain, with Peter Barkworth as private investigator Martin Hewitt; The Mystery of the Amber Beads by Fergus Hume, featuring Hagar, the Gypsy fortune teller; and The Sensible Action of Lieutenant Holst by Baron Palle Adam Vilhelm Rosenkrantz, with John Thaw as Lieutenant Holst, the Danish sleuth.

John Neville as Dr. John Thorndyke, forensic expert, who
solves a murder and clears an innocent girl's name in "A
Message from the Deep Sea," an episode on the first cycle
of The Rivals of Sherlock Holmes (Thames Television 1975).
(Courtesy Eastern Educational Television Network.)

        The other six adventures in the first cycle were The
Moabite Cipher by R. Austin Freeman, with John Neville as
Dr. Thorndyke; The Problem of Cell 13 by Jacques Futrelle,
with Douglas Wilmer as the Thinking Machine; The Case of
Laker, Absconded by Arthur Morrison, with Peter Barkworth
again as Martin Hewitt; The Woman in the Big Hat by Baroness Orczy, directed by Alan Cooke, with Elvi Hale as Lady
Molly of Scotland Yard, and Ann Beach as her policewoman
partner, Mary Granard; The Assyrian Rejuvenator by Clifford
Ashdown, directed by Jonathan Alwyn, with Donald Sinden as
Romney Pringle, a man-about-town private investigator and
confidence stickster; and Anonymous Letters by Bauldin Grol-
ler, with Ronald Lewis as Dagobert Trotsler, an experienced

man of the world, financially well-off, "whose joy it was to spend his leisure hours acting as an amateur detective."

Actually this period following the making of Keith McConnell's Holmes feature, Murder in Northumberland in 1974, was significant for the emergence of several features, television movies and even television series about various "rivals of Sherlock Holmes." The first of these rivals, ironically enough, was Dr. Watson himself, who had starred in his own mystery teleplay on December 25, 1974. Broadcast by the BBC in England, Dr. Watson and the Darkwater Hall Mystery was written by Kingsley Amis, and starred Edward Fox in a 50-minute exploit that saw the good doctor going it alone to investigate and subsequently solve a cunning murder outside London. Figuring out problems, though, was nothing really very new to Edward Fox because the year before he had starred in The Day of the Jackal, a high-tension suspense film in which he played the role of an international super-assassin who had the job of inventing a foolproof (and very complex) hit on Charles de Gaulle. Of course in The Jackal Fox was working the wrong side of the law, but the character he played did nevertheless prove himself a master reasoner, even a master of disguise.[1]

Before the second cycle of The Rivals of Sherlock Holmes series was released, however--and before other dramatizations featuring other Holmes "rivals" were ready--NBC Television issued a press release on June 23, 1975, announcing that British actor Robert Shaw was going to star as Holmes in a special, two-hour taped program for NBC's spring 1976 season. Officially titled Timex Presents Sherlock Holmes (because Timex Watches had already bought the sponsorship of the show), the Holmes teleplay was going to be produced by Joseph Cates, directed by Alan Bridges, and written by Terence Feely. Cates said he had purchased the rights to three of the Holmes short stories from the Conan Doyle Estate, and that the television special would be a composite adventure of these stories. Donald Pleasence was set to play Watson. But NBC never did make the show, perhaps because Robert Shaw's star had risen so extraordinarily high after his lead role in the movie Jaws. Very much in demand by everyone then, Shaw's price likewise shot up.

But there was another Holmes television special being planned around this same time, and this other project did get into production, although it has never been broadcast.

To be produced by Jack Haley Jr. (of That's Entertainment) and coproduced by Malcolm Leo, That's Hollywood
was going to be a series of one-hour or 90-minute programs
covering the entire history of Hollywood films.   The pilot
show was dedicated to the Sherlock Holmes films with Basil
Rathbone and Nigel Bruce.   Written and directed by John
Vincent, the Holmes show was hosted by actor Tony Franciosa, whose introductory remarks were filmed in color at
the noted Scene of the Crime bookshop in Sherman Oaks,
California.   Complete with a Victorian motif, the Scene of
the Crime specializes in mystery and crime fiction books,
magazines and collectibles, and it was against this appropriate background that Franciosa opened the program, pointing out various Holmes books and publications on the store's
shelves, and averring that interest in the Baker Street characters ever increases; this segued into the main topic of
Sherlock Holmes on screen and specifically the Rathbone and
Bruce films.   John Vincent's pilot show then featured some
thirty minutes' worth of film clips, with some very well-
informed, voice-over commentary by Franciosa.

Edited by Robert Lambert of Life Goes to the Movies,
the Holmes movie history show was a good one and there was
humor every so often when certain pieces of dialogue that
seemed to appear in every film were all edited together to
make a single, one-after-the-other film clip.   One such sequence had Watson over and over again exclaiming, "That
was meant for you/us, Holmes!" after he and Holmes were
variously menaced by falling boulders or building masonry,
knives shooting up out of boxes, and like dangers.   The ending of the program featured a special teaser for what would
have been the second show of the series: all about the mystery films of Charlie Chan, Mr. Moto, and Mr. Wong.   But
unfortunately That's Hollywood, which looked to be a very
worthwhile undertaking covering all kinds of films and stars,
did not sell.   The pilot show is still making the rounds, however, and it seems unlikely that sooner or later it won't be
picked up for full production, possibly as a syndicated series.

THE SECOND CYCLE of The Rivals of Sherlock Holmes
television series, released September 4, 1975, proved equally
entertaining and well produced.   The 13 new stories were
The Absent-Minded Coterie by Robert Barr, with Charles
Gray as Monsieur Eugene Valmont, France's greatest amateur detective; The Missing Witness Sensation by Ernest
Bramah, with Robert Stephens as Max Carrados, the blind

Sir Hugh Greene, editor of The Rivals of Sherlock Holmes
books, looks over the studio callboard for the filming of the
"Madame Sara" episode of the Rivals television series
(Thames Television 1975).   (Courtesy Eastern Educational
Television Network.)

---

detective; The Affair of the Avalanche Bicycle and Tire Co.
Ltd. by Arthur Morrison, with Peter Vaughn as Horace Dorrington, one of several villainous rivals of Holmes to appear
in the series; The Case of the Dixon Torpedo, with Ronald
Hines as Johnathan Pryde, private investigator; The Ripening
Rubies by Max Pemberton, with Robert Lang as Bernard Sutton, the jewel dealer; The Superfluous Finger by Jacques Futrelle, with Douglas Wilmer as the Thinking Machine; and
500 Carats by George Griffith, with Barry Keegan as Inspector Leo Lipinzki.

        The final six adventures were The Secret of the Fox-
hunter by William Le Queux, featuring William Drew of the

Foreign Office; The Looting of the Specie Room with Ronald
Fraser as Mr. Horrocks, the purser; The Missing Q.C.'s
featuring Charles Dallas, private investigator; The Case of
the Mirror of Portugal by Arthur Morrison, with Peter Vaughn
once more appearing as Horace Dorrington; Madame Sara by
L. T. Meade and Robert Eustace, with John Fraser as Dixon
Druce, the private inquiry agent; and The Secret of the Magnifique by E. Phillips Oppenheim, with Bernard Hepton as
Mr. John Laxworthy, the elderly gentleman who conceived a
plan of great international importance.

          THEN CAME a Sherlock Holmes short film, starring
Leonard Nimoy. Nimoy later played Holmes on stage in the
Royal Shakespeare Company's American tour production of
William Gillette's Sherlock Holmes (in late 1975, and then on
through 1976), but his film portrayal of Holmes has received
virtually no mention whatsoever and in fact is very little
known.

          Produced by Kentucky Educational Television, The
Hidden Motive was Leonard Nimoy's first time out as Sherlock Holmes, and no doubt was a good rehearsal for his up-
coming Holmes portrayal on stage. Only 16 minutes long,
The Hidden Motive costarred Burt Blackwell as Watson, and
except for a few private screenings[2] the film was only seen
over the Kentucky Educational Television system. The story
had Holmes trying to deduce the contents of a large-sized
globe of the world without opening it up.

          But according to Nimoy (see "Nimoy as Sherlock: Out
of the Spocklight," by Irv Letofsky, Los Angeles Times,
March 21, 1976), the idea to play Sherlock Holmes had originally come to him in 1968 after reading an article that
showed the similarities between Holmes and his Star Trek
character, Mr. Spock. (Undoubtedly this article was "Did
Sherlock Holmes Have Pointed Ears?" by Barbara Goldfield,
published in Baker Street Pages, a Holmes journal, in December, 1967.) Later he talked with Gene Roddenberry, the
producer of Star Trek, about playing Holmes and they even
discussed some projects, but nothing had ever come of the
idea until 1975 and The Hidden Motive film, and the Gillette
play.

          Around this same time (October 1975) Filmways Inc.
in Hollywood was considering a television series based on
the exploits of Solar Pons. Recently published by Pinnacle

In 1975-1976 Leonard Nimoy played Holmes on stage in <u>Sher-lock Holmes,</u> by William Gillette, produced by the Royal Shakespeare Company. (Courtesy Shubert Theatre, Century City, Calif.)

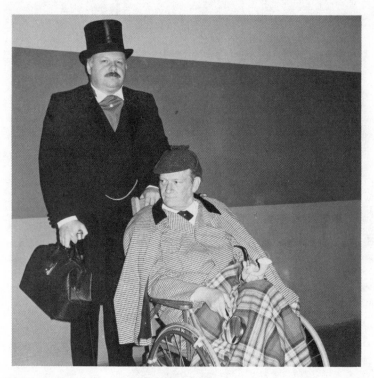

Luther Norris as Holmes, backed by Capt. Cecil A. Ryder, Jr., as Watson, appearing on a KCET-TV found drive (photo by Al Satian 1975).

Books in New York the first time in paperback, the Solar Pons stories were enjoying their first real contact with the world at large, and they were doing very well. Filmways thought the stories would make a good television series, especially since there was a great revival of interest in Sherlock Holmes at that time. Keith McConnell was being considered to star as Pons in the series, and Filmways had even contacted Luther Norris, the renowned bookman and Lord Warden of the Pontine Marsh of the Praed Street Irregulars Society, about serving as technical consultant on the shows. But unfortunately Filmways, who was very enthu-

siastic about doing the Solan Pons programs, received very
little encouragement from the television networks, and so the
project was shelved.

With or without Pons, however, Luther Norris was on
television the following month in another of his many Sherlock
Holmes portrayals.   The occasion was a fund-raising drive
for the publicly-owned KCET television station in Hollywood
and was produced by Steve Miller on November 18, 1975.
After the station ran that night's episode of their Rivals of
Sherlock Holmes series, they cut "live" to the studio where
Ed McMahon of NBC-TV's Tonight show opened the proceed-
ings with a few introductory remarks.   Then McMahon gave
the show over to Gary Owens, the famous announcer from
NBC's Laugh-In show with Rowan and Martin, who then interviewed the special guests.   Two of these special guests were
Holmes and Watson.

Playing Dr. Watson was a tried and true hand at such
performances, Capt. Cecil A. Ryder Jr. , who wheeled in a
121-year-old Sherlock (born January 6, 1854), played by
Luther Norris.   Gary Owens' interview with the Baker Street
duo focused primarily on how in the world Sherlock was able
to keep himself so healthy after all these years.   In reply,
Holmes told Owens and the audience that he attributed his
longevity to eating honey.

GENE WILDER'S The Adventure of Sherlock Holmes'
Smarter Brother was released in late 1975 for the holidays
and subsequently went on to become one of the big hit comedies of the season.   Written and directed by Wilder himself,
the 10th Century-Fox film starred Wilder as Sigerson Holmes,
the so-called "smarter brother" of the title; Marty Feldman
as Sergeant Orville Scaker (Sigerson's "Watson")[3] of the records bureau at Scotland Yard; Madeline Khan as Jenny Hill,
a music hall singer; Dom DeLuise as Gambetti, a conniving
opera star; and Leo McKern as Professor Moriarty.   Holmes
and Watson were played by Douglas Wilmer and Thorley Walters.

As written by Wilder, the story[4] had Sherlock Holmes
telling Watson for the first time that he had an insanely jealous, younger brother named Sigerson.   The reason Holmes
was now telling Watson about Sigerson was because of the theft
of a secret document on which Queen Victoria said rested the
fate of all England.   Holmes had been called into the affair

by the Queen (Susan Field) herself, and he had decided now
on a specific course of action in his efforts to try and retrieve the valuable secret document.

Because his prime suspect in the theft was his old
enemy, Professor Moriarty, Holmes decided he would let it
be known that he and Watson were leaving England for the
Continent to search for the stolen document, which had been
swiped from a safe in the bedroom of Lord Redcliffe (John
Le Mesurier). [5] In reality, however, Holmes and Watson
were merely going to doubleback to England in disguise, and
then search out Moriarty and the document in secret.   Meanwhile, though, while he was supposedly gone from London,
Holmes was going to leave all his pending cases in charge
of his brother Sigerson.   One of these cases involved Jenny
Hill, a blackmailed music hall singer; the case would eventually lead both Sherlock and Sigerson to the stolen document.
The story had the amusing twist that every time Sigerson
thought he was actually getting somewhere on the case by his
own talents, or had saved himself from some predicament,
it was in fact brother Sherlock (acting behind the scenes)
who was responsible.

The climax showed Sigerson and Moriarty having it
out high above the Thames River, a fine scene that reminded
one of the earlier, more serious confrontation between Holmes
and Moriarty in The Adventures of Sherlock Holmes (1939)
with Basil Rathbone and George Zucco.

According to Gene Wilder, he had been wanting to do
a film about Sherlock Holmes for a long time.   In fact while
he was still working in Mel Brooks' Young Frankenstein in
1974, in which he had the title role (with Marty Feldman
playing Igor, his hunchback servant), Wilder said that his
friend, producer Richard Roth, asked him point blank if he'd
ever thought about Holmes for the basis of a film comedy?
"Once a week for the past year," Wilder said.   But still he
had fears that Sherlock Holmes was much too revered a figure
to make fun of; to which Roth had said, "Well, all I'm telling
you is if you could ever find a way to do it, that would be a
picture for us."   They met a week later and again Roth asked

---

Opposite: Gene Wilder (left) as Sigerson Holmes and Marty
Feldman as Sgt. Orville Sacker, Scotland Yard, in The Ad-
venture of Sherlock Holmes' Smarter Brother (20th Century-
Fox 1975).

if Wilder had given any more thought to it.   "No," Wilder
had said, "but I have given a great deal of thought to Sherlock Holmes' insanely jealous younger brother, Sigerson."
(The Adventure of Sherlock Holmes' Smarter Brother, 20th
Century-Fox Press Interview, 1975).

Roth liked the idea of Sigerson right away, and while
Wilder was still finishing his work in Young Frankenstein,
he began writing The Smarter Brother.

The film was shot on location in London and at the
Shepperton Studios where production designer Terry Marsh
created impressive sets such as the mammoth throne room
at Buckingham Palace, the Tivoli Music Hall (which was
largely based on the now-decrepit Wilton Music Hall in Mile
End Road), the interior of an opera house, a huge outdoor set
that was a composite of many London streets at the turn of
the century, and of course the rooms at 221B Baker Street.

The overwhelming success of Wilder's film urged some
other producers and studios to make some of their own Holmes
comedies, of one sort or another.   Playing in adult theatres
around the same time as Wilder's film, though, was Sherlock
Holmes.   This 1975 porno-comedy starred Harry Reems as
Holmes, and it marked Holmes' debut as a Triple X-rated
movie star.   Sherlick Holmes had Reems and Sue Brown ca-
vorting in a story about what happened when "The Master Spy
Stepped Into the Master Bedroom."

On April 20, 1976, ABC Television broadcast Shock-
a-Bye, Baby on their Mystery of the Week program.   It was
a 75-minute, taped play that was not without significant touches
of Sherlock Holmes.

Directed by Lela Swift, and written by the famous mystery writer Henry Slesar, Shock-a-Bye, Baby starred Fritz
Weaver as Alex McQuade, a mystery writer who had just
struck it rich with a sale to Hollywood.   Greta Hysmann
played his wife Victoria, and the plot had their infant son
kidnapped and held for one million dollars' ransom--the same
figure McQuade had made from his sale to Hollywood.   Besides the police, however, two other people were investigating
the kidnapping: Jason and Kate Donahue (Richard Mulligan and
Jill Clayburgh).   They were private eyes, a husband and wife
team who were also friends of McQuade.

Fritz Weaver had played Holmes on stage in Baker

Street: A Musical Adventure of Sherlock Holmes in 1965-1965,
but ABC's Rock-A-Bye, Baby became even more Holmesian
than that when in the opening of the mystery it was revealed
that the name of the McQuade baby was Mycroft; which
McQuade-Weaver, being a mystery writer and all, had taken
directly from the Holmes stories. But there were more
Holmesian allusions coming.

        An otherwise well-directed and very well-acted mys-
tery play, Shock-a-Bye, Baby's denouement actually depended
on certain facts contained in the Sherlock Holmes stories by
Conan Doyle, and ironically was entirely mistaken in its conclusion; the fault of writer Henry Slesar, who should have
known better. According to how the private eye team of Jason and Kate Donahue finally deduced the plot, it went like
this: (1) The baby Mycroft had been kidnapped; (2) the baby
had been named Mycroft in honor of Sherlock Holmes' brother
from the original Holmes stories by Conan Doyle; (3) except
on one occasion, nobody (but the McQuades and their baby's
secretive nurse) had ever been allowed to see the baby;
(4) Mycroft Holmes, although mentioned in the Holmes stories,
never actually appeared in them; (5) therefore, the Donahues
deduced, the baby Mycroft also didn't exist! They figured
out it was all a clever caper pulled by the McQuades so they
could skip the country with the million Alex McQuade had received from his movie sale--money that everyone (including
the Internal Revenue Service) believed had been paid out to
kidnappers, who then presumably murdered the baby and buried him somewhere, never to be found. When the McQuades
were confronted with this theory, they admitted it was all
true.

        But Mycroft Holmes certainly did appear in a few of
the Conan Doyle stories, and so the whole explanation (as
clever as it sounded) was invalid. It's surprising that writer
Slesar didn't know Mycroft Holmes really did step on stage
in the Doyle adventures, or that nobody else connected with
the show ever caught the mistake.

        BROADCAST ON JUNE 16, 1976, was NBC Television's
The Return of the World's Greatest Detective, the first of the
new Holmesian comedies since Gene Wilder's The Adventure
of Sherlock Holmes' Smarter Brother. Filmed by Universal
Pictures in association with NBC, The Return was created,
written and produced by Roland Kibbee and Dean Hargrove,
and directed by Hargrove. A 90-minute show, it starred

Larry Hagman as Sherman Holmes, a policeman; Jenny O'Hare
as Dr. Joan Watson, a psychiatric social worker; Nicholas
Colsanto as Lieutenant Tinker, and Helen Verbit as Holmes'
landlady. It bears a striking resemblance to the earlier
They Might Be Giants film.

Actually a comedy, The Return of the World's Greatest Detective had Larry Hagman playing a bumbling police
officer who was a dyed-in-the-deerstalker Holmes fan, constantly re-reading his book of Holmes stories. One day he
has a slight run-in with a motorcycle (it falls on him, while
he is lying near it reading his Holmes). The result is a
brain concussion, and when he wakes up policeman Sherman
Holmes believes he is the legendary Sherlock. The upshot
is he takes on all the deductive abilities of Holmes, dresses
up like Holmes, and with the help of the psychiatric social
worker named Dr. Joan Watson, who was assigned to his
(mental) case, Sherman Holmes then goes on to aid police
Lieutenant Tinker in solving a baffling homicide. At first
the homicide only looked like a routine automobile accident,
but with Holmes investigating, the pieces of the mystery finally come together to point to an embezzler who had stolen
half a million dollars.

Hagman romped through the show in fine Holmesian
tradition, and he even sounded like Holmes--that is, he
sounded like Basil Rathbone. It was all good fun, and the
reaction from both viewers and critics was very favorable.
But even so--and even though NBC-TV did have hopes to
turn The World's Greatest Detective into a regular series--
they never followed up on the pilot show.

Neil Simon's Murder by Death was another 1976 comedy, this one made for theatres. A Columbia film, it was
produced by Ray Stark, directed by Robert Moore, written
by Robert Moore as a takeoff on the old murder-at-the-man-
sion type mystery film so popular in the thirties and forties.
It was also a satire on detectives, and starred author Truman Capote as Lionel Twain, an eccentric multi-millionaire
who sent out invitations reading, "You are cordially invited
to dinner and murder." Twain sent these invitations to the
world's most famous sleuths, who shortly began arriving at
his isolated, fog-shrouded English manor house in northern
California. The sleuths included the noted Belgian detective,
Milo Perrier (i.e., Hercule Poirot, played by James Coco);
San Francisco's best-known private eye, Sam Diamond (i.e.,
Sam Spade; Peter Falk) and his Girl Friday, Tess Skeffington

(Effie; Eileen Brennan); England's most famous distaff sleuth, Jessica Marbles (Miss Marple; Elsa Lanchester). the inscrutable Oriental detective and ace investigator for the Catalina Island Police Force, Sidney Wang (Charlie Chan; Peter Sellers), accompanied by his ingenious No. 2 adopted son Willie (Richard Narita); and from New York City, Palm Beach and Beverly Hills, the noted and sophisticated urbane crime solvers, Dick and Dora Charleston (Nick and Nora Charles; David Niven and Maggie Smith), and their pet dog Myron.

At dinner Lionel Twain said that someone there would be stabbed to death 12 times at the stroke of midnight, and that as the foremost authority on detective fiction he defied the famous detectives gathered around him to solve the forthcoming murder. Whoever did, however, would receive one million dollars (tax-free) and also be declared the greatest detective in the world. And what all this had to do with Sherlock Holmes was simply this:

Holmes and Watson (played by Keith McConnell and Richard Peel) arrived at Twain's mansion late in the film to figure out the murder that none of the other sleuths had so far been able to solve. But although he does deduce the solution, Holmes refused, then, to divulge that solution to any of the others, and so saying, he left the mansion with Watson. It was a royal putdown. But depending on which print of Murder by Death one sees, the two either do or do not appear in the film. In Oregon and Washington, for example, Holmes and Watson were in, but in most other states in America they were completely cut out of the picture.

There are many reasons for Columbia's double release of Murder by Death. In the first place, trouble started because of actors' egos; ironically, while the biggest star names in the film were playing world famous detectives, when Sherlock Holmes entered the scene their detective characters immediately were dwarfed by the presence of the greatest and most famous of all. Even more ironical is the fact that Holmes was being played by an actor who did not have the famous name the others in the film did. Some of the stars complained about Holmes' upstaging them, especially after filming the scene where the Great Detective solves the crime they couldn't solve, and then walks off without even telling them the solution; pretty much saying, in effect, to go blow in the wind.

Neil Simon did rewrite this climactic sequence,

Keith McConnell (left) as Holmes and Richard Peel as Watson
in their excised roles in <u>Murder by Death</u> (Columbia 1976).
(Courtesy Keith McConnell.)

---

presenting Holmes as not quite as able to solve the crime as
before.   But although this alternate ending was filmed, it
still didn't satisfy some of the players, and so a third ending was filmed, one without Holmes, and this is the ending
as confusing as the events leading to it, that appears in most
of the release prints.   The "rivals," here at least, had won
the day.

Columbia did release (in certain areas) the version
with Holmes in it, but even the problems with some actors'

egos aside, the studio itself had a few difficulties with the
film.   They were never quite sure whether they should adver-
tise that Holmes was in the film.   Holmes' and Watson's en-
trance near the end was supposed to be a surprise for the
audience, and so at one time Columbia thought it best that
advertising not even hint that they were in the film.   But then
with the great resurgence of interest in Holmes at that time,
they began wondering if they weren't missing a good bet by
not advertising it.   Regardless, Murder by Death was a popular film, though not a terribly intelligent one, and seemed to
indicate that audiences really were hungry to see mystery movie comedies.   Of course the Neil Simon name helped at the
box office.

The next Holmes-type comedy was not nearly so confusing: Holmes and Yoyo, a weekly ABC television series
starring Richard B. Schull as Holmes, an old-line cop who
pursued felons in the traditional way, except that he was sad-
dled with a partner, Yoyo (John Schuck), who was a humanoid
robot.   Yoyo's electronic, computerized system would allow
absolutely no room for error.   The series debuted on September 18, 1976, and had some good mystery comedy in it, with
Yoyo usually challenging Holmes' deductions.   It was produced
by Universal Pictures and Leonard Stern, who earlier on television had produced the clever spy comedy Get Smart, with
Don Adams and Barbara Feldon.

The 1976-77 television season in the United States also
brought with it The $128,000 Question, a syndicated quiz pro-
gram that was based on the 1950's network quiz game The
$64,000 Question (which in turn was based on radio's much
earlier $64 Question with Garry Moore).   One of the cate-
gories available to contestants hoping to win the big prize
money in the new version of the game was "Sherlock Holmes."
That season ABC also broadcast The Great Houdinis, a television movie that cast Peter Cushing as Sir Arthur Conan
Doyle--making it the first time in history that the same actor
ever played both Sherlock Holmes and his equally famous creator in drama.

Broadcast in America on October 8, 1976, The Great
Houdinis starred Paul Michael Glaser (of the Starsky and
Hutch television crime show) as the legendary escape artist,
Sally Struthers as his wife Bess, and Ruth Gordon as his
mother Cecelia Weiss.   Written by Melville Shavelson,[6] the
film was supposedly the story of Harry Houdini but was mostly
an inaccurate story of Houdini's overwhelming (but entirely

invented) fixation on his mother. The casting of Peter Cushing as Conan Doyle (who tried to convince Houdini there really was life after death) was also an odd element of the
show.   Cushing was fine in the role, but physically of course
he looked about as much like Conan Doyle as Basil Rathbone
looks like Nigel Bruce.   Maureen O'Sullivan played Lady Jean
Conan Doyle, who had a seance scene with Houdini in which
she believed she had received a message from his dead
mother.

Manny Weltman, a Houdini authority, had been hired
as technical advisor for The Great Houdinis, but obviously
no one there bothered to listen much to whatever he might
have had to say about Houdini's real life, which was certainly
as colorful and dramatic as anything fiction could create.

Others in the cast included Bill Bixby as the Reverend
Arthur Ford; Vivian Vance as Bess Houdini's friend and companion, Minnie Chester; Clive Revill as Dundas Slater, theatrical empressario; Wilfrid Hyde-White as Superintendent Melville of Scotland Yard; Nina Foch as a spiritualist Houdini
soon unmasked; Jack Carter as Houdini's brother, Theo Weiss
(aka Hardeen the magician); Adrienne Barbeau as Daisy White,
a young actress who had an affair with Houdini; and Patrick
Culliton as Houdini's stage assistant. [7]

NOTES

[1] An actor who looks not unlike someone a producer would
cast to play Holmes himself, Edward Fox had costarred with a Sherlock Holmes actor (on television) when
in 1974 he appeared with Douglas Wilmer in the London state production of David Hare's play, Knuckle.

[2] For example, Dr. Watson's Neglected Patients--a Holmes
society headed by Ronald Burt De Waal in Denver--
had a private showing of The Hidden Motive on May 7,
1976.   The occasion was "A Weekend in Denver with
Dr. Watson's Neglected Patients and the Brothers
Three of Moriarty," which also included attending a
performance of Gillette's Sherlock Holmes play with
Nimoy at Denver's Heritage Square Opera House.

[3] Conan Doyle's original name for Watson when he was thinking about writing his first Holmes story, A Study in
Scarlet in 1886, was "Ormond Sacker."

[4] Ballantine Books (New York) published a novelization of The Adventure of Sherlock Holmes' Smarter Brother, written by Gilbert Pearlman, which included scenes from the film.

[5] In 1959 John Le Mesurier had played Barrymore, the butler, in Hammer's The Hound of the Baskervilles with Peter Cushing.

[6] Shavelson also wrote a novelization of his script; The Great Houdinis was published by Fawcett Crest (Greenwich, Conn.) the same month the program was aired.

[7] In 1975, Culliton had the role of Sebastian Grimaldi in a play within a play about a stage actor who was playing Professor Moriarty, in Curley Bradley's Trail of Mystery radio series, produced by Jim Harmon. The episode was entitled "The Man Who Was Not Sherlock Holmes," and featured Kirk Alyn as "Sherlock Holmes," and Richard Gulla as "Dr. Watson."

Sixteen

THE GAME IS AFOOT

It is not given to every actor to play a famous fictional character. But Roger Moore seems to almost have made
a career out of playing famous heroes from literature.

In 1956 Moore played his first famous British hero
when he starred as Ivanhoe in a popular television series of
that same name produced in his native England. Then in
1966 he played Leslie Charteris' Simon Templar in the long-
running television series The Saint, which was not only very
popular, but practically became a cult as well. Then in 1973,
Moore took on the role of Ian Fleming's James Bond in Live
and Let Die, a feature film. He returned to Bond in 1974's
The Man with the Golden Gun, costarring Christopher Lee as
the titled villain, and then played Bond once more in 1977's
The Spy Who Loved Me. Before making his third Bond film,
though, Moore found time to add a fourth illustrious name to
his catalog of impersonations: Sherlock Holmes.

Broadcast over NBC Television on October 18, 1976,
Sherlock Holmes in New York (later released in Europe as a
theatrical feature film) starred Moore as Holmes, Patrick
Macnee as Watson, John Huston as Professor Moriarty, Char-
lotte Rampling as Miss Irene Adler, and David Huddleston as
Inspector Lafferty of the New York City Police Department.
Miss Rampling's association with Conan Doyle stories goes
back to 1967, when she was featured on the BBC's Stories of
Sir Arthur Conan Doyle television series. In the Mystery of
Cader Ifan episode she played Julia Lambert.

Others in the cast of this New York adventure of
Holmes were Gig Young as Mortimer McGraw, president of
the International Gold Exchange; Signe Hasso as Fraulein
Reichenbach, a governess; Leon Ames as Furman, the manager of the Empire Theatre in New York: Jackie Coogan as

a hotel proprietor; Maria Grimm as Nicole, a young ballet
dancer; John Abbott as Heller, Irene Adler's butler; and Roger
Moore's nine-year-old son Geoffrey as Scott Adler, who was
presumably the son of Holmes and Miss Adler.   The executive producer of the film was Jack Haley, Jr., who besides
having brought about such noted film documentaries as Hollywood, the Fabulous Era and That's Entertainment, had also
produced a 1967 television special called The Incredible World
of James Bond.

Produced by John Cutts and directed by Boris Sagal,
Alvin Sapinsley's clever and informed script for Sherlock
Holmes in New York[1] saw Moriarty plotting to avenge himself
on Sherlock Holmes by crushing him in such a way that
Holmes' downfall would become known to the entire world.
This scheme involved blackmail, the kidnapping of Scott Adler, and a devilish plan to relieve New York's International
Gold Exchange of all its gold.   The story opened in London
at Moriarty's headquarters, then moved to Baker Street, and
then went on to New York, where Holmes had been summoned
by Irene Adler, his longtime love, who was appearing on
stage at the Empire Theatre.   It was there in New York that
Sherlock Holmes learned for the first time of the existence
of their son, and then how the boy had been kidnapped.
Holmes also received a message to stay off a sensational
case that would be coming his way shortly, or else he and
Miss Adler would never see young Scott again.   The climax
had Holmes and Moriarty fighting in Moriarty's New York
sanctum, near a trapdoor that opened over the swirling river.
It was a sequence highly reminiscent of the famous Holmes-
Moriarty struggle at the Reichenback Falls in the original
Conan Doyle stories.

For years there has been conjecture about whether or
not Holmes and Miss Adler ("the woman") really ever did
meet again after their initial meeting in Conan Doyle's "A
Scandal in Bohemia."   Some Holmes scholars claim they did,
and can even be specific about dates and places--meetings
that were ultimately kept secret from Watson.   Other scholars
have even claimed Sherlock and Irene not only met again but,
in fact, produced a son.   One popular theory about their son
is that he grew up to become Nero Wolfe, the famous orchid-
loving New York private detective of Rex Stout's novels.
(Wolfe's corpulence and basic laziness can, of course, be
easily traced back to legitimate Holmesian heredity: Mycroft.)
Sapinsley's inclusion of a Holmes-Adler son in Sherlock
Holmes in New York was only one more interesting facet of
an already cleverly worked out, and thoughtfully written script.

Characters in <u>Sherlock Holmes in New York</u> (NBC-20th Cen-
tury-Fox Television 1976) are, left to right, top row: Patrick
Macnee as Watson, Gig Young as Mortimer McGraw, and
David Huddleston as Inspector Lafferty; bottom row: John
Huston as Moriarty, Charlotte Rampling as Miss Irene Adler,
Geoffrey Moore as Scott Adler, and Roger Moore as Holmes.

"We are delighted to have been able to secure Roger [Moore] for this role," said David W. Tebet, senior vice president of NBC. "His elegant charm and talent are ideally suited to the role of Sherlock Holmes...." While making the film at 20th Century-Fox in Hollywood, though, Moore said that at first he hadn't really been too interested in playing Holmes, even though it was true he'd become known primarily because of various heroic film portrayals like the Saint and James Bond. But then he read Sapinsley's script, and said he thought it was funny and original, and so he agreed to do the film. Moore liked the fact he would have a number of disguises to wear (including one as a Doomsday Man parading the streets of New York City), a love affair with a beautiful actress, and he said he also liked the basic plot idea of Moriarty's threatening to steal all the gold.

"But," Moore said, "what I like most about playing Holmes is that there is more dialogue in this script than I ever had in 120 Saint episodes and two Bond films. The script is campy, but I play it straight." The business of Sherlock Holmes' disguises, however, was for Moore much more appealing to read about than to put in actual practice before the movie cameras.

"The disguises take forever to put on, and take off," he said. "I know they work better in fiction than in reality" (NBC Press Release, January 12, 1976).

Generally speaking, Sherlock Holmes in New York, which was a coproduction between NBC and Fox Television, received very favorable notices, but some critics wished that director Sagal would have let Moore and Patrick Macnee (John Steed of The Avengers TV series) simply be themselves in the film, rather than come off as actors trying to play Holmes and Watson. Both Moore and Macnee have developed rather subtle acting styles, and to see them trying to act like a more dynamic Holmes and Watson, as portrayed by others before them, was especially irritating. Moore, for example, seemed to be doing a bad job of a Basil Rathbone, while Macnee actually lowered and hoarsened his voice to try a Nigel Bruce type. Too, Sapinsley's dialogue certainly called for an actor well-schooled on the stage to play Sherlock Holmes, and Moore had never been known for his stage work. Director Sagal would have done better by all concerned had he tailored the script to fit Moore and Macnee's own personal, winning, individual acting styles.

And for some reason the sound quality was not very good throughout much of the film. It gave one the impression that in many scenes the actors were using throat mikes, instead of working off a boom mike. For one thing, there was a consistent rustling of clothing heard when someone might move around in a scene. The sound tended to distort dialogue at times, and came across, in fact, exactly like the kind of rustling sounds heard primarily on television talk shows whenever someone wearing a mike would be talking and moving around, sometimes if even ever so slightly.

" 'THE SEVEN-PER-CENT SOLUTION' is one hundred percent entertainment," said Gene Shalit of NBC-TV's Today Show. "A case of an ingenious novel being turned into a terrific movie...."

Released for the holiday season in late 1976, Universal's The Seven-Per-Cent Solution was a grand, first-class adventure that easily ranks as one of the best Sherlock Holmes films ever made; in its own way, perhaps the best one of all. It's not really fair, though, to compare the film with Holmes movies like Basil Rathbone's The Hound of the Baskervilles, or his Adventures of Sherlock Holmes, because The Seven-Per-Cent Solution really wasn't so much an exploit of Sherlock Holmes as it was a story about Sherlock Holmes.

Produced and directed by Herbert Ross, The Seven-Per-Cent Solution was based on Nicholas Meyer's best-selling novel, and was scripted by Meyer himself. It starred Nicol Williamson as Sherlock Holmes, Robert Duvall as Dr. Watson, Alan Arkin as Dr. Sigmund Freud, Sir Laurence Olivier as Professor Moriarty, Vanessa Redgrave as Lola Devereaux, and Charles Gray as Mycroft Holmes. Others in the stellar cast included Alison Leggatt as Mrs. Hudson, Jeremy Kemp as the scoundrel Baron von Leinsdorf, Samantha Eggar as Mrs. Mary Watson, Joel Grey as the evil Lowenstein, Georgia Brown as Mrs. Freud, and Regine as the Madame of a very fashionable turn-of-the-century Viennese house of pleasure. Leon Greene played Holmes' father, Jill Townsend played Holmes' mother, and Michael Blagdon played Holmes as a boy in a special flashback sequence.

The film opened with a charming title sequence featuring various Sidney Paget illustrations of Holmes from the original Strand Magazine stories, and then told you: "In 1891, Sherlock Holmes disappeared and was presumed dead for three

years thereafter.   This is the true story of that disappearance.   Only the facts have been made up. . . . "

        The reference here was to Conan Doyle's story, "The
Final Problem," and the line about only the facts having been
made up was an intentional laugh-getter that effectively put
the audience into the proper frame of mind for all that was
to come.   For while the film was played straight, and certainly had a basically serious enough storyline, it was supposed to be, after all, entertainment and only to be taken as
such.   A good time at the movies.

        A tale of addiction, abduction, detection, and action,
The Seven-Per-Cent Solution told how Dr. Watson had lured
his friend Sherlock Holmes to Vienna, where Sigmund Freud
was to try to break Holmes of his cocaine habit.   Watson
was extremely concerned about Holmes' mental well-being,
what with Holmes raving about a certain Professor Moriarty,
whom he called "the Napoleon of Crime," and also barricad-
ing himself inside his quarters at Baker Street.   Watson
thought narcotics were at last affecting Holmes' sanity, and
something had to be done, quickly.

        In Vienna, Freud did eventually effect a cure--during
which however Holmes suffered a long and torturous ordeal,
including hallucinating frighteningly about leaping hounds of
death and snakes slithering down bellcords by his bed.   Then
a woman, a former patient of Freud's, entered the picture,
and shortly Holmes, Watson and Freud himself were off and
running on a rousing adventure.   The lady, Lola Deveraux,
was an internationally famous actress who was soon kidnapped,
and a chase sequence involving steam engines racing to the
Austrian border was just one of the smashing highlights at
the climax of the tale.   It was an especially exciting sequence
that had Holmes leaping from one train to another, and then
engaging the villainous Baron von Leinsdorf in a life and
death swordfight that has to be seen to be appreciated.

        The film also showed Freud, through hypnosis, getting
down to the reasons Holmes became a detective in the first
place, why he came to rely on drugs, why he mistrusted
women, and why Moriarty loomed so large to him; a flashback sequence showing Holmes as a boy was particularly well
handled--even shocking.   All in all, it was a terrific film:
the acting was impeccable, the sets and costuming superb,
and its grand sense of humor and adventure left audiences
feeling good after the picture was over.

Left to right: Alan Arkin as Sigmund Freud, Nicol Williamson as Sherlock Holmes, and Robert Duvall as Dr. Watson
in The Seven-Per-Cent Solution (Universal 1976).

One other great accomplishment was that Nicol Williamson and Robert Duvall played a Holmes and Watson fully as
original and believable as, though completely different from,
the Holmes and Watson of Rathbone and Bruce.   Williamson
and Duvall made the parts their own, related to one another,
and no matter how strong and lasting an impression Rathbone
and Bruce ever made on an audience, ten minutes into The
Seven-Per-Cent Solution you forgot there ever was another
Holmes film.   Judith Crist hit it right on the head when in
Saturday Review she said it has a "very high class character
that neither winks an eye nor stoops to simplistics.   It con-
quers on its own level...."

A Shakespearian actor of note, Nicol Williamson himself characterized the film as "Victoriana James Bond...."
He had come to Broadway from London as the attorney in
John Osborne's Inadmissable Evidence, and his prior films
included the 1970 Hamlet, in which he had the title role, and
also that same year The Reckoning with Rachel Roberts,
Douglas Wilmer (BBC-TV's 1965 Holmes), and Peter Sallis
(the musical stage's Watson in the 1964 Baker Street).   Williamson had also appeared in The Wilby Conspiracy with
Michael Caine, and Robin and Marian with Sean Connery and
Audrey Hepburn.

"Everyone has had a go at Sherlock Holmes," Williamson was quoted as saying in a press interview, "but my
Holmes is different, a man in the grip of a terrible affliction,
a man in a state of collapse.   Serious, but with spice and
dash and humor.   Above all, a living man to whom things
are happening, not just a hat and a pipe...."

Williamson also said that playing Holmes was "a re-
sponsibility, but it's okay when you have a director like Herb
Ross.   He works intensely and inventively and, best of all,
economically, so that you don't waste a lot of time.   Movie
sets are notorious for wasting time.   During that time, you
often lose the spark.   You strive to reach a certain peak
moment when the flame is burning brightly.   Ross is a director who comprehends that, and is able to orchestrate all
the elements that go into picture-making so that he can shoot
when the actors are at that peak...."

And realistically speaking, Robert Duvall's Watson in
the film was about as close as anyone had ever gotten to the
Watson of the original Conan Doyle stories.   Duvall even
looked like the Watson of Sidney Paget's original Strand

Magazine illustrations. The ironic part about it, of course,
was that Duvall was about as British as Vivien Leigh was
American when she played Scarlett O'Hara.

"I wanted an original for the part of Watson," director
Ross said. "An English actor who could surprise us by doing a Watson who didn't bumble in the traditional way. Then
one day this unsolicited tape was sent in. I listened to it
without knowing who the actor was, and I was enchanted.
When I was told it was Bob Duvall, I was amazed.... Vanessa Redgrave thought the man [on the tape] was South African. Others pinpointed the voice as coming from one remote
part of England or another. One man guessed Canadian,
which brought him closest, but nobody said American...."

Duvall himself said that he always did have "a mimic
ear. We were a military family, and we moved from one
part of the country to another very often as my dad would
shift from one base to another. That's typical of service
families, and also explains why nobody can tell whether I'm
from New York or California or Texas. I'm from all of
them, so to speak....

"In any case, I've fooled around with languages for
years. And I've always wanted to play English. The first
time I tried Watson, I was winging it, but I knew right away
that I could do it...."

Even before The Seven-Per-Cent Solution was released,
Universal Pictures optioned Nicholas Meyer's second Sherlock
Holmes novel for filming. The West End Horror is another
posthumous memoir of Dr. Watson, this one telling about the
bizarre murder of theatre critic Jonathan McCarthy. In the
story, Sherlock Holmes meets up with assorted real-life, Victorian-era theatre personalities like George Bernard Shaw,
Henry Irving, Ellen Terry, and Bram Stoker, the creator of
Dracula. And there are other new Sherlock Holmes films
planned for the future as well.

"Frank Saletri [Hollywood producer] and I have been
discussing a new series of Sherlock Holmes films," Keith
McConnell said recently. "Frank has already written the
first one, Sherlock Holmes and the Golden Vampire, and I
like the idea very much. For one thing, it's filled with in-
jokes between Holmes and Watson, and I have always thought
good dialogue like that between Holmes and Watson was one
reason in particular why the Basil Rathbone and Nigel Bruce
films have been so popular."

Sherlock Holmes and the Golden Vampire pits the
sleuth against Count Dracula, the vampire, who is in London
and being controlled by none other than Moriarty.   The professor can make the vampire do anything he wants.   Saletri's
plans, though, call for more than a dozen new Holmes films
to be made in Hollywood over the next few years, and besides
the Dracula adventure he's already written The Werewolf of
the Baskervilles and The Black Creature so far.   The films
are planned purposely to thrust Holmes into supernatural exploits, and The Werewolf of the Baskervilles is a direct sequel to The Hound of the Baskervilles, taking up where the
original story left off and showing that although Holmes had
destroyed the giant dog on the moors, the real menace that
has been plaguing the Baskerville family is a werewolf.

"Originally, Frank simply wanted me to star in the
films," McConnell said, "but now we've had quite lengthy
meetings about Holmes, and Frank has decided I should be
Associate Producer as well.   He'd also like me to play in
some straight horror films.   Perhaps Dr. Frankenstein or
the Edgar Allan Poe type of stories...."

Another new Sherlock Holmes film project is The Return of Moriarty, based on the novel by John Gardner.   Actually the first book in a trilogy about the doings of the infamous professor, The Return of Moriarty tells the exploit
from Moriarty's viewpoint--an innovative slant.   There's
also a new British Silver Blaze film with Christopher Plummer and Thorley Walters in the offing, while Bill Warren's
A Study in Identity is making the rounds of the studios.   Warren's script has Holmes meeting up with a Jekyll-Hyde-type
murderer in Victorian England.   And producer Jerry Courneya
is reviving his 1953 series of Holmes chimpanzee television
films, re-editing them into a feature length color comedy to
be called The Adventures of Chimplock Hulmes and Doctor
Watsup.

The story of Holmes on screen is hardly over.

NOTES

[1] To coincide with the television broadcast, Ballantine Books
(New York) published a special paperback novelization
of the script, adapted by D. R. Benson.

BIBLIOGRAPHY*

The Baker Street Journal. Edited by Dr. Julian Wolff (33
  Riverside Drive; New York 10023). Quarterly. (America's foremost Sherlock Holmes publication. $10 per
  year.)

Baker Street Miscellanea. Edited by John Nieminski. The
  Sciolist Press, P.O. Box 2579; Chicago 60690. Quarterly. (Holmesiana. $4 per year.)

Baring-Gould, William S., ed. The Annotated Sherlock
  Holmes. New York: Clarkson N. Potter, 1967. (The
  landmark two-volume set of all the Sherlock Holmes
  short stories and novels arranged in chronological order,
  with illustrations and commentary.

_____. Sherlock Holmes of Baker Street: A Life of the
  World's First Consulting Detective. New York: Bram-
  hall House, 1962. (The leading biography of the life and
  adventures of the world's most famous sleuth.

Benedict, Stewart H., ed. The Crime Solvers: 13 Classic
  Detective Stories. New York: Dell, 1966. Anthology
  featuring Conan Doyle's "The Lost Special," and also
  Mark Twain's "The Stolen White Elephant."

Bensen, D. R. Sherlock Holmes in New York. New York:
  Ballantine, 1976. (Novelization of the NBC-TV movie of
  the same name.)

Biograph Bulletins: 1908-1912. Introduction by Eileen Brewster. New York: Octagon, 1973. (Reproductions of the
  original Biograph Film Bulletins that were distributed to
  theatres at the time.)

---

*Note also that numerous issues of such trade magazines as
Bioscope, Boxoffice, The Hollywood Reporter, Motion Picture
News, Motography, The Moving Picture World, TV Guide, and
Variety contain information related to Holmesian endeavors.

The British Film Catalogue, 1895-1970. Edited by Denis Gif-
     ford. London: McGraw-Hill, 1973. A chronological
     listing of British films, with cast and credits.

Butler, Ivan. Cinema in Britain. New York: A. S. Barnes,
     1973. (A pictorial history of British films that concen-
     trates on the more important ones. Includes commentary
     on the Eille Norwood-Sherlock Holmes films of the 1920s.)

Carr, John Dickson. The Life of Sir Arthur Conan Doyle.
     New York: Dolphin, 1949. (The definitive history of
     Conan Doyle.)

Conan Doyle, Adrian, and John Dickson Carr. The Exploits
     of Sherlock Holmes. New York: Pocket Books, 1976.
     (The further adventures of Sherlock Holmes and Dr. Wat-
     son, based on cases referred to--but never told--by Wat-
     son in the original Doyle books.)

Conan Doyle, Sir Arthur. The Complete Sherlock Holmes.
     Introduction by John Dickson Carr; Preface by Christopher
     Morley. New York: Doubleday, 1953. (All the original
     56 Holmes short stories and four novels in one volume,
     with the famous Preface by Morley.)

Cullen, Tom A. When London Walked in Terror. New York:
     Avon, 1968. (A well-documented history of Jack the Rip-
     per that includes observations made at the time by Conan
     Doyle, and recollections of his father's involvement with
     the Ripper case by Adrian Conan Doyle.)

Derleth, August. Regarding Sherlock Holmes: The Adven-
     tures of Solan Pons. Introduction by Vincent Starrett.
     New York: Pinnacle, 1974. (The first book in the fa-
     mous Solan Pons series.)

De Waal, Ronald Burt. The World Bibliography of Sherlock
     Holmes and Dr. Watson. Boston: New York Graphic
     Society, 1975. (An indispensable classified and annotated
     list of materials relating to the adventures of Holmes
     and Watson: an item-by-item checklist of books, maga-
     zines, films, television and radio programs, memorials,
     societies, comic strips, games and puzzles, and every-
     thing else too.)

Druxman, Michael B. Basil Rathbone, His Life and His
     Films. Cranbury, N.J.: A. S. Barnes, 1975. (A

complete history of Rathbone's films, with a long chapter
devoted to his life.)

Everson, William K. The Detective in Film. Secaucus,
N. J. : Citadel Press, 1972. (A pictorial history of movie sleuths with one chapter, "The Master," devoted exclusively to Sherlock Holmes.)

Greene, Hugh, ed. Cosmopolitan Crimes: The Foreign Rivals of Sherlock Holmes. Baltimore: Penguin, 1972.
(Early detective stories about non-British sleuths following in the Victorian footsteps of Sherlock Holmes.)

_____, ed. The Further Rivals of Sherlock Holmes. Bal-
timore: Penguin, 1974. (Early detective stories about
sleuths following in Holmes' tradition.)

_____, ed. The Rivals of Sherlock Holmes. Baltimore:
Penguin, 1971. (Greene's first anthology of early detec-
tive stories about sleuths following in the footsteps of
Sherlock Holmes.)

Haining, Peter, with G. Kenchapman, eds. The Sherlock
Holmes Scrapbook. Introduction by Peter Cushing. New
York: Clarkson N. Potter, 1975. (A large-sized collection of Holmes memorabilia, including random articles,
newspaper clippings, letters, and photos and drawings
relating to Holmes, Watson, and Conan Doyle.)

Hardwick, Michael, and Mollie Hardwick. The Private Life
of Sherlock Holmes. New York: Bantam, 1971. (Novelization of the 1970 film of the same name.)

Harmon, Jim. The Great Radio Heroes. New York: Doubleday, 1967. (A nostalgic history of radio, with one
chapter, "For Armchair Detectives Only," highlighted by
a remembrance of the Sherlock Holmes shows.)

_____, and Donald F. Glut. The Great Movie Serials,
Their Sound and Fury. Preface by Kirk Alyn. New
York: Doubleday, 1972. (A comprehensive history with
illustrations of the sound era cliffhangers.)

Harrison, Michael. In the Footsteps of Sherlock Holmes.
New York: Berkley Windhover, 1976. (A scholarly,
illustrated recreation of the Victorian era, and what it
was like back in Holmes' day.)

Haydock, Ron, ed. <u>The History of Sherlock Holmes in Stage,</u>
<u>Films, TV & Radio Since 1899.</u>　Sherman Oaks, Calif.:
E-Go Enterprises, 1975.　(A pictorial magazine history
of Holmes and Watson in all media.)

_____, ed. <u>Sherlock Holmes.</u>　Sherman Oaks, Calif.:
E-Go Enterprises Inc., 1976.　(E-Go Collectors Series
3.)　(A Sherlock Holmes magazine with articles, features
and illustrations on films, television, and various other
aspects of Holmes, past and present.)

Heard, H. F.　<u>A Taste for Honey.</u>　New York: Avon, 1946.
(A Mr. Mycroft and Sydney Silchester mystery.)

Lahue, Kalton C.　<u>Bound and Gagged.</u>　New York: Castle,
1970.　(A history of silent movie serials.)

Leblanc, Maurice.　<u>Arsene Lupin, Gentleman Burglar.</u>　Preface by Jules Claretie.　New York: J. S. Ogilvie, 1910.
(A collection of short stories about Arsene Lupin, France's
national thief, that includes the story "Herlock Sholmes
Comes Too Late.")

_____.　<u>Arsene Lupin Versus Herlock Sholmes.</u>　Chicago:
M. A. Donohue, 1910.　(The book on which the 1910
<u>Arsene Lupin vs Sherlock Holmes</u> silent movie series
was based.)

Meyer, Nicholas.　<u>The Seven-Per-Cent Solution.</u>　New York:
E. P. Dutton, 1974.　(A further exploit of Sherlock
Holmes, "Being a Reprint from the Reminiscences of
John H. Watson, M.D.")

Pointer, Michael.　<u>The Public Life of Sherlock Holmes.</u>
New York: Drake, 1975.　(A history of Holmes on
stage, in films, radio and television; particularly noted
for its coverage of the foreign Holmes films and stage
presentations.)

<u>The Pontine Dossier.</u>　Edited by Luther Norris.　The Pon-
tine Press, P.O. Box 261, Culver City, Calif. 90230.
Annual.　(The leading publication about Solan Pons, the
sleuth who followed directly in Holmes' footsteps.　Includes articles and stories on Holmes and other Holmes-
related material as well.)

Rathbone, Basil.　<u>In and Out of Character.</u>　New York:

(The autobiography of the most famous Sherlock Holmes
player of all.)

Reeve, Arthur B. The Poisoned Pen. New York: Harper
& Bros., 1911. (A collection of stories about Craig
Kennedy, America's scientific Sherlock Holmes.)

Starrett, Vincent. The Private Life of Sherlock Holmes.
Introduction by Michael Murphy. New York: Pinnacle,
1975. (The most famous book about Holmes ever written. Includes Starrett's equally famous Holmes short
story, "The Adventure of the Unique Hamlet. ")

Stedman, Raymond William. The Serials: Suspense and
Drama by Installment. Norman: University of Oklahoma
Press, 1971. (A comprehensive history with illustrations
of the serial form in films, radio and television; includes
a tribute to the Holmes radio programs with Basil Rathbone and Nigel Bruce.)

Steinbrunner, Chris, and Otto Penzler, eds. Encyclopedia of
Mystery and Detection. New York: McGraw-Hill, 1976.
(A one-volume reference work covering mystery writers
and famous fictional sleuths. Includes checklists of published works and appearances in media.)

Tuska, Jon. Philo Vance: The Life and Times of S. S.
Van Dine. Bowling Green, Ohio: Bowling Green University Popular Press, 1971. (The history of author
Van Dine and his sleuth Philo Vance in books, film,
and broadcast media.)

United States. Library of Congress. Motion Pictures 1894-
1912: Catalogue of U. S. Copyright Entries. Washington,
D. C. (Also Volumes 1912-39; 1940-49; 1950-59; and
1960-69; indexed catalog of all films copyrighted through
1969.)

Van Ash, Kay, and Elizabeth Sax Rohmer. Master of Villainy. Bowling Green, Ohio: Bowling Green University
Popular Press, 1962. (The life and times of Sax Rohmer, creator of Fu Manchu.)

INDEX

compiled by Donald F. Glut

(Note: for Conan Doyle's works and their adaptations look up under their main title <u>and</u> "Adventure of ...," "Case of ...," and "Sherlock <u>Holmes</u>.... ")

"Abbas Ruby, The" 165
<u>Abbey Grange, The</u> (film) 55; (TV film) 219
Abbott, Bud 163
Abbott, John 149, 273
<u>Abbott and Costello Meet the Invisible Man</u> 163
<u>Absent-Minded Coterie, The</u> 256
Acklund, Joss 220
Adair, Molly 49
Adam, Ronald 233
Addams, Dawn 189
Addinsell, Geoffrey 179
<u>Adventure of Sherlock Holmes' Smarter Brother, The</u> (film) 249, 261-5, 271; (novel) 271
"Adventure of the Black Baronet, The" 165
<u>Adventure of the Black Baronet, The</u> 165-6
"Adventure of the Black Narcissus, The" 201
"Adventure of the Blue Carbuncle, The" 201
"Adventure of the Dancing Men, The" 62, 133
"Adventure of the Empty House, The" 77, 144, 150-1
<u>Adventure of the Empty House, The</u> 161
"Adventure of the Engineer's Thumb, The" 184
"Adventure of the Gloria Scott, The" 180, 182
"Adventure of the Greek Inter-
preter, The" 185
"Adventure of the Mazarin Stone, The" 62
<u>Adventure of the Mazarin Stone, The</u> 161
"Adventure of the Musgrave Ritual, The" 136, 186
"Adventure of the Naval Treaty, The" 27-8
"Adventure of the Norwood Builder, The" 9
"Adventure of the Reigate Squires, The" 174
"Adventure of the Seven Clocks, The" 163, 165
"Adventure of the Six Napoleons, The" 141
"Adventure of the Speckled Band, The" 39, 80, 172, 201, 215
"Adventure of Wisteria Lodge, The" 49
<u>Adventures of Chimplock Hulmes and Doctor Watsup, The</u> 281
<u>Adventures of Dick Tracy, The</u> 106
<u>Adventures of Nick Carter, The</u> 13
<u>Adventures of Sherlock Holmes</u> 16
<u>Adventures of Sherlock Holmes, The</u> (book) 28; (films) (1905) see <u>Adventures of Sherlock Holmes--Held for Ransom</u>, (1911) 16; Stoll

289

series 19, 47-52, 54, 63;
(1939) 116-21, 133, 263,
276; (radio) NBC 121-4,
150, 155-6, 168; BBC 221;
(record) 201
Adventures of Sherlock Holmes
--Held for Ransom 4-5
A-Feudin' and a-Fightin' 165
Affair of the Tortoise, The
253
Affected Detective, The 59
Aitkins, Maria 246
Albers, Hans 101
Albertson, Frank 91
Alexander, Dick 144
Alexis, Martine 179, 194
Alias the Lone Wolf 52
Alibi 82
Allen, Irwin 210
Alwyn, Jonathan 253-4
Alyn, Kirk 125, 271
Amateur Detective, The 33
Amateur Sleuth, The 18
Ames, Leon (Leon Waycoff)
92, 272
Amis, Kingsley 255
Anderson, Arline 246
Anderson, Helen 16
Andrews, David 219
Andrews, Robert D. 127, 130
Angel, Heather 83
Ankers, Evelyn 127-9, 131,
141
Anonymous Letters 254
Archdale, Sybil 55
Archer, John 136
Arkin, Alan 276-278
Arlen, Michael 168
Arnold, Grace 232
Arnold, Nero 100, 105
Arsene Lupin 14-5
Arsene Lupin's Escape 14
Arsene Lupin vs Sherlock
Holmes 13-5
Arsenio Lupin 144
Arthur, Jean 74
Arundell, Dennis 143
Arundell, Edward 48
Ashdown, Clifford 254
Ashton, Jimmy 317
Assyrian Rejuvenator, The
254
Astor, Gertrude 141

At It Again 17
Atherley, Frank 67
Atkin, Ian 161
Atwill, Lionel 113-5, 132-3
Atwood, Richard 55
Aukin, Lionel 217
Ault, Marie 81
Austin, Sam 61

Baby Sherlock 18
Bach, Reginald 83
Baddeley, Angela 81-2
Bain, William 233-4, 253
Baker, Robert S. 208
Baker Street: A Musical
Adventure of Sherlock
Holmes 95, 225, 236,
264-5, 279
Baker Street By-Way, A 208
Baker Street Journal, The
158, 169
Baker Street Pages 258
Balfour, Eve 33
Banfield, George J. 67
Bannon, Jim 148-9
Barbeau, Adrienne 270
Barcroft, John 219
Barkworth, Peter 253-4
Barlow, Jeff 46
Baron, Alexander 233
Barr, Robert 256
Barrie, Nigel 64
Barringer, Michael 97
Barry, Ivory 249
Barry, Russell 12
Barrymore, Ethel 53
Barrymore, John 41, 55-9,
80, 182
Barrymore, Lionel 41
Bartlam, Dorothy 91
Bartrop, Rowland 170, 172
Barumer, Artur 212
Basil Rathbone Mystery Thea-
tre, The 215
Baskerville, Harry 22
Baxter, Beryl 160
Baxter, Warner 137, 149
Beack, Ann 254
Bear Escape, A 17
Beaudine, William 202
Beaumont, Tom 61
Beck, James 234

Becker, Rolf 247
Beckett, Joe 65
Beckinsale, Richard 253
Beebe, Ford 19
Beery, Wallace 65, 210
Bell, Ann 234
Bell, Arnold 184, 186
Bell, Arthur 48, 63
Bell, Dr. Joseph iv
Bellamy, George 55, 59
Benda, Kenneth 228
Benedict, Howard 127, 130
Bennett, Charles 210
Berger, Senta 213
Berkeley, Ballard 217
Berle, Milton 167
Benge, Wilson 144
Benham, Harry 20
Bennett, Leila 93
Benson, D. R. 281
Benson, George 237
Bentley, Thomas 98
Berman, Monty 208
Beryl Coronet, The (films)
  (1913) 28; (1921) 49; (TV)
  219
Besson, Violet 102
Bevan, Billy 93
Bevan, Isla 88
Beverley, Joan 48
Biggers, Earl Derr 66
Bildt, Paul 101
Birch, Derek 219
Bishop, Edward 232
Bishop Murder Case, The
  80-1
Bixby, Bill 270
Black Coffee 82
Black Doctor, The 228
Black Peter (film) 54; (TV)
  233-4; (record) 235
Black Room, The 134
Black Sherlock Holmes, A 46,
  59
Blackie's Redemption 52
Blackton, J. Stuart 4, 19
Blackwell, Carlyle 69-70
Blackwood, Burt 258
Blake, the Lawbreaker 67
Blakeley, Colin 237, 239, 242
Blazdon, Michael 276
Blazing Launch Murder, The
  97

Bloch, Robert 228-9, 236
Blom, August 7
Blood of Fu Manchu, The 220
Bloom, Harold J. 175, 180,
  184
Bloomer Tricks Sherlock
  Holmes 34
Blue Carbuncle, The (film) 61;
  (radio) 250; (TV) 234;
  (record) 235
Blue Diamond, The 14
Blue, White and Perfect 125
Blum, Edwin 116
Blyth, Harry 12, 67
Bobby the Boy Scout; or, The
  Boy Detective 12
Bogus Governess, The see
  Sherlock Holmes Captured
Bond, Philip 233
Bonn, Ferdinand 32-3, 52
Boothby, Guy 253
Borland, Barlowe 113
Bosco, Wally 47, 49, 62
"Boscombe Valley Mystery,
  The" 100
Boscombe Valley Mystery,
  The (film) (1922) 55;
  (radio) 80; (TV) 68, 233
Boston Blackie's Little Pal
  52
Boucher, Anthony 123
Boulton, Matthew 145
Bowery Boys 202
Boyle, Jack 52
Boyne, Chifton 55
Braban, Harvey 48
Bradley, Curley 125
Braginton, James 31-2
Braine, Robertson 47
Bramah, Ernest 256
Bramble, A. V. 94
Brandt, Aage 7
Brantford, Mickey 67
Branville, Yves 190
Bredell, Woody 130
Bree, James 219
Brekendorff, Kurt 52
Brendon, Herbert 52
Brennan, Eileen 267
Brice, Monte 94
Brides of Fu Manchu, The
  220
Bridges, Alan 255

Brigadier Gerard 29, 59
Bright, John 126-7
Britain's Secret Treaty 33
Brodie, Robert N. 227
Brook, Clive 72-6, 86, 89-
    90, 92
Brooke, Hillary 137, 145-6,
    149
Brooks, Louise 74
Brown, Earl 56
Brown, Georgia 233, 276
Bruce, Nigel 14, 19, 28, 38,
    54, 67, 72-3, 79, 83, 89,
    98, 107-26, 128-9, 131-2,
    134-5, 137, 139, 142-4,
    148, 150-5, 159-60, 166-8,
    170, 172, 201, 215, 225,
    242, 252, 256, 270, 275,
    279-80
Bruce-Partington Plans, The
    (film) 55; (TV) 218-9
Brulier, Nigel de 113
Bryan, Peter 203
Bryce, Alex 97
Bryson, Tom 146
Buckler, Hugh 48
Buckley, Keith 227
Bulldog Drummond 70
Bunnage, Avis 250
Burgardt, Theodore 34
Burge, Eugene 24
Burger, W. Germain 50
Burgess, Christopher 233
Burian, Vlosta 91
Burke, David 219
Burke, John 95
Burleigh, Bertram 55, 61
Burns and Allen 156, 158
Burrell, Daisy 38
Burrell, Richard 200
Burson, Greg 249
Burstup Homes 18
Burstup Homes' Murder Case
    18
Burton, Langhorne 67
Butler, Alexander 38
Butler, Daws 164
Butt, Johnny 41
Byrd, Ralph 104, 106
Byrne, Eddie 208

Cab No. 519 6-8

Cabot, Sebastian 161
Caillou, Alan 246
Caithness, Wilfred 96
Calvert, Charles 12
Calvert, E. H. 74
Campbell, Catina 49
Campbell, Dr. Maurice 245
"Canary" Murder Case, The
    74
Canine Sherlock Holmes, A
    18
Canning, Thomas 33
Capote, Truman 266
Cardboard Box, The 62
Cardinal's Snuffbox, The 52
Carlile, C. Douglas 12-3,
    15, 29
Carlos, Christopher 233
Carlton, Lewis 33
Carr, Jane 96
Carr, John Dickson (John Keir
    Cross) 38, 65, 87, 163,
    165-6, 169, 202, 221
Carradine, John 113
Carsten, Peter 223, 225
Carter, Jack 270
Carter, Rudolph 160
Carter Case, The 46
Caruso, Anthony 182
Carver, Emilio 177
Case for Sherlock Holmes, A
    16
Case of Harry Crocker, The
    180-1
Case of Hypnosis, A 165
Case of Identity, A 48
Case of Lady Beryl, The 175
Case of Laker, Absconded,
    The 254
Case of the Baker Street
    Bachelors, The 195-6
Case of the Baker Street
    Nursemaids, The 192
Case of the Belligerent Ghost,
    The 178-9
Case of the Blind Man's Bluff,
    The 180, 198
Case of the Careless Suffragette,
    The 189
Case of the Chemical Fumes,
    The 12
Case of the Cunningham Heri-
    tage, The 172, 174-5

Case of the Deadly Prophecy, The 190

Case of the Diamond Tooth, The 198-9

Case of the Dixon Torpedo, The 257

Case of the Eiffel Tower, The 194

Case of the Exhumed Client, The 194-5

Case of the French Interpreter, The 185-6

Case of the Greystone Inscription, The 186-7

Case of the Haunted Gainsborough, The 196-7

Case of the Imposter Mystery, The 193-4

Case of the Impromptu Performance, The 195

Case of the Jolly Hangman, The 193

Case of the Laughing Mummy, The 187-198

Case of the Metal-Sheathed Elements, The 246

Case of the Mirror of Portugal, The 258

Case of the Missing Girl, The 18

Case of the Neurotic Detective, The 197-8

Case of the Pennsylvania Gun, The 175, 177

Case of the Perfect Husband, The 192-3

Case of the Red-Headed League, The 181-2, 198

Case of the Reluctant Carpenter, The 189-90

Case of the Royal Murder, The 196

Case of the Shoeless Engineer, The 184-5, 187

Case of the Shy Ballerina, The 179

Case of the Singing Violin, The 186

Case of the Split-Ticket, The 185

Case of the Stuttering Bishop, The 163

Case of the Texas Cowgirl, The 177-8

Case of the Thistle Killer, The 187-8

Case of the Tyrant's Daughter, The 200

Case of the Unlucky Gambler, The 198

Case of the Vanished Detective, The 188

Case of the Violent Suitor, The 192

Case of the Winthrop Legend, The 175-7

Casebook of Sherlock Holmes, The 66, 201

Casebook of Solar Pons, The 202

Cash on Demand 221

Castle, William 149

Castle of Fu Manchu, The 220

Cates, Joseph 255

Caught 4-5

Caught with the Goods 16-7

Cavanagh, Paul 141, 144-5, 202

Cazes, Clive 233

Cecil, Evelyn 61

Challenge, The 168

Champeen Detective, The 33

Chaney, Lon 135

Chanslor, Roy 144

Chaplin, Charles Spencer 53

Charles Augustus Milverton (film) 54; (radio) 219-20; (record) 235

Charlie Chan Carries On 84

Charlie Colms 18

Charlton, Althea 219

Charteris, Leslie 105, 124, 272

Chemistry of Love, The 228

Chester, Betty 55

Chimplock Holmes see Professor Lightfoot and Dr. Twiddle

Christie, Agatha 82, 84

Christmas Pudding, The 190-1

Chronicles of Solar Pons, The 202

Churchill, Berton 97

Clayburgh, Jill 264

Clive, E. E. 113, 116

Clue of the Second Goblet, The 67

Clutching Hand, The 100
Clyde, David 141
Coco, James 266
Coffee, Lenore 52
Coffin, Adeline 67
Cohen, Alexander H. 95
Cohen, Herman 223-4, 229, 235
Coleby, A. E. 16, 71
Collins, Edwin J. 210
Collins, Lewis D. 97
Collins, Ray 221
Colonel March of Scotland Yard 202
Colsanto, Nicholas 266
Compson, J. W. 18
Conabere, Sydney 234
Conan Doyle, Adrian ix, 163, 165-6, 169, 225-6, 250
Conan Doyle, Sir Arthur iv, viii-x, 2-3, 8, 11, 13, 19-22, 24-5, 27-9, 32, 34, 36-41, 43-4, 47-8, 51-4, 59, 62, 64-7, 69, 72, 74, 76-7, 82, 84, 86-7, 89, 91-4, 96, 98, 100-2, 104-5, 107, 109-10, 113, 116, 122-3, 127, 129-30, 135, 138-9, 142, 147, 160-1, 163-4, 168-9, 172-4, 180, 182-3, 200-1, 203, 207-15, 217, 221, 227-8, 231, 236, 242, 245-7, 249-50, 255, 265, 269, 270, 272-3, 277, 279
Conan Doyle, Denis 250
Confidence Trick, The see Sherlock Holmes in the Claws of the Confidence Men
Confidence Tricksters, The 205
Conrad, Robert 246
Conspirators, The see The Murder at Baker Street
Conway, Booth 38
Conway, Tom 70, 155-6, 168-9
Coogan, Jackie 272
Cook, Donald 97
Cooke, Alan 253-4
Cooper, George A. 67, 97, 232
Cooper, Giles 215, 217, 219
Cooper, Melville 160
Cooper-Cliffe, H. 39

Copley, Peter 175-6
Copper Beeches, The (films) (1912) 27, (1921) 49; (radio) 80; (TV) 219
Corbett, Harry H. 250
Cording, Harry 133, 144, 153
Corri, Adrienne 222
Corydell, John Russell 13
Cosmopolitan Crimes: The Foreign Rivals of Sherlock Holmes 253
Cossins, James 253
Costello, Lou 163
Costello, Maurice 4-5
Council of Three, The 13
Counterfeiters, The 34-5
Courneya, Jerry 164, 165, 281
Court, Hazel 205
Courtland, Van 61
Cox, Morgan 104
Crabbe's Practice 228
Craft, William 65
Craig, Alex 140
Craig, Frank 65
Craig Kennedy, Criminologist 163
Crane, Barry 245
Cranshaw, Frank 219
Crawford, H. Marion 170, 172, 175-7, 179, 184, 199-200, 220-1
Crawford, June 197
Crazy House 137
Cregeen, Peter 219
Crime Doctor, The 137
Crime Doctor's Courage, The 149
Crime Doctor's Diary, The 149
Crime Doctor's Gamble, The 149
Crime Doctor's Manhunt, The 149
Crime Doctor's Warning, The 149
Crime Is My Business 208
Criminals Always Blunder 205
Cringley, William 65
Crisp, Donald 67, 72, 74
Croker-King, C. H. 49
Crooked Man, The 62
Cropper, Anna 219

Cross, Larry 232
Croxley Master, The (film)
    52; (TV) 228
Cullin, Arthur M. 62, 64
Cullin, M.   38
Cullitan, Patrick 125, 270-1
Curley Bradley's Trail of Mys-
    tery 125, 271
Curse of Frankenstein 205
Curtis, Donald 67
Curwin, Patric 148
Curzon, George 97, 104
Cushing, Peter 48, 73, 77,
    203-21, 230-6, 269-70
Cutcliffe-Hyne, C. J. 33
Cuthbertson, Allan 219
Cutts, Graham 88
Cutts, John 273

D'Alby, Edward 96
Daly, Arnold 36-7, 40
Dancing Men, The 232
Dane, Cecil 54
Dane, Frank 46
Daneman, Paul 233
Daniell, Henry 127, 131, 136,
    144-7
Dannay, Frederic 97
D'Aragon, Lionel 39, 62
D'Arcy, Roy 90
Dark Castle, The 245
Darkest Africa 165
Darling, W. Scott 133
Dastor, Sam 247
Date with the Falcon, A 168
Daughter of the Dragon 84
Davenport, Nigel 246
Davidson, Lawford 55
Davies, Bernard 245
Davies, Cliff 62
Davies, Gareth 219
Davis, Gilbert 88
Day of the Jackal, The 255
"Daydream" 168
Deadly Bees, The 228-9
Dean, Basil 72, 88
Deane, Alica 232
De Becker, Harold 133
"Decapitation of Jefferson
    Monk, The" 148
Deckers, Eugene 181-2, 191,
    197

De Cordoba, Pedro 64
Decqumine, Jacques 196
De Forrest, Charles 33
Delamar, Mickey 105
Del Baye, Paulette 49, 112
Delevanti, Cyril 144
Delevanti, Winifred 40
Del Ruth, Ray 182
DeLuise, Dom 261
"Demon Angels, The" 165
Dempster, Carol 56
Denham, Maurice 220
Denny, Ivan 176, 213
Denny, Reginald 56, 127, 131,
    149
De Normand, George 125
Denton, Jack 59
"Deptford Horror, The" 165
Derleth, August 201-2
Desert Sheik, The see Fires
    of Fate
Detectives in Fiction 104
Dethlefsen, Otto 6
Devil's Foot, The (film) 48;
    (TV) 219
Devil's Mask, The   149
Devine, Jerry 56
De Wolf, Francis 206
Dexter, John 177
Diabolical, More Diabolical,
    and The Most Diabolical 29
Diamond, I. A. 237
Diamond, Marian 217
Diamond Swindler, The 8
Dick Tracy 104
Dick Tracy Meets Gruesome
    106
Dick Tracy Returns 106
Dick Tracy vs Crime Inc. 106
Dick Tracy's Dilemma 106
Dick Tracy's G-Men 106
Dickey, Basil 91
Dignon, Edward 97
Dillon, Brendan 246
Dillon, Tom P. 151, 153
Dineheart, Alan 93-4
Disappearance of Lady Frances
    Carfax, The 61
Disguised Nurse, The 8,
    10-1
Dixon, Conway 96
Dr. McDonald's Sanitarium
    24-5

Dr. Sin Fang 71
Dr. Watson and the Darkwater
    Hall Mystery 255
Dodsworth, John 167
Doleman, Guy 229
Doniger, Walter 160
Donlan, James 80
Doomed to Die 106
Doran, Hetty 49
Doran, Sonny 191
Dorington Diamonds, The
    59
Dotrice, Roy 253
Dougherty, Jack 66
Downing, Rupert 205
Downing, Vernon 157
Doyle see Conan Doyle
Drake, Colin 182, 185
Drake, William 116
Drayton, Alfred 48-9
Dressed to Kill (Sherlock
    Holmes) 151, 153-4, 156,
    168; (Michael Shayne) 125
Duchess of Wiltshire's Dia-
    monds, The 253
Dudley, Philip 219
Duguid, Peter 219
Duncan, Archie 174-5, 177
Dunning, Fred 40
Durant, Claude 174
D'Usseau, Leon 100
Duvall, Robert 276, 278-80
"Dying Detective, The" 72
Dying Detective, The (film)
    47-8; (TV) 161

Eames, Charles and Ray 220-1
Earle, Fred 49
Early, Charles M. 179, 189,
    194, 196
Early, Joseph 189, 194, 196
Earthquake Motor, The 51
Eaton, Charles 68-9
Echo Murders, The 148
Edalji, George 247
Edison, Thomas Alva 1-2, 4,
    11-2, 17-8
Edwardians: Conan Doyle, The
    246-7
Edwards, Kenneth R. 104
Edwards, Olga 161
Eggar, Samantha 276

Elementary, Mr Dear Watson
    246
Elliott, Duncan 198
Elliott, June 187
Elliott, William J. 48-9, 112
Elsom, Isobel 63
Elvey, Maurice 48-9, 62,
    112
Emerton, Roy 88, 96
Emney, Mrs. Fred 67
Empty House, The 49
Engels, Erich 101
Engholm, Harry 31, 38, 52
Engineer's Thumb, The 61
English, Robert 49, 112
Enter Arsene Lupin 19
Episode of the Sacred Ele-
    phants, The 12
d'Esterre, Mme. 47-9, 54,
    61-2
Eustace, Robert 258
Evans, Fred 35-7, 40-1
Evans, Graham 232
Evans, Joe 35-6, 40
Evans, Rex 147
Evans, Wee Willie 147
Eveleigh, Leslie 67
Exploits of Brigadier Gerard,
    The 67
Exploits of Elaine, The 36,
    41
Exploits of Sherlock Holmes,
    The 169
Exploits of Three-Fingered
    Kate, The 12
Eyes in the Night 105

Face of Fu Manchu, The 220
Fairbanks, Douglas 34, 76
Fairman, Austin 49
Fake Rembrandt, The 14
Falcon and the Coeds, The
    168
Falcon in Danger, The 168
Falcon in Mexico, The 168
Falcon in San Francisco, The
    168
Falcon Strikes Back, The 168
Falcon Takes Over, The 168
Falcon's Adventure, The 168
Falcon's Alibi, The 168
Falcon's Brother, The 168

Falk, Peter 266
Fane, Dorothy 55
Farrar, David 143, 148
Fass, George 190
Fass, Gertrude 190
Fatal Hour, The 106
Fate of Renate Yongk, The
    52
Fawcett, Robert 165
Fealich, Allen 34
Feldman, Marty 261-3
Feely, Terence 255
Felton, Felix 217
Fer-de-Lance 100
Fetchit, Stepin 69
Fialova, Vlasta 245
Fichtner, Erwin 22
Field, Susan 263
Fielding, Edward 41, 44
Fields, Stanley 90
Fighting Eagle, The 67
"Final Problem, The" 61,
    77-8, 118, 138, 215, 277
Final Problem, The (film)
    61-2, 64; (radio) 221
Finish of Arsene Lupin, The
    14
Finley, Frank 222, 229
Fires of Fate (1923) 64, 91;
    (1932) 91
Firm of Girdlestone, The 29
Fisher, Terence 203, 212-3
Fitzgerald, Aubrey 55
Fitzgerald, Dallas 100
Fitzpatrick, Neil 234
500 Carats 257
$500 Reward 16
"Five Orange Pips, The" 144
Fix, Paul 133
Flag of Distress, The 18
Flea of the Baskervilles, The
    34
Fleming, Ian 77-9, 86, 88,
    96-8, 134
Flink, Hugo 51
Flivver's Famous Cheese Hound
    see Pimple's Million Dollar
    Mystery
Florence, Ilona 233
Florey, Robert 92
Flugrath, Edna 48
Foch, Nina 49, 270
Foley, George 54

Forbes, Mary 116
Forbes, Ralph 113
Ford, Derek 222-3
Ford, Donald 222-3
Ford, Francis 32, 91
Ford, Garret 72
Ford, John (Jack Francis) 32
Forrest, Steve 182-3
Foss, Kenneth 47
Foster, Norma 104
"Foulkes Rath, The" 165
Fox, Bernard 246
Fox, Edward 255, 270
Fox, Reginald 61
Fox, Sidney 92
Franciosa, Tony 256
Francis, Arlene 92
Francis, Derek 219, 233
Francis, Freddie 229
Francis, Raymond 161-2
François, Jacques 190, 196
Frankenstein Created Woman
    215
Frankenstein Meets the Wolf
    Man 135, 221
Frankenstein Must Be Destroyed
    215
Franz, Arthur 163
Fraser, John 222, 258
Fraser, Ronald 258
Freeman, R. Austin 253-4
Frees, Paul 164
Frenchman's Creek 143, 168
Fric, Martin 91
Frohman, Charles 43, 79
Further Adventures of Sexton
    Blake--The Mystery of the
    S.S. Olympic, The 26
Further Adventures of Sherlock
    Holmes, The 54-5
Further Mystery of Fu Manchu,
    The 71
Further Rivals of Sherlock
    Holmes, The 253
Futrelle, Jacques 254, 257

Gabell, Leigh 62
Gage, Jack 172, 175, 189
Galvani, Dino 88
Gamble, Warburton 93-4
Gangelin, Paul 141
Gardner, Earl Stanley 163

Garnwood, William 40
Garris, Roger 194, 196
Gauge, Alexander 182
Gay Falcon, The 168
Gazzolo, Nando 235
Geeson, Judy 253
Geldert, Clarence 80
Gemora, Charles 182
Gertsman, Maury 151
Ghost Talks, The 68-9
Gibbs, Sheila 220
Gielgud, Sir John 220
Gilbert, Lewis 49, 55, 61
Gillette, William vii-viii, 2-4,
    6-8, 40-6, 52-3, 55, 77,
    79-80, 89, 116-7, 124, 203,
    221, 225, 258
Glaser, Paul Michael 269
Gloria Scott, The 61
Glynne, Agnes 31
Goddard, David 217
Goddard, James 253
Goddard, Paulette 175
Godfrey, Renee 150
"Gold Hunter, The" 165
Golden Pince-Nez, The 55
Goldman, James 243, 250
Goldsmith, Frank 62
Goldwyn, Samuel 54-6, 58-9,
    74
Gomez, Thomas 127, 131, 167
Goodie, F. Wyndham 104
Goodman, John B. 146
Goodrich, Louis 78
Goorney, Howard 233-4
Gordon, Mary 113, 116, 126,
    133, 142, 151, 154
Gordon, Michael 137
Gordon, Richard 80, 94-5
Gordon, Ruth 269
Gorno, Ottorino 76
Goss, Helen 206
Gotell, Walter 160
Gouget, Henri 16
Gough, Michael 192
Gould, Beckett 161
Gould, Chester 104
Gould, John 233
Goulding, Alf 88
Goulet, Arthur 98
Graham, John 211
Graham, Violet 62
Grahame, Noel 62

Grain, A. Corney 39
Granger, Stewart 73, 245
Grant, Kirby 140
Granville, Bonita 124
Graves, Fred 29
Graves, Robert 90
Gray, Charles 253, 256, 276
Gray, Eve 100
Gray, Willoughby 233
Gray Dame, The 6, 8
Great Detective, The (film)
    34; (musical) 95
Great Houdinis, The (film)
    269-71; (novel) 271
Great Office Mystery, The 67
Greek Interpreter, The (film)
    54; (TV) 233
Green, Denis 123
Green, Judd 49
Green, Martyn 166
Green, Nigel 220, 233
Green, Seymour 197
Greene, Sir Hugh 252-3, 257
Greene, Leon 276
Greene, Richard 110, 113-5,
    220
Greene Murder Case, The 74,
    76
Greet, Claire 88
Gregaard, Paul 7
Gregers, M. 32
Grey, Joel 276
Grey, Lorraine 97
Grey, Richard M. 160
Grierson, John 76
Griffard's Claw 30
Griffith, George 257
Grimm, Maria 272
Groler, Bauldin 254
Grossmith, Lawrence 98
Grover, Michael 219
Gruber, Frank 150
Guise, Wyndham 65
Gulla, Richard 125, 271
Gundrey, V. Gareth 83
Gunn, Judy 98
Guttner, Bruno 101

Haboush, Victor 249
Haden, Sara 26
Hagen, Julius 77, 86, 96, 98
Hagman, Larry 266

Haldane, Bert 29, 59
Hale, Creighton 36-7, 40
Hale, Elvi 254
Haley, Jack, Jr.   256, 273
Hall, Huntz 202
Hall, Selma 102
Hall, Thurston 136
Hallett, Henry 83
Halliday, Brett 121
Hallman, Adolf 163
Hamer, Gerald 135, 137, 141
Hampden, Buford 41, 44
Hampton, Sandra 219
Hand, The 40
Hand of Fu Manchu, The 71
Handl, Irene 237
Harben, Hugh 104
Harbord, Carl 151, 153
Harding, Kay 141
Harding, Lyn 40, 81-2, 96,
  98
Harding, Rex 97
Hardwick, Michael 232-5
Hardwick, Mollie 232-5
Hardwicke, Sir Cedric 211
Hardy, Robert 235
Hare, Lumsden 56
Hargrove, Dean 265
Harlow, John 143
Harmon, Jim 123, 152, 211,
  271
Harrington, George 49
Harris, Jack H. 211
Harris, Paul 219
Harris, Richard 233
Harrison, David 219
Harrison, Jack 76
Harrison, Kathleen 143
Hartl, Karl 101
Hartmann, Edmund L. 133,
  141
Harvey, Anthony 243-4
Harvey, Elwyn 167
Harvey, John J. 64
Hasse, Camilla 219
Hasso, Signe 272
Hastings, Carey 33
Hatchet Man, The 165
Hathaway, Henry 200-1
Hatton, Rondo 140-1, 143
Haues, Michael 220
Haunted House, The 165
Haven, James C. 264

Hawley, Wanda 64
Hawthorne, David 61
Haydn, Richard 210
Haynes, Roberta 191
Hayward, Louis 105
Heard, H. F. 188, 228-9
Heathcote, Thomas 161
Heatherley, Clifford 48, 91
Hector, Louis 84, 102-3, 158
Hedison, David 210
Hemlock Hoax, the Detective
  15
Henley, Jack 88
Hepton, Bernard 258
Herbert, Bryon 167
Herbert, Holmes 133, 142,
  144
"Herlock Sholmes Comes Too
  Late" 13-4, 144
Herlock Sholmes in "Be-a-
  Live Crook" 76
Herman, Albert 100
Herrick, Hubert 47
Heuer, Hans 101
Hewitt, Violet 49
Hewland, Philip 47, 78, 86
Hidden Eye, The 100
Hidden Motive, The 258, 270
"Highgate Miracle, The" 165
Hill, James 222-3
Hines, Ronald 257
"His Last Bow" 72, 127
His Last Bow 61
Hiscott, Leslie 77, 82, 88,
  96
Hobbs, Carlton 100, 164, 235
Hobbs, Halliwell 93, 137
Hobbs, Jack 55, 62
Hodgson, Hope 253
Hodgson, Leyland 127, 131
Hoey, Dennis 133, 135-7,
  139, 141, 150, 152-3, 221
Hohl, Arthur 116, 140-1
Holden, Stanley 95
Holder, Mary 217
Holger-Madsen, Forrest 6
Holman, Vincent 97
Holmes, Ben 105
Holmes and Yoyo 269
Homlock Shermes 18
Hooded Terror, The 104
Hopper, Hedda 56, 70
Horner, Penelope 219-20, 232

Hornung, E. W. 6-7
Horror of Dracula 205
Horton, Robert 98
Hotel Mystery, The see
  Sherlock Holmes' Last
  Exploit
Houdini, Harry 180, 269-71
Hound of the Baskervilles, The
  (novel) 20, 24-5, 203, 207;
  (films) (1914) 20, 22-5, 30,
  69; (1921) 49-51, 62, 112,
  (1929) 54, 69-71, 101, (1932)
  82-4, (1937) 101, (1939) 21,
  67, 98, 107-8, 110-6, 121,
  141, 220, 276; (1959) 203-8,
  211, 271, 281, (1968) 235;
  (radio) (1942) 123, (1957)
  250, (1969) 235; (TV) (1968)
  232-3; (1972) 245-6
"Hound of the Baskervilles,
  The" 164
House of Distemperley, The
  37
House of Fear, The 143-5
House of Horrors, The 143
House of Temperley, The 29,
  37, 53
House of the Invisible, The
  253
House Without a Key, The 66
House Without Any Windows,
  The 24-5
Houston, Donald 222-6
How It Happened 65
How the Hound of the Basker-
  villes Returned 24-5
Howard, Ronald 170-2, 175,
  177, 179, 180, 183-4, 193,
  198-201, 207, 209
Howard, William K. 88, 90
Howes, Anne 246
Howlett, Anthony D. 245
Hoyt, Arthur 65
Hoyt, Harry 65
Huddleston, David 272, 274
Hughes, Lloyd 65
Hulbert, Claude 134
Hume, Fergus 253
Hume, Marjorie 68
Humphreys, Cecil 19, 47
Hunter, Craig 232
Hunter, Ian 88
Huston, John 92, 272, 274

Hutchinson, Thomas H. 102
Hyde-White, Wilfrid 270
Hypnotic Detective, The 9
Hysmann, Greta 264
Hytten, Olaf 55, 131, 137

I Love a Mystery 148-9
I Will, I Will, I Will 46-7
I. B. M. Puppet Shows, The
  220-1
Illustrious Client, The (TV)
  217, 219; (record) 235
Imeson, A. B. 62
"In Re: Sherlock Holmes"--
  The Adventures of Solar
  Pons 202
In the Footsteps of Sherlock
  Holmes 235
In the Grip of the Eagle's
  Claw see Griffard's Claw
In the Money 202
Indian Spider, The 51
Inside India 165
Inspector Hornleigh 85
Inspector Hornleigh Goes to It
  85
Inspector Hornleigh on Holiday
  85
Ireland, Ian 246
Is Conan Doyle Right? 64
Isolated House, The 23-4

Jack the Ripper 208-10, 222
Jackson, Brian 233
Jackson, Louis H. 143
Jacoby, Michael 131
James, Alan 104
Jane, Sybil 83
Jawlock Jones 33
Jazz Hounds, The 59, 61
Jenkins, Roger 233
Jennings, Gladys 62
Jewel Thieves Run to Earth by
  Sexton Blake, The 15
Johnson, Lyle 49
Johnson, Noel 250
Johnson, Van 200-1
Jones, Barry 219, 222
Jordan, Miriam 89
Joyce, Brenda 140
Judd, Alan 161

Jurgensen, Edwin 101
Just Before Dawn 149
Just Off Broadway 125
Justice, Barry 228
Jutke, Herbert 69

Kahn, Madeline 261
Kaiser's Spies, The 33
Kaisertitz, Erich 24
Kallis, Stanley 245
Karen, Guita 177
Karloff, Boris 105-6, 134,
  188, 202, 229
Karoly, Bauman 9
Karr, Cecil 49
Kavanagh 205
Kay, Marjorie 41, 44
Kay, Phillip 33, 49
Kearney, Anthony 233
Kearns, Michael 96
Keaton, Buster 64, 67, 76
Keegan, Barry 257
Keene, Carolyn 124
Keller, Zen 234
Kellino, W. P. 40
Kemp, Jeremy 276
Kemp, Margaret 56
Kemp-Welsh, Joan 94
Kendrick, Bayard H. 105
Kenney, James 233
Kerr, Molly 64
Kerrigan, J. M. 93
Kibbee, Roland 265
Kilburn, Terry 116
Kinder, Stuart 18
King, Claude 40, 90, 105
King, Diane 220
King, George 104
King, Philip 160
Kiss and Kill see The Blood
  of Fu Manchu
Kite Mob, The 205
Klarens, George 69
Knaggs, Skelton 150
Knowles, Patric 131
Komai, Tetsu 93
Korvin, Charles 19
Kosleck, Martin 143, 147,
  149
Kotite, Donald 190
Krakow, Ernst 101
Kreiss, Ludwig 45

Kuhne, Friedrich 22, 25, 33
Kussell, H. D. 94
Kuwa, George 66

Lady Condale's Diamonds 15
Lady Frances Carfax 220
Lagoni, Otto 8, 10-1
Lamac, Karl 91, 101
Lamas, Fernando 210
Lambert, Robert 256
Lanchester, Elsa 267
Landi, Marla 206
Lanfield, Sidney 113
Lang, Robert 257
Larsen, Viggo 6-9, 13-5, 46
Last Adventures of Sherlock
  Holmes, The 59, 61-3
Last of the Lone Wolf, The
  52
Latest Triumph of Sherlock
  Holmes, The 12
Latimer, Michael 227
Laurel, Stan 65
Lawford, Betty 72
Leach, Inspector 205
Leach, Rosemary 217
Leake, Barbara 222
Lease, Rex 100
LeBlanc, Maurice 13-4, 106,
  144
Lee, Christopher 56, 203-21,
  229, 236-7, 239, 242, 272
Lee, Leonard 147
Lee, Manford B. 97
Lee, Rowland V. 88
Leeds, Charles 205
Leeds, Howard 89
Leggatt, Alison 276
Leigh, Suzanna 229
Leigh, Terry 219
Lejeune, C. A. 161
Leland, David 233
Lelicek in the Service of Sher-
  lock Holmes 91, 101
Le Mesurier, John 161, 206,
  263, 271
Lemonnier, Meg 177
Lennox, Dorothy 52
Leo, Malcolm 256
Leonard, Hugh 232-3
Le Queux, William 257
Leslie, Laurie 61-2

Lester, Henry E.   222, 225
Levin, Henry   148
Levine, Joseph E.   208-10,
   222
Lewis, Ronald   254
Liable, Andre   13
Licundi, Gabriella   233
Liebler, Theodore   4
Liebman, Robert   25
Life of Sherlock Holmes, The
   235
Lift, The   228
Lindsay, Kevin   233
Lindsay, Margaret   137
Lindsay, Richard   62
Lindsey, Enid   217
Lipscomb, W. P.   82, 88
Litel, John   124
Little Sherlock Holmes, The
   12
Livesay, Donald   96
Livesay, Roger   94
Livesey, Sam   83
Lloyd, Frederich   83-4
Lockwood, Preston   247
Lomas, Herbert   88
Lone Wolf, The   52
Lone Wolf Returns, The   52
Lone Wolf's Daughter, The   52
Longden, John   160
Longing of Sherlock Holmes,
   The   245
Looting of the Specie Room,
   The   258
Lord, Marjorie   136
Lord Edgeware Dies   84
Lorenzen, Henry   101
Lorraine, Harry   34-5, 46
Lorre, Peter   104, 106, 121,
   208
Lost Special, The   91
Lost World, The   (novel) 65,
   210; (films) (1925) 65, 104,
   210, (1960) 208, 210-1, 236;
   (radio) 87
Lot 249   228, 236
Love, Bessie   65
Love, Montagu   127, 131
Love, Robert   253
Lovell, Leigh   80, 84, 94,
   124
Lowe, Edward T.   133
Lowry, Morton   113

Lucas, William   232
Lugg, William   62
Lugosi, Bela   92, 135, 149,
   249
Lukavsky, Randovan   245
Lukschy, Wolfgang   213
Lumley, Arthur   55
Lumont, Roger   247
Lupino, Ida   116-7, 119
Lynds, Ernest   96
Lyons, H. Agar   64, 71
Lytell, Bert   52

Maben, Alvys   161
McAllister, Ward   61
Macauley, Jack   39
McCarey, Ray   95
McClenahan, Rue   243
McConnell, Keith   vii-x, 247-
   50, 255, 260, 267-8, 280-1
MacDonald, Edmund   136
MacDonald, Philip   200
McDougall, Rex   49-50
Mace, Fred   16-7
Mack, H. S.   18
Mackay, Barry   187
McKern, Leo   261
McKim, Edwin   34
McKinnell, Norman   77-8
Mackintosh, Mary   61
McKnight, Thomas   130
MacLaren, Ian   113
McLaren, Tony   232
McLauchlin, Russell   158, 169
McLeod, Gordon   143
McMahon, Ed   261
Macmillan, Kenneth   95
Macnee, Patrick   272, 274-5
McNeile, H. C. ("Sapper")   70
Macrae, Arthur   98, 100
MacRae, Henry   91
Macready, George   148
Madame Sara   257-8
Madden, Peter   217
Maine, Lorie   247-9
Maitland, Arthur   102-3
Maitland, Lauderdale   64
Majeroni, Mario   41, 44
Malden, Karl   182
Malins, Geoffrey H.   54, 61-2,
   65
Malkowski, Arthur   101

Malleson, Miles 88, 206
Malyon, Elly 113
"Man Who Was Not Sherlock
    Holmes, The" 125, 271
Man Who Was Sherlock Holmes,
    The 101
Man Who Wouldn't Die, The
    125
Man with the Twisted Lip, The
    (film) 49; (radio) 80; (TV)
    (1951) 160-1, (1965) 219
Mander, Miles 88, 141, 149
Mankum, Philip 228
Mannering, Cecil 38, 59
Mannock, Patrick L. 54, 61-2,
    343
Manson, Helena 190
Marcin, Max 137
Marechal, Lois Perkins 187
Margetson, Arthur 137
Marin, Edwin L. 92
Marko, Andreas 219
Marlen, Trude 101
Marquand, John P. 104
Marriott, Anthony 228
Marsh, Sam 61
Marsh, Terry 264
Marshall, Alan 116
Marshall, Herbert 211
Martin, Hal 55, 62
Martin, Ian 156, 168
Martin, Sobey 160
Martin, Trevor 219
Martinek, H. O. 12
Marvelous Misadventures of
    Sherlock Holmes: A Musical
    Mystery for Children, The
    96
Marvin, Arthur 2
Massey, Daniel 232
Massey, Raymond 81-2
Masterpiece Theatre 246-7
Mather, Aubrey 144
Matthews, Christopher 227
Matthews, Lester 91
Maturin, Eric 161
Maude, Charles 29
Maude, Lillian 97
Maupin, Ernest 41-4
May, Dezma du 62
May, Nancy 55
Maye, Nartina 186
Meade, L. T. 258

Mear, H. Fowler 86, 96, 98
Medford, Harold 182
Medina, Patricia 182
Meet Nero Wolfe 100
Meet Sexton Blake 143
Meinert, Rudolph 22
Melford, Jill 208
Member of the Black Hand,
    The see The Murder at
    Baker Street
Memoirs of Sherlock Holmes,
    The 28
Mercer, Beryl 113
Merrow, Jane 246
Merson, Billy 40
Mesier, Edith 123-4
Message from the Deep Sea, A
    253-4
Meyer, Nicholas 197, 276,
    280
Michael Shayne, Private Detec-
    tive 124
Micklewood, Eric 186
Middlemass, Frank 234
Midget Sherlock Holmes, A
    18
Midgley, Robin 215
Midivani, Princess Nina 250
Miles, Juliet 233
Miles, Peter 233
Milford, Bliss 18
Millenson Case, The 149, 155,
    248, 280
Miller, Walter 66
Miller, Minston 104
Miller, Stanley 233-4
Miller, Steve 261
Millhauser, Bertram 19, 135-
    6, 138-9, 141, 144
Millinship, William 181
Million Dollar Bond, The 8
Mills, Kim 253
Millward, Charles 39
Mirror of Death, The 51
Miss Sherlock Holmes 9, 11
Missing Q.C.'s, The 258
Missing Rembrandt, The 73,
    86-8, 91
Missing Three-Quarter, The
    62
Missing Witness Sensation,
    The 256-7
Mr. Moto in Danger Island
    106

Mr. Moto Takes a Chance 106
Mr. Moto Takes a Vacation
   106
Mr. Moto's Gamble 106
Mr. Moto's Last Warning 106
Mr. Sherlock Holmes of Lon-
   don 245
Mr. Wong, Detective 105
Mr. Wong in Chinatown 106
Mix-Up in Mexico 165
Moabite Cipher, The 254
Moffat, Alice 55
Monsieur Sherlock Holmes 247
Montez, Maria 131
Moore, Geoffrey 273-4
Moore, Harry 233
Moore, Joyce 82
Moore, Robert 266
Moore, Roger 73, 272-4
Morell, Andre 203-6
Morey, Harry T. 72
Morgan, George 91, 104
Morgan, Richardson 232
Morhaim, Joe 195, 197-8
Morheim, Lou 181-2, 185
Morley, Robert 222
Morrison, Arthur 253-4,
   257-8
Morrison, Patricia 151
Morse, Carlton E. 148
Mortimer, Charles 96
Morton, Gabrielle 67
Morton, Gregory 167
Morton, Judee 232
Moseley, Alice 12
Moss, Hugh 29
Mother Hubbard Case, The
   181
Mowbray, Alan 89, 93, 150,
   153
Mower, Jack 65
Moyse, Mr. 25
Muir, Gavin 137
Mulhall, Jack 100
Mulligan, Richard 264
Mummy, The 205
Murder at Baker Street, The 9
Murder at Site Three 208
Murder at the Baskervilles
   see Silver Blaze (1936
   film)
Murder by Death 249-50,
   266-9

Murder in Northumberland
   viii, 247, 255
Murder in the Hotel Splendid,
   The 52
Murder of Roger Ackroyd, The
   82
"Murder Will Out" 76
Murdered Constable, The 205
"Murders in the Rue Morgue,
   The" 11, 182
Murders in the Rue Morgue,
   The 92
Murdock, Janet 150
Murray, Thelma 67
Mursky, Alexander 69
Murtagh, Cynthia 61
"Musgrave Ritual, The" 136,
   186
Musgrave Ritual, The (films)
   (1912) 28, (1922) 55; (TV)
   233
Mysterious Casket, The 51
Mysterious Death on the Under-
   ground Railway, The 253
Mysterious Dr. Fu Manchu,
   The 84
Mysterious Mr. Moto 106
Mystery of Boscombe Vale,
   The 27
Mystery of Cader Ifan, The
   228, 272
Mystery of Fu Manchu, The
   (book) 71; (film series)
   63, 70-1
Mystery of Marie Roget, The
   131
Mystery of Mr. Wong, The
   106
Mystery of the Amber Beads,
   The 253
Mystery of the Dancing Men,
   The 62
Mystery of the Diamond Belt,
   The 33, 46
Mystery of the Leaping Fish,
   The 34
Mystery of the Lost Cat, The
   18
Mystery of the Silent Death,
   The 67
Mystery of the Week 264
Mystery of Thor Bridge, The
   (film) 62; (TV) 233

Mystery Theatre   169

Naish, J. Carroll   19
Nancy Drew and the Hidden
  Staircase   124
Nancy Drew, Detective   124
Nancy Drew, Reporter   124
Nancy Drew, Troubleshooter
  124
Napier, Alan   159-60
Narita, Richard   267
Nash, Percy   47, 52, 59
"Naval Treaty, The"   9
Naval Treaty, The   (film) 55;
  (TV) 233
Nederlander, James   203, 225
Neilan, Marshal   33
Neill, Roy William   133-5,
  138-41, 151
Neilsen, Hans   213
Net of Fate   165
Nettleton, John   247
Neuss, Alwin   8-11, 22-4, 33,
  40
Nevers, Ernie   91
Neville, John   222-5, 253-4
New Adventures of Sherlock
  Holmes, The   31, 170-84,
  202, 220
New Catacombs, The   228
New Exploits of Elaine, The
  37
New Exploits of Sherlock
  Holmes, The   169
Newall, Guy   47
Nick Carter   246
Nigh, William   105
Night of Terror   32
Night Train Riddle, The   191
Nimoy, Leonard   258-9, 270
Niven, David   267
Noble Bachelor, The   49
Nolan, Lloyd   121, 124
Norfolk, Edgar   88, 97
Norris, Luther   109, 202,
  260-1
Norwood, Ellie   48-51, 54,
  61-4, 78, 112
"Norwood Builder, The"   147
Norwood Builder, The   (film)
  54, 88, 105; (record) 235
Notched Hairpin, The   188

Novotna, Jarmilla   167

Oakie, Jack   76
O'Brady, Frederick   187, 189
O'Brien, Manning   208
O'Brien, Willis   65
Obzina, Martin   146, 151
Odemar, Fritz   101
O'Hare, Jenny   266
Oland, Warner   76, 84, 121
Old Secretaire, The   14
Olivier, Sir Laurence   276
Olsen and Johnson   137
Omanoff, Ben   186
On Top of the Underworld
  205
O'Neill, Ella   91
$128,000 Question, The   269
Oppenheim, E. Phillips   258
Orczy, Baroness   253-4
Orr, Mary   167
Osborne, Andrew   160
Oscar, Henry   97, 161, 169
O'Sullivan, Duncan   198
O'Sullivan, Maureen   270
Oswald, Richard   22-3, 25,
  69, 71
Otterson, Jack   151
Otto, Paul   13, 15
Out West   165
Owen, Bill   161
Owen, Reginald   89, 92-4
Owens, Gary   261
Oxley, David   206
Oxley, Roy   217

Padlock Bones   33
Page, Genevieve   239-41
Page, Norman   63
Paget, Sidney   276, 279
Painful Predicament of Sher-
  lock Holmes, The   45
Pallette, Eugene   74, 76
Palmer, Nicholas   219
Paramount on Parade   75-6
Parker, Albert   56
Parker, Cecil   232
Parker, Cecilia   91
Parkinson, H. B.   65
Pascal, Ernest   113
Patocka, Joseph   245

Paul, Fred 31, 54, 64, 71
Paulo, Harry 31
Payne, Douglas 33, 46-7, 59, 61
Payne, Sandra 219
Pearl of Death, The 141-3, 159
Pearlman, Gilbert 271
Pearson, George 31, 40
Pearson, Winifred 31
Peel, Richard 267-8
Pemberton, Mox 257
Percival, Cyril 49
Perrins, Leslie 67-8, 78, 96
Phantom of the Rue Morgue, The 182
Phillips, Minna 137
Pierre, Carlos 233
Piggott, Temple 93
Pimple's Boy Scout 35
Pimple's Clutchy Hand 35
Pimple's Million Dollar Mystery 35
Pimple's the Case of Johnny Walker 35
Pio, Elith 6, 8, 10-1
Pitt-Chatham, C. 49
Pleasence, Donald 253, 255
Plummer, Christopher 287
Plummer, George Marsden 67
Plympton, George 91
Podmore, William 102
Poe, Edgar Allan 11, 71, 92, 131, 179, 182, 281
Poisoned Seal, The 52
Ponto, Erich 101
Porter, Carole 233
Porter, Nyrea Down 219
Post, William, Jr. 133
Postance, William 44
Powell, William 56, 74-6
Power, Ronald 55
Previn, Steve 190, 196
Price, Dennis 148, 233
Priory School, The 49
Prisonnière, La 79
Private Life of Sherlock Holmes, The (film) 221, 237-43, 250; (novel) 250
Problem of Cell 13, The 254
"Problem of Thor Bridge, The" 62

Professor Lightfoot and Dr. Twiddle 163-5
Pseudo-Quartette, The 12
Purdell, Reginald 134
Pursuit to Algiers 134, 147-8, 150

Quayle, Anthony 223
Queen, Ellery 96-7, 169, 227

Racina, Thom 95
Radd, Ronald 220
Radio Detective, The 656
Radio Murder Mystery, The 94-5
Raffles Escapes from Prison 6-7
Raine, Jack 167
Rains, Claude 210
Rampling, Charlotte 272, 274
Ramsey, Nelson 48, 61
Randolph, Anders 56
Rasmussen, Holger 9
Rasp, Fritz 69, 101
Rathbone, Basil vii-viii, 4, 14, 19, 21, 28, 38, 48, 54, 56, 67, 72-3, 77-81, 89, 98, 107-26, 128-34, 137, 139, 142-4, 146, 149-61, 166-8, 170, 182, 201-3, 207-9, 211, 215, 220, 227, 229, 231, 242, 245, 252, 256, 263, 266, 270, 275, 279-80
Rathbone, Ouida 166
Rawlins, Lester 243
Rawlinson, A. R. 104
Rawlinson, Herbert 46
Ray, Allene 66
Raymond, Charles 33-5
Raymond, Cyril 54
Raymond, Gary 233
Raymond, Jack 55, 82
Raymond, Roy 61, 67
Rayner, Albert 62
Rayner, Minnie 78, 86, 94, 96, 98
Raynham, Fred 49-50, 55, 63, 67, 112
Read, Anthony 219
Read, Ian 219-20

Reals, Grace 41, 44
Receivers, The 205
Red Circle, The 55
Red Handed 228
"Red Window, The" 165
Regine 276
Redgrave, Corin 233
Redgrave, Vanessa 276
"Red-Headed League, The" 4,
    89, 93, 182, 201
Red-Headed League, The
    (film) 48; (radio) 30; (TV)
    (1951) 161-2, (1965) 219
Reed, Maxwell 232
Reed, Tom 92
Reems, Harry 264
Reeve, Arthur B. 36
Reeves, Kynaston 88
Regas, George 116
Reigate Squires, The (films)
    (1912) 28, (1922) 55; (TV)
    161
Reminiscences of Solar Pons,
    The 202
Rendel, Robert 83-4
Rennie, Michael 210
Reply Paid 188
Resident Patient, The 49
Retired Colourman, The 220
Return of Fu Manchu, The
    (book) 71; (film) 84
Return of Moriarty, The 28
Return of Sherlock Holmes,
    The (film) 70-4, 76, 88;
    (play) 64, 105
Return of Solar Pons, The
    202
Return of the World's Greatest
    Detective, The 265-6
Return to Hampstead 211
Revill, Clive 270
Rex, Bert 34-5
Reynolds, Sheldon 170, 172,
    174, 177, 183
Richards, Kenneth 189
Richardson, Ralph 220
Ridgwell, George 54-5, 59
Riggs, Lynn 126-7, 130, 135
Riordan, Marjorie 147
Ripening Rubies, The 257
Ritelis, Viktors 233
Rival Sherlock Holmes see
    Sherlock Holmes' Enemy

Rivals of Sherlock Holmes,
    The (book) 253, 257; (TV)
    252-71
Roach, Paul 247
Robbery at the Railroad Station,
    The 18
Robbins, Stewart 41
Roberts, George 245
Robertshaw, Jerrold 94
Robinson, B. Fletcher 20-2
Robinson, John 161
Rock, Charles 29
Rodgers, Anton 219
Rodney, June 191
Rodney Stone (story) 29, 65;
    (film) 47
Rohmer, Sax 63, 71, 84
Rohr, Tony 233
Rolf, Karl Heinz 51
Roman Hat Mystery, The 97
Romance of Elaine, The 40
Romances of the Prize Ring
    65
Ronay, Edina 232
Rooke, Irene 49, 112
Room for a Night 165
Rose, Arthur 64
Rose, Cleo 196
Rosen, Milton 151
Rosen, Phil 131
Rosenberg, Max J. 229, 236
Rosenhaym, Paul 25
Rosenkrantz, Baron Palle
    Adam Vilhelm 253
Rosenzweig, Joel 249
Ross, Hector 160
Ross, Herbert 276, 279-80
Rossitto, Angelo 140
Roth, Richard 249, 263-4
Rotmund, Ernest 101
Rotterdam-Amsterdam 46
Rowland, William 94
Rowlins, John 126, 130
Ruhmann, Heinz 101
Rushton, William 246
Russell, Margaret 185
Ryan, Madge 234
Ryder, Cecil A. 1, 109,
    260-1

Sachs, Leonard 219
Saffan, Henri 232

Sagal, Boris 273, 275
Sage of Baker Street, The
    163
Saint, The 272, 275
Saint in New York, The 105
St. John, Jill 210-1
Saint's Girl Friday, The 105
Saintsbury, H. A. 38-40,
    105
Saire, David 233
Saletri, Frank 280-1
Sallis, Peter 95, 225, 279
Samuelson, G. B. 31, 38-40
Sanders, George 105, 168
Sandox, Henry 177
Sangster, Jimmy 208
Sannon, Emile 32
Sapinsley, Alvin 273, 275
Sasdy, Peter 217
"Scandal in Bohemia, A" 153,
    159, 163, 201, 227, 273
Scandal in Bohemia, A (film)
    48-9; (radio) 80; (TV)
    161
Scarab, The 211
Scarlet Claw, The 38, 140-1
Scarlet Ring, The see A
    Study in Scarlett (1953 film)
Schable, Robert 56
Schaffer, Natalie 179
Schofield, Susan 59
Schonberg, Lilly 101
Schuck, John 269
Schull, Richard B. 269
Schulyze-Westrum, Edith 213
Scotland Yard's Inspector
    Burke 156, 158
Scott, George C. 243-5
Scream in the Night, A 33-4
"Sealed Room, The" 165
Second Stain, The (film) 55;
    (TV) (1951) 161, (1968) 232
Secret Document, The 6-7
Secret of the Fox-hunter, The
    257
Secret of the Magnifique, The
    258
Seefelu, Edward 34
Seerl, Anthony 247
Seiler, Lewis 68
Sellers, Peter 267
Semon, Larry 40
Sennett, Mack 16-8

Sensible Action of Lieutenant
    Holst, The 253
Seroff, Georges 69
Seven-Per-Cent Solution, The
    (novel) 197, 276; (film)
    253, 276-80
Seward, Leslie 220
Seward, Sidney 49, 65
Sexton Blake 12
Sexton Blake and the Bearded
    Doctor 97-8
Sexton Blake and the Hooded
    Terror 104-5, 143
Sexton Blake and the Mademoi-
    selle 97-8
Sexton Blake, Gambler 67
Sexton Blake vs Baron Kettler
    29
Sexton Pimple 36
Seyford, Michael 182
Seymour, Madeline 55
Seyrig, Delphine 181
Shadows in the Night 149
Shatner, William 246
Shavelson, Melville 269, 271
Shaw, Montagu 90
Shaw, Harold 29
Shaw, Robert 255
Shelley, Barbara 208
Shelly, Norman 100, 164,
    215, 235
Shepherd, Sally 144, 146
Shepley, Michael 96
Sherlick Holmes 264
Sherlock Ambrose 46
Sherlock Bonehead 33
Sherlock Boob, Detective 34
Sherlock Brown 52
Sherlock Holmes (films) (1909)
    12, (1916) 40, 42-6, (1921
    series) 51-2, (1922) 54-9,
    74, 80, (1932) 88-92, (1953)
    see Professor Lightfoot and
    Dr. Twiddle; (plays) (1897)
    41-2, (1906) 33, (1953) 167-
    8; (radio) (1933) 94-5,
    (1959) 215, 235; (TV) (1951)
    161-2, (1954) see The New
    Adventures of Sherlock
    Holmes, (1965) 216-20, 231,
    (1968) 230-5
Sherlock Holmes: A Drama in
    Four Acts (play) 2-3,

7-8, 40-1, 43, 45, 52, 55,
79, 89, 116-7, 203, 225,
258-9, 270; (radio) 221
Sherlock Holmes and the Deadly
Necklace 56, 212-3, 251
Sherlock Holmes and the Golden
Vampire 280-1
Sherlock Holmes and the Great
Murder Mystery 9, 11
Sherlock Holmes and the Grey
Lady 101
Sherlock Holmes and the Mid-
night Meeting 40
Sherlock Holmes and the Secret
Weapon 132-5, 143
Sherlock Holmes and the Voice
of Terror 126-31, 134,
167-8
Sherlock Holmes Baffled 1-2,
4, 11
Sherlock Holmes Captured 8,
10-1
Sherlock Holmes Cheated by
Rigadin 16
Sherlock Holmes Detective Kit
250
Sherlock Holmes' Enemy 9
Sherlock Holmes Explained by
His Creator, Sir Arthur
Conan Doyle and Presented
in Action by William Gillette
53
Sherlock Holmes Faces Death
135-7
Sherlock Holmes' Fatal Hour
see The Sleeping Cardinal
Sherlock Holmes "Follow the
Clues" Jigsaw Puzzle 250
Sherlock Holmes in Deadly
Danger 6-7
Sherlock Holmes in New York
(film) 272-6, 281; (novel)
281
Sherlock Holmes in the Claws
of the Confidence Men 8
Sherlock Holmes in the Gas
Cellar see The Secret
Document
Sherlock Holmes in Washington
135-6
Sherlock Holmes, Jr. 16
Sherlock Holmes' Last Exploit
9

Sherlock Holmes' Masterpiece
see The Million Dollar
Bond
Sherlock Holmes on Leave 40
Sherlock Holmes Risks His
Life see Sherlock Holmes
in Deathly Danger
Sherlock Holmes Saves London
see Sherlock Holmes and
the Voice of Terror
Sherlock Holmes Solves "The
Sign of the Four" 30
Sherlock Holmes vs Dr. Mors
32-3, 52
Sherlock Holmes vs Jack the
Ripper see A Study in
Terror (novel)
Sherlock Holmes vs Professor
Moriarty 15
Sherlock Holmes vs the Black
Hood 30
Sherlock, Jr. 64, 67
Sherlock Sleuth 65
Sherlock's Home 88
Shine, Wilfred 83
Shipman, Barry 104
Shirley, Alfred 156
Shock-a-Bye, Baby 264-5
Shoscombe Old Place (TV)
233; (record) 235
Showcase 160
Sign of Four, The (novel)
see The Sign of the Four
(film) 88, 91
Sign of the Four, The (novel)
30, 62, 88, 140, 247;
(film) 62-4, 88; (TV)
233-4
Silken Threads 67-8
"Silver Blaze" 98, 227
Silver Blaze (films) (1912)
26-7, (1923) 61 (1936) 20,
98-100; announced 281;
(radio) 104
Silver Blaze--From the Mem-
oirs of Sherlock Holmes
235
Simon, Neil 249, 266-7, 269
Sinclair, Hugh 105
Sinclair, Mary 192
Sinden, Donald 254
Singer, Campbell 160
Singer's Diamonds, The 6-7

Siodmak, Curt 213, 221
Sir Arthur Conan Doyle 53,
    66-7, 71
Six Napoleons, The (film) 55;
    (TV) 219
Slaughter, Tod 105
Sleepers West 124-5
Sleeping Cardinal, The 77-9,
    82
Slesar, Henry 265
Sleuths at the Floral Parade,
    The 18
Sleuths' Last Stand, The 18
Small, Knighton 61
Smith, H. Reeves 72, 74
Smith, Maggie 267
Smith, Ormond G. 13
Smith, Sebastian 61
Snake Ring, The 51
Snowden, Eric 156
Society Sherlock, A 40
Sohnker, Hans 213
Solan Pons: Mr. Fairlie's
    Final Journey 202
Solitary Cyclist, The (film)
    49; (TV) 233
Solon, Ewen 206
Sondergaard, Gale 19, 138-40,
    149
Soutten, Ben 88
Spanish Cape Mystery, The 97
"Speckled Band, The" 39, 80,
    172, 201, 215
Speckled Band, The (films)
    (1912) 25-7, (1923) 61,
    (1931) 81-2; (radio) 249-
    50; (TV) 160, 215-7;
    (record) 235
Speckled Band: An Adventure
    of Sherlock Holmes, The
    39-40, 82, 105, 169
Speelmans, Hermann 101
Spider Woman, The 19, 137-
    40
Spider Woman Strikes Back,
    The 140
Spina, Harold 95
Spot 18
Spottswood, James 102
Squeedunk Sherlock Holmes, A
    12
Stander, Lionel 100
Standing, Percy Darrell 61,
    64

Standing, Wyndham 93
Stanley, Eric 64
Stanley, John 156
Stapleton, Beryl 110
Stark, Ray 266
Starkle, Martin 161
Starrett, Vincent 201
Steele, Geoffrey 150
Steerman, A. Harding 62
Stemmle, Robert 101
Stenning, Arthur 167
Stephens, Robert 73, 237,
    239, 241-2, 253, 256
Stephenson, Henry 116
Sterling, William 232-3
Stern, Leonard 269
Steven, Anthony 253
Stewart, Athole 81-2
Stiles, Leslie 55
Sting of Death, The 188
Stirling, Pamela 148
Stock, Nigel 215-7, 219,
    230-1, 234-5
Stock-Broker's Clerk, The
    55
Stoker, H. G. 64
Stolen Heirlooms, The 34-5
Stolen Necklace, The 16
Stolen Papers, The 27-8
Stolen Purse, The 18
Stolen Treaty, The 9
Stolen Wallet, The see Sher-
    lock Holmes in the Claws
    of the Confidence Men
Stone, Lewis 65
Stone, Milburne 137
Stone of Mazarin, The 62
Stories of Sherlock Holmes,
    The 215
Stories of Sherlock Holmes,
    v. 3 and v. 4 227
Stories of Sir Arthur Conan
    Doyle, The 227-8, 272
Story of Waterloo, A 94
Stout, Rex 100, 215, 273
Stowe, Percy 12
Strange Case of Hennessy, The
    95
Stratton, John 228, 233
Stricklyn, Ray 211
Struthers, Sally 269
Stuart, Jennifer 232
Stuart, John 83

Study in Identity, A 281
Study in Scarlet, A (novel)
  31-2, 38, 172-3, 270;
  (films) (1914 Samuelson)
  31-2, 40, (1914 Universal)
  31-2, 38, 52, (1933) 73,
  92-4; (TV) 232
Study in Skarlit, A 36, 38
Study in Terror, A (film)
  222-7, 229; (novel) 227;
  (record) 235
Subotsky, Milton 229, 236
Sullivan, Francis L. 87
Sullivan, Pat 67
Superfluous Finger, The 257
Surelock Jones 18
Sure-Locked Homes 67
Sutton, Shawn 219-20
Swain, Mack 46
Swarbrick, Stephen 190
Swift, Lela 264
Sylvester, R. D. 49
Sympson, Tony 97, 104
Syngarde, Peter 217
Syrig, Delphine 186

Tales of Fatima 159
Taste for Honey, A 188-9,
  228-9
Tate, John 233-4
Tate, Nick 233
Tawase 88
Taylor, Alma 69
Taylor, Eric 219
Taylor, Grant 233
Taylor, Ray 104
Teatime in Baker Street 158-9,
  169
Tebet, David W. 275
Teed, G. H. 97
Terrible 'Tec, The 40
Terriss, Tom 64
Terror by Night 38, 147,
  150-3
Terror by Train 165
Terry, Don 136
Terry, J. E. Harold 64
Texaco Star Theatre 166-7
Teynac, Maurice 190, 196
Thank You, Mr. Moto 106
That's Hollywood 256
Thaw, John 253

Theft of the Diamonds, The
  see The Singer's Diamonds
Theft of the State Document,
  The see The Secret Docu-
  ment
Their First Divorce Case
  16-7
Their First Execution 18
Their First Kidnapping Case
  17
They Might Be Giants (play)
  243, 250; (film) 243-5,
  251, 266; (novel) 250-1
They Shall Repay 97
Thief in the Night 165
Think Fast, Mr. Moto 104
Thirteen Lead Soldiers 168
Thomas, Frankie 124
Thompson, Hugh 45
Thompson, Robert E. 246
Thomson, David 189
Thornton Jewel Mystery, The
  34-5
Three Days Dead 46
Three-Fingered Kate, Her
  Second Victim 12
Three-Fingered Kate, Her
  Victim the Banker 12
Three Garridebs, The 102-3,
  158
Three Students, The 62
Tiger of San Pedro, The 49,
  55
Time to Kill 125
Timex Presents Sherlock
  Holmes 255
Tingwell, Charles 233
Tiseley, Vincent 219-20
Tober, Sidney 121, 124
Todd, Malcolm 55
Tomb, Harry 185
Toone, Geoffrey 208
Torrence, David 56
Torrence, Ernest 89
Tosh, Donald 233
Toumanova, Tamara 238
Towers, Harry Alan 220
Townley, Toke 219
Townsend, H. 48
Townsend, Jill 276
Tragedy of Korosko, The 64,
  91
Trailing the Counterfeiter 16

Trapped in a Trunk   165
Travers, Roy   67
Tree, Madge   61
Treville, M. Georges   25-8
Trevor, Austin   82, 84
Triumph of Sherlock Holmes,
   The   73, 96
Tubley's Clutching Hand   41
Turnbull, John   97-8
Tuttle, Frank   76
Twelvetrees, Helen   68-9
23 Paces to Baker Street
   200-1, 208
Twisted Tales   65
"Two Women, The"   165
Twyford, Cyril   77, 86, 96

Uncanny Room, The   24-5
Unknown, The   149

Valley of Fear, The   (novel)
   30, 38, 96, 177, 213-4;
   (films) (1916) 31, 38-40,
   52, 62, 65, (1935) see The
   Triumph of Sherlock Holmes,
   (1968) 235
Vallis, Robert   49
Van Atta, Lee   104
Van Avery, Dale   92
Vance, Louis Joseph   52
Vance, Vivian   270
Vandeleur, Iria   161
Van Dine, S. S.   74, 80
Van Horne, Andreas   22, 25
Van Zandt, Phillip   133
Varley, John   143, 148
Varnel, Max   219
Vaughn, Bernard   39
Vaughn, Peter   257-8
Veiller, Bayard   52
Vengeance of Fu Manchu, The
   220
Verbit, Helen   266
Verne, Kaaren   133
Verne, L.   62
Veteran of Waterloo, The   94
Vevan, Billy   153
Vibart, Henry   49
Victor, Joseph   195
Villainous Villain, A   40
Vincent, John   256

Vincent, Leslie   147
Viper, The   134
Von Seyffertitz, Gustav   56,
   74
Von Stackelberg, Carla   101
Voska, Vaclaw   245
Voss, Peter   101

Walcott, Arthur   49
Walker, (Miss)   49
Walker, Lewis   29
Walker, Martin   100
Wallace, Edgar   83-4, 93
Walters, Thorley   212-5, 251,
   261
Ward, Cecil   55
Ward, Ernest C.   33
Warrant for X   200
Warren, Bill   281
Warrick, Guy   245
Warrington, Neil   46
Warwick, John   208
Wasserman, Vaclav   91
Waters, Russell   177
Watson, June   233
"Wax Gamblers, The"   165
Weaver, Fritz   95, 236-4
Webb, Dick   52
Webb, James   182
Wedding Presents, The   12
Weisberg, Brenda   141
Weiss, Hanni   22
Welden, Ben   88, 96
Welles, Orson   221
Welsh, Jane   78, 86
Weltman, Manny   270
Wendeley, Richard   167
Wentworth, Robin   233
Werewolf of the Baskervilles,
   The   281
Werker, Alfred   116, 124
West End Horror, The   280
Whalley, Norma   48, 55
Wheatley, Alan   161-2
When Giants Fought   65
Where Is She?   32
White, Madge   49
White, Pearl   18, 36-7, 40
Wilde, William   220
Wilder, Billy   237, 241-2
Wilder, Gene   249, 261-5
Wiley, Hugh   105

Willard, John 56
Willes, Peter 116
William Voss 34
Williamson, Nicol 73, 276,
    278-9
Willis, Hubert 46-50, 53, 61,
    88, 112
Willis, J. Elder 76
Willis, Marjorie 46, 54
Wilmer, Douglas 215-20, 231,
    253-4, 257, 261, 270, 279
Wilmer, Geoffrey 55
Wilson, Frank 41, 71
Wilson, Henry 61, 63
Wincott, Geoffrey 219
Winton, Dora de 62
Wisteria Lodge 233
Withers, Grant 105
Witting, Clifford 219
Wolf, Maud 62
Wolheim, Louis 56
Woman in Green, The 144-7
Woman in the Big Hat, The
    254
Wong, Anna May 84, 93-4
Wontner, Arthur 28, 47-8,
    72, 76-9, 82, 86-8, 94,
    96-100, 134, 203, 221
Wood, John 203
Woodland, Norman 233
Woods, Donald 163, 169
Woodthorpe, Peter 233
Woodward, Joanne 243-4
World of Sherlock Holmes,
    The 211
Worlock, Frederick 136, 150,
    153
Wormald, S. 13, 15
Would-Be Detective, The 30
Wright, Ben 156
Wright, Humbertson 63
Wright, Marie 97, 104
Wright, Michele 181
Wyatt, Eustace 102
Wymark, Patrick 219

Yanai, Aka 181
Yarborough, Barton 148-9
Yellow Face, The 48
York, Cecil Morton 52, 55,
    61
Young, Gig 272, 274

Young, Roland 56, 70, 80

Zanuck, Darryl F. 113, 116
Zehn, Willy 25
Zerbe, Anthony 246
Zucco, George 116, 136,
    149, 263